T0178998

Real-time Systems Scheduling 1

*Series Editor*
*Abdelhamid Mellouk*

# Real-time Systems Scheduling 1

*Fundamentals*

*Edited by*

## Maryline Chetto

WILEY

First published 2014 in Great Britain and the United States by ISTE Ltd and John Wiley & Sons, Inc.

ISTE Ltd
27-37 St George's Road
London SW19 4EU
UK

www.iste.co.uk

John Wiley & Sons, Inc.
111 River Street
Hoboken, NJ 07030
USA

www.wiley.com

Library of Congress Control Number: 2014946161

British Library Cataloguing-in-Publication Data
A CIP record for this book is available from the British Library
ISBN 978-1-84821-665-5

# Contents

## CHAPTER 5. ESTIMATION OF EXECUTION TIME
## AND DELAYS.
Claire MAIZA, Pascal RAYMOND and Christine ROCHANGE

## CHAPTER 6. OPTIMIZATION OF ENERGY
## CONSUMPTION
Cécile BELLEUDY

# Preface

We refer to a system as real-time when it has to meet deadlines when reacting to stimuli produced by an external environment. Punctuality therefore constitutes the most important quality of a real-time computer system, which, moreover, distinguishes it from conventional computer systems. We refer to a system as embedded when it is physically integrated into a physical device whose control and command it ensures, which have a particular impact on its sizing and the selection of its components.

The rapid evolution of microelectronic techniques and communication infrastructures in recent years has led to the emergence of often-miniaturized interconnected embedded systems (wireless nodes processing data coming from sensors), leading to the birth of the concept of the "Internet of things". The real-time qualifier therefore remains relevant for all these autonomous and intelligent objects as it was in the 1970s with the advent of microcomputers, when this qualifier was restricted to industrial process controlling systems.

The large variety of appliances in which real-time systems are now integrated requires increasingly strict constraints to be taken into account in terms of physical size, computational power, memory capacity, energy storage capacity and so on, in their design. It is therefore in this direction that research efforts have turned for several years.

Every piece of software with real-time application is composed of tasks, programs whose execution requires a concurrent access to shared resources limited in number (processor, memory, communication medium). This raises the central issue of scheduling whose solution leads to a planning of tasks that respects the time constraints.

Since the early 1970s, in particular following the publication of the crucial article by Liu and Layland, research activity in the field of real-time scheduling, both through its theoretical results and integration in operating systems, has allowed us to overcome numerous technological barriers.

*Real-Time Systems Scheduling* constitutes a learning support regarding real-time scheduling intended for instructors, master's degree students and engineering students. It also aims to describe the latest major progress in research and development for scientists and engineers. The book groups together around 30 years of expertise from French and Belgian universities specialized in real-time scheduling. It was originally published in French and has now been translated into English.

This book is composed of two volumes with a total of 13 chapters.

Volume 1 entitled *Fundamentals* is composed of six chapters and should be of interest as a general course on scheduling in real-time systems. Reading the chapters in order, from 1 through to 6, is recommended but not necessary. Volume 1 is structured as follows: Chapter 1 constitutes a conceptual introduction to real-time scheduling. Chapters 2 and 3, respectively, deal with uniprocessor and multiprocessor real-time scheduling. Chapter 4 discusses results on scheduling tasks with resource requirements.

Chapter 5 relates to the scheduling issue in energy-constrained systems. Chapter 6 presents the techniques of computing the worst-case execution time (WCET) for tasks.

Volume 2 entitled *Focuses* is composed of seven chapters. This volume aims at collecting knowledge on specific topics and discussing the recent advances for some of them. After reading Chapter 1 of Volume 1, a reader can move to any chapters of Volume 2 in any order. Volume 2 is structured as follows: Chapter 1 highlights the newer scheduling issues raised by the so-called energy-autonomous real-time systems. In Chapter 2, the authors consider a probabilistic modelization of the WCET in order to tackle the scheduling problem. In Chapter 3, the authors show how automatic control can benefit real-time scheduling. Chapter 4 deals with the synchronous approach for scheduling. In Chapter 5, the authors focus on the optimization of the Quality-of-Service in routed networks. Chapter 6 is devoted to the scheduling of messages in industrial networks. Finally, Chapter 7 pertains specifically to resolution techniques used in avionic networks such as AFDX.

Maryline CHETTO
July 2014

# List of Figures

# List of Tables

# Introduction to Real-time Scheduling

The aim of this chapter is to introduce real-time scheduling. To do this, after a presentation of the context, we focus on material and software architectures commonly employed in the programming of real-time systems. Next, from a few examples of programs, classical task models are introduced. The techniques implemented to validate these models are developed throughout the chapters of this book.

## 1.1. Real-time systems

Real-time systems are very extensively used: from wide-consumption technological products (smartphones, games) to terrestrial transport systems (trains and cars) as well as aerial (aeroplanes) and spatial (satellites, shuttles and rockets) transport systems, through non-embedded critical systems such as power plant control, factory machinery control, or bank transaction systems. These are computer programs subject to temporal constraints. Non-compliance with the temporal constraints can lead to a discomfort of use for some programs referred to as *soft* real-time constraint programs (games, vehicle comfort

---

Chapter written by Emmanuel GROLLEAU.

functionalities such as air conditioning), or it can have catastrophic consequences for *strict* real-time constraint programs (such as the braking system of a vehicle or the control functionality of an aeroplane).

A real-time system can be either embedded or not: an embedded system embeds its own computing hardware and its own energy source. The energy sources can be electrical batteries, motors fed by fuel, ambient energy such as solar power, or even a combination of several sources. Embedded systems are characterized by low energy consumption computing capabilities in favor of autonomy, small size compared to non-embedded computing capabilities in order to reduce the footprint and the weight of the control system.

In the remainder of the chapter, we will call the global entity *system*, for instance, the control system of a vehicle. A system provides various *functionalities*, such as, for example in the case of a vehicle, braking, controlling the on-board radio, autonomous parking, and so on. The functionalities are generally ensured, on complex systems, by subsystems, which can be distributed over several CPUs and networks.

The functionalities and systems can be subject to temporal constraints. We can distinguish between local constraints and end-to-end constraints: an end-to-end constraint is typically derived from high-level requirements on the functionalities. A requirement describes what a functionality has to perform (functional requirement), or what properties it has to have (non-functional requirement). Generally, temporal constraints are considered non-functional since they characterize the response time the functionality has to have. A very widespread requirement in critical systems is segregation, which enforces two implementations of a same functionality to use different computing and communication resources.

EXAMPLE 1.1 (Braking and steering control system).– The following example, taken from a vehicle case study, illustrates the concepts of system, functionality, subsystem and requirements.

We consider a subset of the braking and steering correction functionalities on a passenger vehicle. Figure 1.1 represents different CPUs (called ECU for electronic control units in this context) as well as the main sensors and actuators, and the communication bus allowing the calculators to exchange information. The antilock braking system (ABS) functionality consists of measuring the speed of the various wheels and calculating a slip ratio. Above a certain value, the ABS control unit has to act on the hydraulic pressure regulating valve in order to reduce the exerted pressure, thus allowing the skidding wheels to regain traction, and therefore to reduce the braking distance. A non-functional requirement concerning this functionality could be that the maximum delay between the moment when the wheels skid and the moment when the pressure is reduced to be lower than 50 ms. In a simplified view, we could envision that the ABS functionality is performed by the subsystem that is running on the ABS control unit.

Let us now consider the steering correction functionality. This has to take into account the driver's intent (the angle of the steering wheel), as well as the speed of the vehicle, and can use gyro meters (measuring the angular speed) or an inertial unit (measuring the attitude using the measures of angular speed, heading and acceleration) in order to measure the rotational speed of the vehicle. Depending on the speed of the vehicle, the difference between the command attitude (angle of the steering wheel) and the rotational angle of the vehicle the extra sensory perception (ESP) control unit is able to determine whether the vehicle is in oversteer (the vehicle starts to go into a spin since the rear is drifting) or understeer (the front has a tendency to skid and the vehicle continues forward instead of following the curve). The outputs of the ESP control unit, interpreted by the ABS control unit, are translated as a braking of the front outside wheel in order to compensate an oversteer, or the rear inside wheel for an understeer. We can thus see that the ESP functionality is distributed over several subsystems, running on several ECUs. The ESP can also be subject to end-to-end temporal constraints, which will be translated as local temporal constraints on the ECUs and communication buses involved in the functionality.

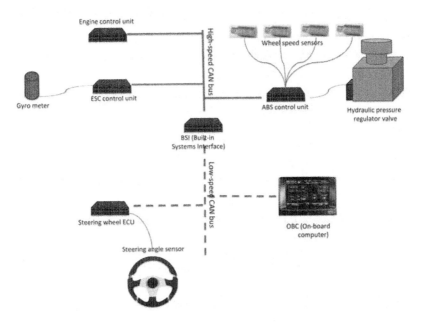

**Figure 1.1.** *Distributed system ensuring the braking and steering correction functionalities*

Some temporal constraints can be purely local: the pieces of information circulating in a network are typically cut up into frames (series of bytes). Embedded CPUs typically do not have a memory of more than a single received frame. Consequently, a requirement that we could expect to have would be for a CPU to be able to read and memorize a frame before the reception of the next frame, under penalty of losing a frame.

On each subsystem running on a CPU, the requirements are mirrored by temporal constraints. A temporal constraint is a time frame in which a process must always be executed in its entirety.

## 1.2. Material architectures

From example 1.1, we have an overview of the main material elements composing a real-time system: CPUs, communication networks, sensors and actuators.

### 1.2.1. *CPUs*

In this section, we consider central processing units (CPUs) based on a Van Neumann or Harvard architecture, in other words CPUs that separate the memory and calculation units. Most of the CPUs in use since the invention of computing are indeed based on one of these architectures.

A CPU is a processor allowing the execution of programs. A program, while running, has its instructions copied into memory: it then becomes a process. A process can be composed of several algorithms that need to be run in parallel, these are tasks. A task is composed of a series of instructions to be executed sequentially. An instruction can be arithmetical and logical, a conditional or unconditional jump, movements between the memory and the registers, access to an input/output device, etc.

CPUs can be single- or multi-core: each computing core allows the execution of a task at a given time. A process is thus parallelizable since several tasks of the same process can be run simultaneously, on the other hand we generally consider tasks not to be parallelizable. This means that a task cannot simultaneously be run on several cores.

The execution of an instruction consists of loading the instruction from memory, decoding it and running it. The time-stepping of the execution of the instructions is ensured by a clock, used as a time reference called the cycle, in the cores.

If all these operations were executed sequentially, then the processor cores would be underutilized. Indeed, the circuits specialized in the processing of instructions are available during the loading and decoding of the instruction. Moreover, the memory could be slower to respond than the execution time of an instruction. This is called a memory bottleneck, since the processor can be led to wait several cycles before the instruction arrives from memory. CPUs can therefore integrate local optimizations, or have particular architectures allowing, on average, the acceleration of certain processes. For instance, cache memory allows the storage of central memory data in rapid-access memories. These memories are closer to the processor and faster, but are of smaller size than the central memory and can therefore only memorize a part of the data. The working principle is that when the processor wants to read from an address in memory, the cache, if it has stored the content of that address, sends the content to the processor, which then does not have to wait for the central memory. When the requested address is not present in the cache, the cache stores it for an ulterior use. If it is full, a cache-managing strategy has to be used to decide which content will be replaced. This optimization brings, on the architectures on which it is employed, very significant increases in performance. This is due to the locality principle: a program often contains loops and manipulates the same data, consequently when the processor has to load an instruction or a piece of data, it is often to be found in cache memory. On newer architectures, there are several levels of cache memory depending on the size and the speed. Moreover, on multi-core architectures, certain levels of cache memory can be shared by certain cores. In consequence, the parallel execution by several cores has an effect on the shared cache memory.

A CPU can be associated with specific circuits (*application specific integrated circuit* (ASIC)) allowing it to be relieved from time-costly functions, such as for example polling the arriving data on a communication bus, or computing the attitude (pitch angles, roll and heading) depending on the sensors of an inertial unit.

When an input/output device needs to communicate an event to the processor, as, for example, pressing a key on a keyboard or the arrival of a message on a communication bus, a hardware interrupt is triggered. After processing each instruction, a processor has to check whether a hardware interrupt has occurred. If this is the case, it has to process the interrupt. It stops the current processing, and executes the instructions of an interrupt handler routine.

From a real-time point of view, a CPU is thus a computing resource that runs tasks. The execution of each instruction takes time, expressed in cycles. Though the execution is sequential, numerous factors (material optimizations, interrupts) interfering with the execution of a task complicate the study of the duration of these processes. The field of study of the duration of tasks is called *timing analysis*.

### 1.2.2. *Communication networks*

A communication network is a medium allowing CPUs to communicate by sending each other data. The communication networks used in critical real-time systems have to be able to give guarantees regarding maximum delays in the transmission of messages. We therefore use deterministic networks, generally with a decentralized arbitration (no CPU is indispensable for the network to work). This is the case of a *controller area network* (CAN), which is a synchronous deterministic network used mainly in vehicles and aeroplanes, or a switched Ethernet such as *avionics full duplex* (AFDX) employed in civil avionics that enables us to reach high throughputs.

From a general point of view, CPUs connected by communication networks transmit, on a physical level, frames (i.e. a series of bytes). From a real-time point of view, a transmission medium is seen as a frame-transmitting resource, the transmission time of a frame is obtained simply from the throughput and the length of the medium. The main difficulty, from a message transmission point of view, is to take into account the utilization of the shared media (see Chapter 6, Volume 2), or the wait in queues in the case of a switched network (see Chapter 7, Volume 2). We consider that the emission of a frame cannot be interrupted.

With the recent emergence of multi-core and *manycore* CPUs (we refer to several tens or hundreds of cores as *manycores*) a new kind of communication network has appeared: *networks on chip* (NoC). These networks connect computing cores. As it is not physically possible to directly connect all the cores, we could consider that the cores are the vertices of a two-dimensional grid, and that communication media (the NoC) connect a core to its four neighbors. In order to facilitate the integration on a single chip, this grid can have more than two dimensions, and constitute a cube or a hypercube. In this case, the transmitted packets are relatively small in size in order for them to be easily stored in the cores, which will then work as routers transferring the frames from one source core to a destination core.

### 1.2.3. *Sensors and actuators*

A sensor is a device capable of reading a physical quantity (temperature, pressure, speed, etc.). There is a very large variety of sensors, their common feature is that in order to interface with a computer system, they have to offer at least a digital or analog interface, or have a communication bus interface. A digital or analog interface uses an electric quantity to represent the measured physical quantity. A communication bus interface allows the sensor to transmit frames containing measures in a binary format.

An actuator is a device which allows us to control a physical element (flight control surfaces, solenoid valves, engines, etc.). Just like a sensor, it has to have a digital or analog interface or a bus.

It may be noted that digital and analog inputs as well as buses that can be found on CPUs can be of two types: polling and interrupt-based. Polling inputs allow a program to read the binary representation of an electrical signal in input. Interrupt-based inputs trigger, on certain events, a hardware interrupt on the CPU, which will then have to execute an interrupt handler routine.

### 1.3. Operating systems

To facilitate the exploitation of material resources (CPUs, networks, memories, etc.) by an application, the operating system provides services and primitives that ease the programming. The aim of this section is to present the general aspects of operating systems and to characterize what makes an operating system real-time. It also aims to present the primitives that can be found in real-time applications.

### 1.3.1. *Generalities*

An operating system can be broken down into three layers:

– The kernel manages the memory, the processor and the hardware interrupts. The time sharing of the cores of a CPU between the tasks and/or processes is called scheduling.

– The executive is a kernel combined with device drivers, high-level access functions at the inputs/outputs, and protocol-related drivers (TCP/IP, CAN, etc.).

– An operating system is an executive that also integrates an organ of dialog with the system (such as a *shell* or a windowing system), diagnostics, surveillance, adjustment, updates and development, etc.

Since this book deals with real-time scheduling, we will focus, in the following, on the functioning of the operating system kernel. A kernel provides the necessary primitives for the creation of tasks and for communication and synchronization. If it is a multi-process kernel, it also provides the corresponding primitives for the processes. Kernels in embedded systems, which represent a large part of critical real-time systems deal, for the most, with only one process, and consequently, we will mainly focus on the handling of tasks.

### 1.3.2. *Real-time operating systems*

Operating systems can be generalist or real-time. A generalist operating system prioritizes flexibility, ease of use and average processing speed. It has to be noted that accelerating the average processing speed using local optimizations can cause instances of tasks whose processing time would be longer than without any optimization. For instance, the principle of instruction preloading will preload and pre-decode the next instructions during the processing of an instruction. However, if the next instruction depends on the result of an operation (conditional jump), the next preloaded instruction could correspond to the wrong operational branch. In this case, which happens rarely for well-designed prediction algorithms, the length of the instructions in time without any optimization could be shorter than the length of instructions with preloading optimization. Moreover, the determinism of the processing time is very much affected by the optimizations. This is the same for devices that prioritize flexibility (for example virtual memory, with the exchange mechanism between central memory and mass storage), or ease of use (for example the automatic update which will use up resources at moments difficult or impossible to predict).

The two most widespread generalist operating systems are *Microsoft Windows* and *Unix*. Both of these occupy a large disk space (around a gigabyte) and have a significant (several hundreds of megabytes) memory footprint (central memory usage).

Embedded CPUs, usually having a small amount of memory (a few kilobytes to a few megabytes of central memory) and a limited computing power (a few megahertz to a few hundreds of megahertz), for a mass storage round one gigabyte, real-time operating systems (RTOS) prioritize memory footprint and simplicity. Moreover, as we will see throughout this book, real-time is not fast, it is deterministic. Indeed, with a few exceptions, the temporal validation methods are conservative: when the system is validated, it is validated for the worst case. Indeed, an important metric characterizing an RTOS is kernel latency: this duration describes the worst delay in time that can elapse between a task-release event and when it is effectively being taken into account by the kernel. The internal architecture of an RTOS is designed to minimize this delay; to the detriment of the average processing speed.

There is a very large number of RTOSs and numerous standards defining RTOSs, implemented in various operating systems. We can point to the *portable operating system interface* (POSIX) standard *pthreads* 1003.1, which defines generalist RTOSs, the Ada standard that is very well adapted to very critical applications such as those which can be found in military and aerospace avionics, the OSEK standard developed by a consortium of European vehicle manufacturers, characterized by a very small memory footprint and a low increase in cost, and proprietary RTOSs such as VxWorks of WindRiver, or *real-time executive for multiprocessor systems* (RTEMS), which define their own primitives and provide a POSIX 1003.1-compliant interface.

### 1.3.3. *Primitives provided by the kernel*

Regardless of the generalist or real-time operating system, a certain number of primitives are provided for the management of parallelism. Since most RTOSs are mono-process, we will focus on the management of tasks. Figure 1.2 represents the possible states of a task such as they are perceived by the kernel. Only the ready tasks compete for the acquisition of computing resources, in other words for a core of a CPU.

– Task creation/deletion: the creation of a task consists of an initialization phase, followed by a launch phase. Initialization consists of designating the entry point of the task, which is generally a subprogram, attributing a control block that will serve to memorize the information important to the kernel in order to manage the task, (identifier, location to save the context of the task when it is preempted, such as the core registers of a CPU) and, except for special cases, allocating a stack for it which it will use to call subprograms and allocating its local variables. The launch phase consists of moving the process to the *ready* state, in other words notifying the scheduling that it is ready to be executed and needs computing resources.

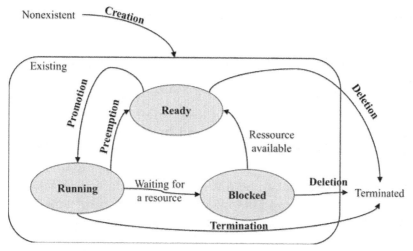

**Figure 1.2.** *Possible states for a task*

– Time management: most operating systems provide wait primitives either until a given date, or during at least a certain amount of time. A task running a wait primitive is moved to the *blocked* state and no longer competes for the acquisition of computing resources. At the given date, the operating system moves the task back into the *ready* state. Let us note that on most material architectures, the management of time is based on programmable clock systems (*timers*) allowing it to trigger a hardware interrupt after a required number of clock cycles. The kernel therefore uses the hardware interrupts generated by the clock in order to wake up the tasks at the end of their wait. There is therefore no computing resource usage by a task during the wait.

– Synchronization: when tasks share critical resources (same memory zone, material element that cannot be accessed in a concurrent manner, etc.), it is necessary to protect access to the critical resources by a synchronization mechanism that guarantees the mutual exclusion of access. Current operating systems propose at least the semaphore tool and some, such as those based on the Ada standard (protected objects) or the POSIX standard (conditional variables), propose the Hoare monitor. When a task is blocked during the access to its critical section, it is moved to the *blocked* state, in other words it is the task that will release the critical section which will move another blocked task to the *ready* state.

– Message-based communication: most operating systems propose mailbox mechanisms based on the producer/consumer paradigm. A producer task generates messages into a buffer and can possibly move to a *blocked* state if the buffer is full. The consumer task can be put to wait for data: it is blocked if the buffer is empty and is woken up at the arrival of a message in the buffer.

– Inputs/outputs: when a task needs to perform blocking input/output, for instance accessing a mass storage unit, reading input from the keyboard, waiting for a frame on the network, etc., it starts the input/output, which moves it to the *blocking* state. The kernel, following the hardware interrupt corresponding to the expected answer from the input/output device moves the task to the *ready* state.

## 1.4. Scheduling

Scheduling, given a set of ready tasks, consists of choosing, on each core, at most one task to run.

### 1.4.1. *Online and offline scheduling*

Scheduling is based on a strategy of choice, which can be static or be based on an algorithm.

In the static case, we use a table in which we have predefined the allocation times of the tasks to the cores, the scheduler is then called a sequencer since it merely follows an established sequence; we then refer to offline scheduling. This type of scheduling is only possible when the times the tasks will be ready are known beforehand, in other words the sequence-creation algorithm has to be clairvoyant.

When we use a selection algorithm on the task(s) to be executed based on the immediate state of the system, we refer to online scheduling. Online schedulers consider the set of ready tasks at certain moments of time in order to choose between them the allocation of the computing resources. No matter the method used to design the online strategy, it has to be resource-efficient. Indeed, the time spent by the computing resources for the scheduler to execute its strategy is called the processor overhead, since it does not directly contribute to the execution of the functionalities of the system. The computational complexity of schedulers must be linear, or even quadratic, in the worst case, depending on the number of tasks.

The moments when the scheduler has to make a choice correspond either to the moments when a task changes state (wakeup, blocking), in other words when there is a change of state in a task of the system, or to moments that are fixed by a time quantum. In the second case, the scheduler is activated at each time quantum and makes a decision depending on the immediate state of the tasks.

In RTOSs, most proposed scheduling algorithms are based on priorities. As we will see later, these priorities can be fixed-task (assigned to a task once and for all its jobs), fixed-job (assigned to a job once it is released) or dynamic.

A scheduling sequence can be represented on a Gantt diagram, such as in Figure 1.3. The time is in abscissa, each line represents the execution of a task, an ascending arrow represents the activation of a task whereas a descending arrow represents a deadline. In this figure, we consider two tasks $\tau_1$ and $\tau_2$ executed once on a processor, with respective durations of 2 and 3 units of time. $\tau_1$ is woken up at time 1 and $\tau_2$ at time 0. We assume that the strategy of the scheduler is based on priorities, and that $\tau_1$ is of higher priority than $\tau_2$. Thus, at time 0, only $\tau_1$ is ready and is given a processor. When $\tau_1$ is woken up, the scheduler preempts $\tau_2$, since the set of ready tasks is $\{\tau_1, \tau_2\}$ with $\tau_1$ of higher priority than $\tau_2$. At the termination of $\tau_1$, the only ready task is $\tau_2$, it therefore obtains the processor. At time 4, $\tau_2$ misses its deadline.

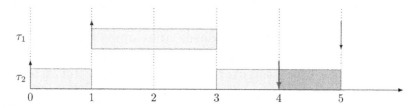

**Figure 1.3.** *Gantt diagram*

### 1.4.2. *Task characterization*

In a real-time system, most processing is recurrent, or even periodic. Each recurrent execution is called an instance or a *job*. Thus, in example 1.1, the reading of the gyro meter will presumably be periodic. Ideally, this would happen continuously, but since we are using a processor, our only choice is to discretize the process. The same applies to most of the input rhythms of the system, which are either periodic when the system needs to scan the state of a sensor, or triggered by the arrival of a message on the network or by another external event.

Each job of each task executes instructions, and consequently, uses up time on the computing resources. A task is therefore characterized by the duration of its jobs. Given that there could be loops with a number of iterations depending on the data, conditional paths, more or less efficient material optimizations determined by the execution time or the data values, etc., the duration of the jobs of a task cannot be considered fixed. In a real-time context, it will be characterized by a *worst-case execution time* (*WCET*). The techniques used to determine the WCET are presented in Chapter 5.

Compliance with time-related requirements is mirrored on tasks by deadlines. In most models, each job is given a deadline that it has to comply with. Since every task can generate a potentially infinite number of jobs, each with a deadline, the temporal constraints are generally represented on a task $\tau_i$ by a relative deadline, often denoted by $D_i$. The relative deadline represents the size of the temporal window in which a job has to be executed from its activation.

Following their activation types, we distinguish between three kinds of tasks:

– Periodic tasks: tasks activated in a strictly periodic manner. A periodic task $\tau_i$ of period $T_i$ is characterized by an initial release time, denoted $r_i$ (as in *release*) or $O_i$ (as in *offset*) in the literature. The first job starts at time $r_{i_1} = r_i$, and the task potentially generates an infinity of jobs, $\tau_{i,k}, k \geq 1$. The $k^{th}$ job $\tau_{i,k}$ is woken up at time $r_{i,k} = r_i + (k-1)T_i$, and its deadline is $d_{i,k} = r_{i,k} + D_i$.

– Sporadic tasks: tasks activated by an event, in such a way that there is a minimal delay between two successive activations. This delay is seen as a minimal period $T_i$. In general the release time $r_{i,1}$ of the first job of a sporadic task $\tau_i$ is unknown, the activation time $r_{i,k} \geq r_{k-1} + T_i$, for all $k > 1$.

– Aperiodic tasks: tasks for which there is no known minimal delay separating two successive activations. In the case where an aperiodic task is given a deadline, we generally retain the right to accept or to refuse processing depending on whether or not we can guarantee compliance with the deadline. When it is not given a deadline, our goal will often be to minimize its response time without affecting the deadline-compliance of the tasks under temporal constraints.

When an external event is periodic, before declaring a task triggered by this event as periodic, it has to be ensured that the timebase (material clock) used by every periodic task of the system is identical. Indeed, let us assume that a task run by a CPU is activated by a periodic message coming from another distant CPU, even if the sending of the message is completely regular from the point of view of the distant CPU, there is a drift, even a small one, which undermines the periodicity hypothesis. Indeed, as we go along, the effective release times of the task woken up by these messages will be more and more offset with respect to a periodic release.

The typical implementation of a periodic task on a RTOS is given in Figure 1.4, and that of a sporadic or aperiodic task is given in Figure 1.5. In the sporadic or aperiodic case, the trigger event is typically indicated by the occurrence of a hardware interrupt, for example, the arrival of a frame on an input/output bus or on a communication network. The distinction between sporadic and aperiodic comes from what characterizes the event expected by the wake-up of the task. In certain cases, the trigger event is characterized by a minimal delay between two successive activations. In case that the minimal delay between two successive activations cannot be determined, the task is aperiodic.

```
periodic task τi
    release=origin+ri // origin gives the time reference
    do
        wait for release
        // code corresponding to a job of the task
        release=release+Ti
    while true
```

**Figure 1.4.** *Typical implementation of a periodic task*

In the case of periodic tasks, the initial release time is usually known, and we then refer to concrete tasks, whereas in the sporadic and aperiodic cases, the trigger event often being external, it is difficult to know in advance the moment when the first job is triggered. We then refer to non-concrete tasks.

```
sporadic or aperiodic task τᵢ
    do
        wait for trigger event
        // code corresponding to a job of the task
    while true
```

**Figure 1.5.** *Typical implementation of a sporadic task and an aperiodic task*

For periodic or sporadic tasks, the relationship between period and relative deadline is of great importance in the temporal study of the systems. We therefore distinguish between three cases for a task $\tau_i$:

– Implicit deadline ($D_i = T_i$): this is historically the first model that has been studied. The deadline of a job corresponds to the release time of the next job.

– Constrained deadline ($\exists i, D_i < T_i$): the deadline of a job precedes the activation of the next job. In this case and in the implicit deadline case+, two jobs of the task $\tau_i$ can never be in competition for the computing resources.

– Arbitrary deadline ($\exists \tau_i, D_i > T_i$): jobs of $\tau_i$ can potentially be in competition for a processor. However, in general, we consider that a job has to be completely terminated before the next job can be executed. We refer, in this case, to the non-reentrance of tasks. Most RTOSs implicitly offer the principle of non-reentrance. For example, on Figure 1.4, a job, which corresponds to an iteration of the "While true" loop, cannot be executed before the end of the preceding job (iteration).

### 1.4.3. *Criticality*

In most temporal analyses, tasks are considered to have strict constraints, in other words in no circumstance can a deadline be violated. Various studies have, however, been carried out on systems with fewer constraint tasks. For instance, the model $(m, k) - firm$ considers that $m$ deadlines out of $k$ have to be respected. More recently, the multi-criticality model was inspired by the criticality levels in civil avionics proposed by the DO178B/C. These levels of criticality represent the cohabitation of more or less strict-constraint tasks in a system of tasks.

### 1.4.4. *Metrics related to scheduling*

The main problem dealt with in the temporal study of an application concerns the deadline-compliance of the tasks, but several other metrics are of interest. In order to illustrate a few typical metrics used to describe a scheduling process, Figure 1.6 represents a fixed-task priority scheduling (the priority is assigned to the tasks, each job of a task is given the priority of the task). Considering the system of tasks, $S$, is composed of three periodic tasks with implicit deadlines (deadline equal to the period) $\tau_1$, $\tau_2$, $\tau_3$ with respective WCETs of 3, 3, 3, with respective periods of 6, 9, 18 and with respective release times of 0, 1, 2. Given a system execution log, which can be called a scheduling sequence, we could characterize for example:

– Start time of a job: time at which the job acquires a computing resource for the first time. For example, in Figure 1.6, the second job $\tau_{2,1}$ of the task $\tau_1$ has a starting time of 3.

– End time of a job: the job $\tau_{1,1}$ has an end time of 3.

– Response time of a job: corresponds to the difference between the end time and the release time. The response time of the job $\tau_{2,1}$ is thus 5. A job complies with its deadline if and only if its response time is not greater than its relative deadline.

– Response time of a task: corresponds to the maximum response time among the jobs of the task. Since there is a potentially infinite number of jobs, we will see in the next chapters how to determine this response time. In Figure 1.6, since the state of the system is the same at time 0 and at time 18 (all the jobs are terminated with the exception of a job of task $\tau_1$ which arrived at that moment), then the infinite scheduling sequence is given by the infinite repetition of the sequence obtained in the time interval [0..18[. Consequently, the response time of the task $\tau_2$ is given by the worst response time of its jobs, in other words 6. For $\tau_1$, we can observe a response time of 3, and for $\tau_3$ a response time of 16. Therefore, since every job complies with its deadline, the scheduling sequence is valid. We say that the system is schedulable by the chosen scheduling policy.

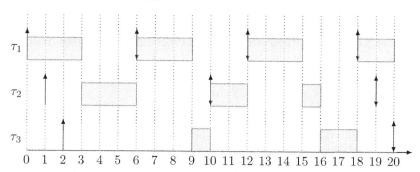

**Figure 1.6.** *Fixed-task priority scheduling of the system S*

– Latency of a job: difference between the current time instant and the deadline of the job. At time 5, the latency of the job $\tau_{2,1}$ is 5.

– Laxity or slack of a job: given by the difference between the latency and the remaining processing time to finish the job. At time 5, the laxity of the job $\tau_{2,1}$ is 4.

– Input/output delay of a job: difference between the start time and end time. Indeed, we often consider for tasks that the inputs are performed at the beginning of the task, and the outputs at the end of the task. The input/output delay of $\tau_{2,1}$ is 3.

– Sampling jitter, response time jitter, input/output jitter: represents the variation, respectively, of the starting time (taking input, sampling for an acquisition task), of the response time of the jobs, and of the input/output delay. The jitters have an impact mainly on the quality of control performed by a corrector from the field of automatic control.

### 1.4.5. *Practical factors*

Various elements influence the behavior of the tasks, mainly the mutual exclusion during the access to critical resources, the synchronous communications between tasks implying precedences between jobs of different tasks, or the access to input/output devices which lead to the suspension of jobs.

#### 1.4.5.1. *Preemptibility and mutual exclusion*

In real applications, tasks may have to share critical resources (shared variables, communication networks, a particular material element, etc.). In this case, as in every parallel application, the resources are protected in order to guarantee the mutual exclusion of their access. Typically, we use mutual exclusion semaphores or Hoare monitors which encapsulate the access to critical resources. This implies that parts of tasks cannot be mutually preempted. Figure 1.7 presents a typical task using a critical shared resource through a semaphore. In this case, we will differentiate between the duration of the code before, during and after the critical section.

Let us consider a system $S_2$ of three periodic tasks $\tau_1$, $\tau_2$, $\tau_3$ run in parallel. Their temporal parameters, of the form $r_i$ (release time), WCET ($C_i$, worst-case execution time), $D_i$

(relative deadline) and $T_i$ (period), are given in Table 1.1. Tasks $\tau_1$ and $\tau_3$ share a critical resource for their entire duration. The mutual exclusion can for instance be ensured by a semaphore $s$. Thus, the entry into the critical section is subject to taking the semaphore $s$, and when a job tries to take $s$ when it is already taken, it is moved to the *blocked* state. At the release of the semaphore, a job waiting for it is moved to the *ready* state and is thus put back into competition for a computing resource.

```
task τ₁:
  release=origin
  do
    wait for release time
    // code before critical section  }— Duration C₁,α
    take resource(s)
    // critical section              }— Duration C₁,β
    release resource(s)
    // code after critical section   }— Duration C₁,γ
  while true
```

**Figure 1.7.** *Typical implementation of a task using a critical resource*

|        | $r_i$ | $C_i$ | $D_i$ | $T_i$ |
|--------|-------|-------|-------|-------|
| $\tau_1$ | 0 | 2 | 6 | 8 |
| $\tau_2$ | 0 | 6 | 15 | 16 |
| $\tau_3$ | 0 | 6 | 16 | 16 |

**Table 1.1.** $S_2$ *system parameters*

We assume that the scheduler is fixed-task priority based, and that the task $\tau_1$ has higher priority than $\tau_2$ which has higher priority than $\tau_3$. Figure 1.8 represents a scheduling of the system when every task lasts as long as their WCET. The dark parts represent the critical sections, which prevent $\tau_1$ and $\tau_3$ from preempting each other.

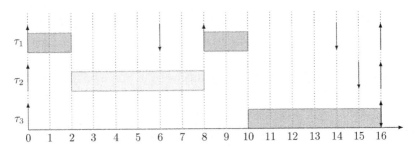

**Figure 1.8.** *Scheduling of system $S_2$*

The scheduling sequence is valid, and the system is in the same state at time 16 as at time 0. In consequence this scheduling sequence can be indefinitely repeated. However, if the system is scheduled online, it would be a serious mistake to conclude that the system is schedulable, since during the execution of the system, it is possible, and even very frequent, that the duration of the tasks is lower than their WCET. Therefore, if the task $\tau_2$ only uses 5 units of time to run, we obtain the sequence in Figure 1.9.

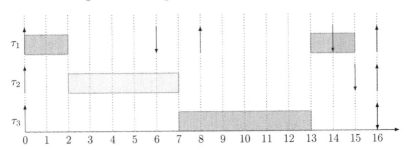

**Figure 1.9.** *Scheduling of system $S_2$ with $\tau_2$
being shorter than expected*

In this sequence, at time 7, $\tau_{3,1}$ is the only active job, it therefore acquires the processor and begins its critical section. At time 8, even though $\tau_{1,2}$ is the active job with the highest priority, it will move into the *blocked* state since it cannot enter into its critical section. It is only at the end of $\tau_{3,1}$'s critical section that $\tau_{1,2}$ is woken up and acquires the processor.

The observed phenomenon is called a scheduling anomaly: while the tasking system needs less computing resources, the created scheduling sequence is less favorable, in the sense that the response time of some tasks increases. When the scheduling is online, several parameters can vary: the parameter which can always vary in the online case is the execution time. When the tasks are sporadic, the period can also vary. In most realistic systems, tasks are likely to share critical resources. An online scheduling of tasks which shares resources can be subject to anomalies when the durations decrease. We say that it is not $C-$sustainable: the concept of sustainability is presented in section 1.5.2. This is the same for the period: if it increases, some response times might increase. Consequently, the online scheduling of tasks under resource constraints is not $T-$sustainable.

The non-preemptive case can be seen as a specific case of critical resource sharing: everything happens as if every task shared the same critical resource, preventing them from being mutually preempted.

### 1.4.5.2. *Precedence constraints*

When tasks communicate by messages, mainly when the messages are transmitted through mailboxes, also called message queues, a task waiting for a message has to wait for the transmission of a message by another task. The receiving task is thus subject to a precedence constraint. On the left-hand side of Figure 1.11, a system of four tasks communicating by messages is presented. The simple precedence model is such that two tasks subject to a precedence constraint (predecessor and successor) have the same period. In every known real-time model, precedence constraints form an acyclic graph. The typical code of the task $\tau_1$ is given in Figure 1.10.

```
task τ₁
    do
        // code before transmission of m₁
        send message m₁
        // code after transmission
        wait for message m₂
        // code after reception of m₂
    while true
```

**Figure 1.10.** *Typical implementation of the task $\tau_1$ presented in Figure 1.11*

A reduction to normal form consists, when every task has the same period, in cutting the tasks around the synchronization points, in other words putting the transmission at the end of task and the wait for messages at the beginning of task. On the right-hand side of Figure 1.11, the task $\tau_1$ is thus cut into three tasks $\tau_{1,1}$, $\tau_{1,2}$ and $\tau_{1,3}$. The reduction is such that, from a scheduling point of view, the systems before and after the reduction are equivalent.

When the communicating tasks have different periods, we refer to multi-periodic precedence constraints. In this case, the reduction is done on job-level instead of task-level, since the jobs of a same task are subject to different precedence constraints.

### 1.4.5.3. *Activation jitter*

The activation jitter is a practical factor commonly employed in cases where the tasks wait for messages coming from a network, or to model the delay that can be taken up by the messages in switched networks. The activation jitter represents the uncertainty regarding the possibility to execute a task as soon as it is woken up. Usually denoted as $J_i$, from a task model point of view, the jitter is such that, given the release time $r_{i,j}$ of a job of the task $\tau_i$, it is possible that it is only able to start its execution at an uncertain moment of time, between $r_{i,j}$ and $r_{i,j} + J_i$. For instance, let us consider a periodic task executed on a distributed system, supposed to be waiting for the message $m_k$ with same period coming from the network. We could pose $J_i$ = response time($m_k$) to represent the fact that the arrival delay of the message $m_k$ with respect to the expected release time of the job can vary between $0$ and $J_i$.

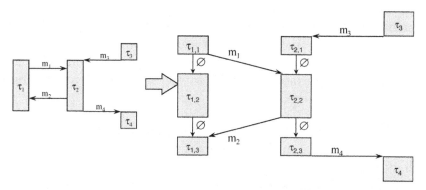

**Figure 1.11.** *Reduction to normal form of precedence constraints when the periods are identical*

### 1.4.5.4. *Suspensions*

Suspensions are another practical factor considered by some task models. Indeed, a task performing, for example, an input/output, is suspended during the operation. For instance, a task which accesses a file on a mass storage device first initiates the input/output and is then suspended, in other words moved to the blocked state, and is reactivated when the input/output device responds. The task is thus suspended during the input/output. The duration of suspension is usually difficult to predict exactly, and is generally bounded by an upper limit.

### 1.4.6. *Multi-core scheduling*

Recent material architectures build on the miniaturization of transistors in order to integrate several computing cores on a single chip. We refer in this case to multi-core processors.

These architectures are already present in non-critical fields, from personal computers to smartphones. They are also to be generalized in critical systems, since from a technological point of view, the miniaturization of transistors approaching the size of an atom, the propagation speed of electric current in the circuits for a reasonable energy and therefore the computing frequency of the processors will soon reach a limit. Since 2005, the increase in processor computing power is therefore mainly ensured by the increase of the number of computing cores and no longer by the increase of computing frequency as before.

Multi-core architectures are more and more complex, and with the increase in the number of cores, the passage of data between the cores is becoming a real problem and can even become a bottleneck. In real-time scheduling, we are therefore not only interested in the scheduling of processes in the cores, but also in the internal network traffic of the processors, which is called *network-on-chip* or NoC. Finally, let us note that numerous multi-core architectures use hierarchical cache memories, which complicates the computing of the WCET.

Figure 1.12 presents these three views: in part $(a)$, a completely abstract architecture, assuming uniform access to memory, is used by the task-scheduling analysis on the processors. In this architecture, we generally ignore the data transmission delays between the cores as well as the migration delays. The migration of a task consists of starting it on one core and continuing on another core. In the mono-core case, the preemption delay is usually assumed to be included in the WCET of the tasks. However, the architecture presented in part $(c)$ shows that this hypothesis is very restrictive, since in the case that a task migrates from core 1 to core 2, only the data from the task present in level 1 cache has to be synchronized, whereas if a task migrates from core 1 to core 3, the data in the level 1 and 2 caches has to be synchronized, which would take more time. In case $(c)$, the data will have a different path to travel depending on the original core and the destination core, which would take a different amount of time. It is therefore important to consider the effective hypotheses after reading the results presented in the multi-processor chapter.

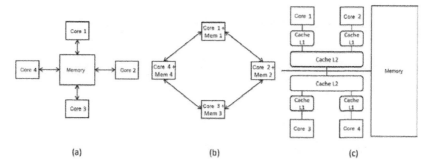

**Figure 1.12.** *Three multi-core views: (1) simplified view of scheduling in the cores, (2) NoC and (3) cache hierarchy and WCET*

One way to reduce the impact of the restrictive material architecture-accounting hypotheses is to limit, or even to remove, migrations. In the multi-processor case, we therefore consider several hypotheses of migration:

– Total: every job can migrate at any given moment in time.

– Task-level: a job can not migrate, but a task can migrate between its jobs.

– None: tasks are assigned to a single core.

These hypotheses result in three types of multiprocessor schedulers:

– Global scheduling: there is a single scheduler for all cores, and a single set of ready tasks. For $m$ cores, the scheduler chooses, at every moment in time, up to $m$ ready jobs to be assigned to a computing core.

– Partitioned scheduling: there is a scheduler for each core. Tasks are assigned to a single core which is then managed as a uniprocessor core. The issue of scheduling is in this case an issue of assignment, which is a knapsack-type of problem.

– Semi-partitioned scheduling: only certain jobs are allowed to migrate, in such a way as to increase scheduling performance with respect to partitioned scheduling, while limiting the impact of migration cost.

We usually consider, even in the multi-core case, that the tasks and the jobs are not parallelizable. However, in some cases, parts of jobs can be simultaneously executed on several cores. For example, we may find *directed acyclic graph* (DAG) task models or parallelizable tasks. In the case of DAG tasks, each graph node is a part of a task which can be parallelized with relation to the other parts of tasks while respecting the precedence constraints between parts of tasks.

## 1.5. Real-time application modeling and analysis

### 1.5.1. *Modeling*

This section summarizes the different parameters and practical factors commonly employed in temporal analysis. These elements are based on the way tasks work in reality.

– BCET, WCET $C_i$: best and worst execution time of each job of a task, also used to represent the transmission time of messages on a communication medium.

– $r_i$: release time of the first job of a task, only known when the task is concrete.

– $D_i$: relative deadline of a task. We distinguish between constrained deadlines, implicit deadlines and arbitrary deadlines.

$-T_i$: period of a task, minimum delay between the activation of two successive jobs of a sporadic task.

$-J_i$: release jitter of a task.

– Critical resources: represents mutual exclusion.

– Precedence constraints: expressed as a DAG, these constraints represent the precedence, often linked to the data, between jobs. Simple precedences link tasks with same periods, while multi-periodic precedences link tasks with different periods.

– Suspensions: represent the suspension time linked to input/output accesses.

Various models have been proposed to closely represent the relationships between the tasks. Thus, for instance, for some sporadic tasks, even if we do not know the activation time of a task in advance, we know the activation scheme of some tasks if we know the activation of the first. Let us assume, for example, that a task is activated by the arrival of a frame on the network, and that this frame is always followed, after a certain delay, by a second frame activating a second task. The activation of the second task is therefore conditional to the activation of the first.

### 1.5.2. *Analysis*

We can break down the view of a real-time system into three parts:

– Computational resources: processors, networks, or switches, these resources allow the execution of jobs or the transmission of messages.

– Scheduling or arbitration: technique implemented to rationally distribute the resources to the jobs or messages.

– Jobs or messages: of recurrent nature, jobs or messages represent the need in computational resources of the application. If the application is real-time, these elements are subject to temporal constraints represented by deadlines.

We will call configuration the set of computational resources, scheduling policies (or arbitration), and jobs or messages together with their constraints.

The temporal analysis of the system can be broken down into several problems:

1) Scheduling: consists of ensuring that for a given configuration, the temporal constraints of the jobs or messages are always respected.

2) Sensitivity analysis: based on a configuration in which certain parameters of jobs or messages are ignored, consists of establishing a domain for these parameters such that the configuration obtained for any value of the domain is schedulable.

3) Dimensioning: based on a configuration in which the computational resources are unknown or partially known, consists of choosing the minimum number of resources such that the configuration is schedulable.

4) Choice of policy: consists of choosing a scheduling policy such that the configuration obtained is schedulable.

5) Architecture exploration: given computational resources, find a task assignment, and communication mapping into messages, mapped into networks, such that the temporal constraints are met.

Every problem is based on the scheduling problem, which is therefore of central importance in this book. The standard definitions related to this problem are as follows:

DEFINITION 1.1 (Schedulability).– *A system of tasks is schedulable by a scheduling algorithm if every job created will meet its deadline.*

DEFINITION 1.2 (Feasibility).– *A system of tasks is feasible if it is schedulable by at least one scheduling algorithm.*

DEFINITION 1.3 (Schedulability test).– *A schedulability test is a binary test returning yes or no depending on whether the configuration is schedulable, or whether the system is feasible.*

Schedulability tests are usually conservative, and we then refer to sufficient tests: if the answer is yes, the configuration is schedulable, but if the answer is no, then it is possible that the configuration is schedulable but the test cannot prove it. In some simple academic cases, accurate tests are available, in other words tests that are necessary and sufficient.

We have seen that in certain cases, such as in the presence of critical resources, scheduling anomalies may occur. In consequence, the sustainability of schedulability tests should be defined.

DEFINITION 1.4 (Sustainability).– *A schedulability test is $C-$sustainable ($T-$, $D-$, $J-$ sustainable, respectively) if, in the case that the answer is yes, the configuration remains schedulable if we reduce the execution times (increase the periods or relative deadlines, reduce jitter, respectively).*

The concept of sustainability, mainly $C-$sustainability, is paramount for every online scheduler. A schedulability test has to be $C-$sustainable in order to be used online. In the case that a test is not $C-$sustainable, for example a simulation for a system sharing resources, then it can only be used offline. Indeed, the scheduling sequence in Figure 1.8 remains valid if it is indefinitely played offline by a sequencer.

## 1.6. System architecture and schedulability

The challenges of temporal analysis are strongly linked to the real-time systems design engineer whose role, during the design of the system, is to fashion the CPUs and the networks and to assign the functionalities of a system to the tasks. This section therefore creates the link between the choice of assigning two communicating functions on tasks, CPUs, networks and the worst-case delay between the beginning of the first function and the end of the second function, assuming, for the sake of simplicity, that the tasks will have an implicit deadline. To simplify things, let us consider two functions $A$ and $B$ running periodically with same period $T$, represented at the center of Figure 1.13. Function $A$ precedes function $B$. For each choice of architecture, we compute the worst-case end-to-end delay $D$, in other words the worst-case delay between the release of $A$ and the end of $B$.

In case (a), the resulting architecture is the sequence in the same task. The task having an implicit deadline and the system deemed schedulable, the worst-case response time of the task is less than or equal to the period, the worst-case end-to-end delay is therefore less than or equal to the period of the task: $D \leq T$.

In case (b), the function $A$ is executed in a periodic task $\tau_A$ with period $T$, which precedes the task $\tau_B$ executing $B$, with the same period. The end of execution of $\tau_A$ triggers task $\tau_B$. There are several possible models to represent the two tasks: the first will presumably be modeled by a periodic task with period $T$. If the system is strictly periodic, the task $\tau_B$ may be modeled by a task whose release time is offset, for example by $T$ with respect to $\tau_A$. In this case, the worst-case execution time is $D \leq 2T$ since each task has to execute in its window of size $T$ and that the two windows are offset one after the other.

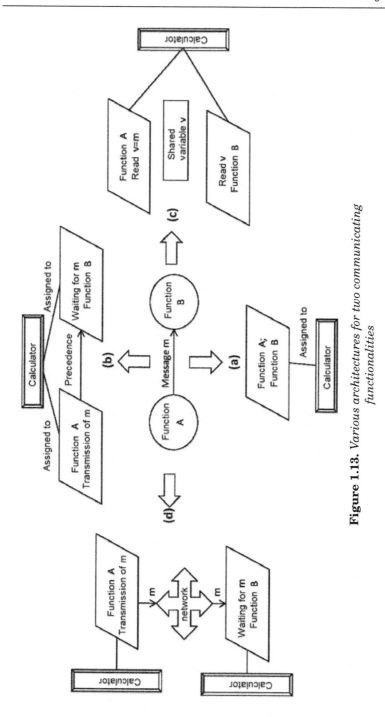

**Figure 1.13.** *Various architectures for two communicating functionalities*

In case (c), the communication of $m$ is carried out in an asynchronous fashion by a shared variable $v$. Assuming that the two tasks are periodic with period $m$, the release case that is the most unfavorable for the end-to-end delay occurs when the task $\tau_A$ which runs $A$ terminates the latest, in other words the variable $v$ is modified $T$ units of time after the release of $\tau_A$. Moreover, we consider that $\tau_B$ has started the earliest possible and read the variable $v$ just before its modification by $\tau_A$. The variable $v$ will be read, at the latest, at the end of the newt period of $\tau_B$, in other words $2T$ later. In consequence, the worst-case delay is $D \leq 3T$.

In case (d), the tasks are placed on two different CPUs, and the message $m$ is transmitted through a communication network. We assume that the message, with period $m$, has a transmission delay less than or equal to $T$ (this will be proven by the schedulability analysis of the network). In the worst case, from the point of view of the processor running the task $\tau_A$, the maximum delay between the release of $\tau_A$ and the transmission of the message on the network is assumed to be $T$ (the system is deemed schedulable), and afterward the transmission delay on the network is at most $T$. At most $2T$ after the release of $\tau_A$, the message arrives on the second processor. Depending on the type of implementation of the task $\tau_B$ running $B$, we could use here several models for this task. If the task is triggered by the arrival of the message, then there has to be $T$ between the moment the message arrives and the moment where $\tau_B$ terminates, which gives $D \leq 3T$. If the task $\tau_B$ is time-triggered, in other words it is executed periodically and at each release it considers the last arrived message, then we are in the case of an asynchronous communication between the arrival of the message on the CPU and its taking into account by the task $\tau_B$, as in case (c), this asynchronism costs at most $2T$, in this case, the end-to-end delay is therefore $D \leq 4T$.

We can thus see that the choice of the software implementation (tasks) and material implementation (allocation to processors and networks) has a very large impact on the end-to-end response time, ranging here from $T$ to $4T$ depending on the choice of architecture. A close analysis of schedulability can strongly help in reducing this delay, for instance by tuning the relative deadlines, it is possible to reduce the windows in which the tasks are executed.

# 2

# Uniprocessor Architecture Solutions

In this chapter, we will take a look at the problems and solutions in real-time scheduling for uniprocessor architectures.

In the first part, we present classical results from the state-of-the-art allowing us to design a real-time system (RTS). These results are based on the expression of feasibility conditions (FCs) that guarantee the compliance with temporal constraints associated with the execution of tasks on a system. We are foremost interested in the characterization of a scheduling problem leading to the definition of task models, temporal constraints and scheduling algorithms for an RTS. We focus on the periodic and sporadic task activation models. We will then look at the main state-of-the-art scheduling algorithms by specifying the contexts for which they are optimal. We will then study the worst-case scenarios as well as the FCs for temporal compliance in a preemptive, non-preemptive context for the scheduling policies based on task-level fixed priorities (FP), job-level fixed priorities (JFP) and dynamic priorities.

Chapter written by Laurent GEORGE and Jean-François HERMANT.

In the second part, we present sensibility analyses that allow us to determine the acceptable limit deviations of task parameters (worst-case execution time (WCET), periods and deadlines), which guarantee the schedulability of tasks. We study in particular the FP- and JFP-type schedulings (the case of Earliest Deadline First (EDF)).

## 2.1. Introduction

Scheduling theory has been widely studied over the past 40 years. Numerous results are available. They allow us to solve the problem of designing an RTS. The design allows us to verify, before its conception, that an RTS complies with timeliness properties associated with the execution of jobs originating from tasks. This design is based on a "worst-case" approach which allows us to guarantee that throughout the lifetime of a system, the tasks will respect their temporal constraints. The worst-case approach is distinguished from average analysis- and simulation-based approaches. Verifying that an RTS is consistent in worst-case allows us to guarantee the property of determinism: for each possible activation scenario, the tasks comply with their temporal constraints.

The methodology usually employed to solve a scheduling problem is the following:

– identify the class of the problem to solve (task model, with temporal constraints and with scheduling considered);

– identify the possible activation scenarios of the tasks in the RTS;

– identify, in the set of possible activation scenarios, the subset leading to the worst cases for the temporal constraint compliance of the tasks;

– determine, for this subset, the associated FCs. An FC is a necessary, necessary and sufficient or simply sufficient test for guaranteeing the compliance of the tasks with the temporal constraint.

– verify that the FCs are met for a given architecture.

The class of a real-time problem is defined by the scheduling model, the task model and the temporal constraint model employed. From the identification of the class of the problem to solve, we can identify the complexity of the problem to solve and deduce the existence of solutions for the problem.

We retrace in a first part the various task models, temporal constraints and schedulings defining the class of a problem. We describe the worst-case scenarios when no particular activation scenario is imposed (non-concrete case). We then study task-level fixed priority schedulings (FP), job-level fixed priority schedulings (JFP) for EDF and First In-First Out (FIFO) schedulers, and dynamic priority schedulings for Least Laxity First (LLF) and round robin (RR) schedulers, and the conditions for which these algorithms are optimal. The optimality property of a scheduling algorithm allows us to deduce the existence of a solution to the scheduling problem. We will then elaborate on the classical FCs for the FP and JFP schedulers.

Most FCs do not allow the deviation of task parameters defined in the specifications of a problem. It could be interesting to study the temporal robustness of FCs, allowing us to guarantee the compliance of the tasks with the temporal constraints, in case of the deviation of parameters of the tasks. This approach, called *sensibility analysis*, has the aim of studying the possibility of introducing more flexibility in the specifications in order to make the FCs more robust, in the design phase. Most state-of-the-art results consider sensibility analyses in which only a single parameter can evolve. We put ourselves in this context in this chapter. The reader interested in multidimensional sensibility analysis may refer to [RAC 06], in which a stochastic approach is proposed when taking into account the variation of several parameters.

This chapter is organized as follows. In section 2.2, we present the various models and concepts that allow us to classify the scheduling problem. We describe the task models, the temporal constraint models, the scheduling models as well as the notations and classical concepts of real-time scheduling. Section 2.3 presents the different state-of-the-art algorithms and specifies the conditions which make them optimal. Section 2.4 introduces the concept of busy period and defines the scenarios which lead to the compliance of temporal constraints of the tasks, for fixed-priority or dynamic scheduling policies. These worst-case scenarios are at the foundation of feasibility tests presented in section 2.5. We will then study the sensibility analyses proposed in the state-of-the-art in section 2.6. We consider the sensibility of WCETs, of periods and deadlines. Finally, we conclude the chapter.

## 2.2. Characterization of a scheduling problem

In this section, we recall a few classical concepts for the characterization of the class of the scheduling problem.

### 2.2.1. *Task model*

We consider a set $\tau = \{\tau_1, \ldots, \tau_n\}$ of $n$ tasks. Various *laws of arrival* have been studied in the state-of-the-art. We distinguish between the following laws of arrival for a task $\tau_i$:

– *periodic* arrival: the activation requests of the jobs of a task $\tau_i$ are periodic, with period $T_i$;

– *sporadic* arrival: the activation requests of the jobs of a task $\tau_i$ have a minimal interarrival time greater than or equal to $T_i$;

– *aperiodic* arrival: single activation request for the duration of the system. This model has been widely studied in presence of real-time periodic tasks. The aim is to allow aperiodic tasks with relative (flexible) temporal constraints in the presence of real-time periodic tasks [SPR 89, STR 95].

In this chapter, we will be looking at the periodic and sporadic laws of arrival.

The *structural model* of a task specifies the constraints associated with the structure of the tasks. We distinguish between:

– *The local structure:*

 - the *sequence*: an elementary task, composed of a sequential code;

 - the task with *precedence constraints*, composed of a set of sequential tasks in a relation of linear precedence or in a graph;

 - the task with *resource constraints*, for which a part of the code accesses a critical resource in mutual exclusion. The critical section is non-preemptive.

– *The distributed structure*, composed of a set of tasks which are executed on several nodes interconnected by a communication network:

 - *the tree*, for which a task executed on a node triggers a set of processes on other nodes, forming a tree (for example multicast tree) without response from the latter ones;

 - *the client / server* (or request/response);

 - *the graph* defined by a set of dependency relations between the distributed tasks.

In this chapter, we will be looking at the task model without precedence or resource constraints. The reader interested in taking into account precedence constraints may refer to the task model called *transaction*, studied mainly in [RAH 12]. We will now introduce the various hypotheses possible in relation with the *activation times* of tasks:

– *Concrete* tasks: a scenario for the first activation times (offset) of the tasks is imposed. When the offsets can be chosen freely by the designer of the system, we refer to offset free systems.

– *Non-concrete* tasks: we do not know the first activation times of the tasks beforehand.

REMARK 2.1.– For the periodic law of arrival, considering a concrete task model means knowing the activation times of all the jobs of the tasks.

We will now introduce the notations specifying the WCET of a task (of sequential type) and the worst-case response time of a task:

– The WCET of a task $\tau_i$ is denoted by $C_i$.

– This worst-case execution corresponds to the execution of the sole task without any preemption from the operating system.

– Several approaches are possible to determine the WCET of a task [PUS 97]. Either by precise analysis of the machine code of the task and the material architecture on which the task is executed, or by benchmark on a real architecture, the value of $C_i$ is more challenging to guarantee, it depends on the conditions of execution (memory, processor cache policy, etc.). An extension of the execution time model has recently been proposed in the framework of probabilistic distributions of execution times (see [BER 02]). Proposing independent execution time distributions, for instance, in the case of cache memory utilization is still a largely open problem.

– The *worst-case response time* $r_i$ of $\tau_i$ is the worst-case duration between the activation request of any job of $\tau_i$ and its termination. $r_i$ depends on the scheduling policy and takes into account the delay introduced by the jobs of tasks with higher priority than $\tau_i$ (see section 2.5). We necessarily have $r_i \geq C_i$.

We now introduce the concept of *jitter* of a task $\tau_i$ denoted by $J_i$:

– The jitter is a delay between an event and its taking into account by the system.

– We refer to activation jitter when this event corresponds to an activation request of a task. Taking the activation jitter into account in the FCs means strengthening the worst-case scenarios (subject the first job of the task to an activation jitter in the case of periodic tasks [TIN 94a]).

– In a networking context, the jitter allows us to model, for a data flow, the variations of the processing times of the nodes visited by this flow and the communication link delays. It is used to compute the end-to-end response time of a flow ([TIN 94b] for the holistic approach, [MAR 04b] for the trajectory-based approach and [LEB 97] for network calculus).

In the aim of simplifying the notation, we will not consider the activation jitter in this chapter. The worst-case scenarios of section 2.4.2 and the feasibility tests outlined in section 2.5 can nevertheless be easily adapted to take this parameter into account (see, for example, [TIN 94a, GEO 96]).

### 2.2.2. *Temporal constraint models*

The aim of these approaches is to guarantee the compliance with temporal constraints for the execution of the tasks of the system. We distinguish between various temporal constraint models:

– The *relative deadline* of a task $\tau_i$ denoted by $D_i$: temporal constraint associated with the worst-case response time of any job stemming from the task $\tau_i$.

– The *latest absolute termination deadline*:

- Each job of a task $\tau_i$ with activation time (release time) $t_i$ must imperatively be terminated at time $t_i + D_i$.

- When $\forall \tau_i, i \in \{1, \ldots, n\}, T_i = D_i$, we then refer to implicit deadlines.

- When $\forall \tau_i, i \in \{1, \ldots, n\}, T_i \leq D_i$, we then refer to constrained deadlines.

- When the deadlines dot not have a valid relation for all tasks (all of them are smaller than / equal to / larger than the periods of the tasks), we refer to arbitrary deadlines.

– The *latest absolute starting deadline*:

- Each job of a task $\tau_i$ with first release time $t_i$ must imperatively begin its execution at time $t_i + D_i$. In the particular case of periodic tasks for which every job has to begin its execution exactly at the time of its release, we then refer to strictly periodic tasks [MEU 07] (absolute starting deadline equal to the release time of the job).

In the following, we will look at the latest absolute deadline constraint model.

### 2.2.3. *Scheduling model*

We will now introduce the various possible constraints for the scheduling of tasks.

Preemptive and non-preemptive scheduling of a task:

– *Preemptive* scheduling: the scheduler can interrupt a running task in favour of another task.

– *Non-preemptive* scheduling: the scheduler has to wait for the task to end in order to reschedule the tasks.

We refer to the *non-preemptive effect* when a job of a lower-priority task delays the job of a higher-priority task (see Figure 2.1). This effect occurs when a job of a high-priority task is released while a job of a lower-priority non-preemptive task is running (see Figure 2.1).

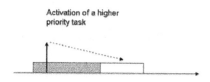

**Figure 2.1.** *Non-preemptive effect*

In this chapter, we consider both kinds of scheduling.

We will now specify the various invocation models of the scheduler:

– Event-driven: the scheduler is invoked upon the reception of an event (new activation of a task, processing of an interrupt, etc.). This scheduling class is traditionally referred to as asynchronous scheduling in the state-of-the-art. It is the subject of this chapter.

– Time-driven: the scheduler determines its invocation times independent of the events taking place in the system. In this class, we distinguish between:

– The periodic scheduler (tick scheduler) which takes into account the arrival of jobs during the last scheduler period. The common period for real-time operating systems is 1 $ms$. The value of the scheduler period has several impacts:

- A delay in taking a task into account is reflected by an activation jitter (see section 2.2.1).

- An additional overhead linked to the execution of the scheduler, limits the value of the period of the scheduler ([BUR 95]).

– The time triggered (TT) approaches [KOP 03] that build a static scheduling table which is imposed on the set of tasks, and this table is periodically run. This scheduling class is also referred to as synchronous scheduling in the state-of-the-art and it assumes, in a distributed context, a synchronization of clocks for interconnected nodes (in FlexRay and TTEthernet networks, for example).

With event-driven scheduling, there is a cost linked to the context switch or to the preemption of the scheduler. In this chapter, we consider that this cost is included in the WCET of the task. Recent works study how to take into account this cost in the FCs [MEU 07], for periodic tasks scheduled with FP. The problem of taking the cost preemption cost into account for non-concrete tasks is still an open one (the case of a synchronous activation is not necessarily the worst-case).

We will consider event-driven scheduling from now on.

The scheduler has to determine the order in which the jobs of the tasks are executed. A very traditional solution is to assign a priority to the jobs of the tasks in order to define this order. The scheduler, once invoked, chooses the job with the highest priority (highest priority first (HPF)). We distinguish between FP, fixed-job priority and dynamic priority scheduling:

– *Fixed-task priority*: the priority of the jobs of a task is identical for every activation, it is inherited from the priority of the task.

– In the following, we will call FP (fixed-task priority) the scheduling algorithms based on fixed-task priorities, with the online algorithm HPF. We will present the more traditional FP algorithms in section 2.3.1.

– *Fixed-job priority*: the priority of a job of a task does not change after being assigned a value, but the priorities of the successive jobs of this task can have different values. We will call JFP this class of algorithms in the following (JFP: job-level fixed priority).

– *Dynamic priority*: the priority of a task can evolve with time.

– In the fixed-job priority scheduling class we will focus, in this chapter, on the FCs for FIFO scheduling (the priority of a job of a task is in fact its activation time even if FIFO does not explicitly need this information) and on EDF in section 2.3.2.

– LLF and RR dynamic priority schedulers are studied in section 2.3.3.

PROPERTY 2.1.– In this chapter, we assume that the priority of a job of a task is higher when its value is smaller.

We will now introduce the concept of idleness of a scheduler:

– A scheduler is said to be *idling* (or non-work-conserving) if it does not necessarily process the tasks as soon as they are activated even though it has nothing to do:

- The EDL server [SIL 99], which executes the tasks at the latest, is an example of idle scheduling which handles aperiodic tasks in the presence of periodic tasks.

- In the networking context, an idling scheduler can generally be used to regulate (shaping) the input and output times of tasks of a communication node.

- We distinguish between two types of regulators: the flow regulator (to avoid overloading the inputs and outputs of a node) and the jitter regulator (to reduce the jitter of tasks in input of a node in a network).

– A *non-idling* scheduler (or work-conserving) is thus a scheduler which cannot delay the execution of a task when it has nothing to do. This type of scheduler corresponds to most schedulers in real-time operating systems.

We will now introduce the concept of the optimality of a scheduling algorithm:

– An algorithm is said to be *optimal* with respect to a class of scheduling problems if it finds a solution to the problem when there is one.

*Contrapositive of this definition:*

– If an optimal scheduling algorithm for a class of problems does not find a solution then there is no solution to the scheduling problem.

### 2.2.4. *Concepts and notations*

Let us recall the traditional concept and notations for uniprocessor real-time scheduling.

The analysis conducted considers time to be *discrete*: the activation times of the tasks as well as the parameters of the tasks are expressed using the same metric: the clock tick. [BAR 90a] show the relevance of this hypothesis using the following facts:

– most schedulers use a clock as temporal reference;

– if every temporal task parameter is expressed using the same clock tick, then, they show that there is a continuous scheduling solution if and only if there is solution in discrete time.

Thus, when the task parameters are integer (multiples of the same clock tick), it is not restrictive to consider that the scheduling times are as well. In the following, we will consider discrete time.

Let $\tau = \{\tau_1 \ldots \tau_n\}$ be a set of $n$ sporadic tasks.

Let us recall a few definitions associated with this set of tasks when the tasks are without activation jitter:

– A set of periodic tasks is called *synchronous* if the first activation request time coincides for every task, and is called asynchronous otherwise.

– $\forall x \in \mathbb{R}$, $\lfloor x \rfloor$ denotes the integer part of $x$ and $\lceil x \rceil$ denotes the ceiling of $x$.

– The *workload* requested by a synchronous task $\tau_i$ in the interval $[0, t[$ is $\left\lceil \frac{t}{T_i} \right\rceil C_i$.

– By analogy, the workload requested by a synchronous task $\tau_i$ in the interval $[0, t]$ is $\left(1 + \left\lfloor \frac{t}{T_i} \right\rfloor\right) C_i$.

– $U = \sum_{i=1}^{n} \frac{C_i}{T_i}$ is the *utilization factor of the processor*, it represents the percentage of utilization of the processor for the execution of a set of tasks [LIU 73].

REMARK 2.2.– An obvious necessary condition is: $U \leq 1$.

– The *demand bound function* [BAR 90b, SPU 96] $dbf(t)$ is the sum of the execution times required by every task in the synchronous scenario in which the activation time and the absolute deadline are in the interval $[0, t]$:

$$dbf(t) = \sum_{D_i \leq t} \left(1 + \left\lfloor \frac{t - D_i}{T_i} \right\rfloor\right) C_i$$

The demand bound function is a measure of the minimum number of jobs that necessarily have to be executed in order to always comply with the deadlines of the tasks.

The scheduling algorithms considered in this article are the following:

– A set of tasks is said to be schedulable by a given scheduling policy if and only if all the tasks comply with their deadlines with this scheduling policy for every possible activation request scenario.

– FP (*Fixed Priority, highest priority first scheduling*), a fixed-task priority scheduling where the priorities are arbitrary:

- for FP, $hp(i)$ represents the subset of tasks with priority higher than or equal to the task $\tau_i$ except $\tau_i$;

- for FP, $\overline{hp_i}$ represents the set of tasks with strictly lower priorities than $\tau_i$;

– EDF scheduling algorithm. EDF schedules the jobs of a task following their absolute deadline. According to EDF, the job of a task with the closest absolute deadline has the highest priority.

## 2.3. Scheduling algorithms/optimality

### 2.3.1. *FP fixed-job priority algorithms*

The optimality of fixed-job priority scheduling algorithms is not general. We can find schedulable task sets with JFP scheduling or with dynamic priority scheduling which respect the deadlines of the tasks even though no fixed-job priority scheduling algorithm is able to do so.

*Rate monotonic (rm) scheduling [LIU 73]*:

– The priority of a job is a function of the period $(T_i)$ of its task. The smaller the period, the higher the priority of the task.

*Optimality*:

– RM is optimal for the preemptive scheduling of non-concrete sporadic or periodic tasks for implicit deadlines.

– RM is not optimal when the deadlines are no longer implicit.

– RM is not optimal for the scheduling of periodic tasks with implicit deadlines but with an offset (free or not) [JOS 82, GOO 97].

– RM is not optimal for the non-preemptive scheduling of tasks [GEO 96].

*Deadline monotonic (DM) scheduling: [LEU 80]*

– The priority of a task is a function of its relative deadline $(D_i)$.

– The smaller the relative deadline, the higher the priority of the task.

*Optimality:*

– DM is optimal for the preemptive scheduling of sporadic or periodic tasks with constrained deadlines. This optimality is dropped when the tasks have offsets (free or not) [JOS 82, GOO 97].

– DM is not optimal in a non-preemptive context.

*fp (Fixed Priority with HPF)*

– This algorithm is to be used when there is no obvious relation valid for all the tasks between the period and the deadline allowing us to infer on the optimality of a particular assignment of priorities;

– or when the priorities are imposed.

*Optimality*:

– Audsley in [AUD 91] proposes an optimal method of assigning priorities: valid with FP for the preemptive scheduling of sporadic or periodic tasks, called optimal priority assignment (OPA) in the state-of-the-art, for non-concrete periodic or sporadic tasks or periodic tasks with an offset (free or not) [AUD 91, MEU 07, GOO 03].

– This method is also optimal in a non-preemptive, non-concrete context (see [GEO 96]).

*Principles of the algorithm:*

– This assignment algorithm operates in an iterative way from the lowest priority ($prio = n$) to the highest priority ($prio = 1$).

– The function search-if-feasible($\tau, prio$) determines whether, in the current set of tasks $\tau$, there exists a task schedulable over the priority level $prio$. It is based on the calculation of the maximum response time of a task (see section 2.5). It returns the first schedulable task $\tau_j$ found or 0 if no task was found, in which case there is no solution to the scheduling problem.

– It has to be noted that if, over a priority level, there are several schedulable tasks, we can arbitrarily choose one of the feasible tasks without undermining the optimality of the assignment of priorities.

We describe the algorithm proposed by Audsley [AUD 91], traditionally called OPA.

---

$\tau = \{\tau_1, \ldots, \tau_n\}$ : **task set**;
prio $\leftarrow$ n : **integer**; j : **integer**
failed$\leftarrow$ false : **boolean**;
**While** ($\tau \neq \emptyset$) **do**
    j=search-if-feasible($\tau$, prio);
    **If** ($j \neq 0$ **AND** failed=false) **then**
        *[we assign the priority $prio$ to the task $\tau_j$]*
        assign-priority(j, prio);
        *[we remove $\tau_j$ from set $\tau$]*
        $\tau = \tau - \{\tau_j\}$;
        prio $\leftarrow$ prio-1;
    **else**
        failed=true;
    **end If**
**done**

---

**Algorithm 1:** *Optimal priority assignment OPA*

Concerning preemptive or non-preemptive fixed-priority scheduling, the non-feasibility of a scheduling problem in a preemptive context does not imply that the problem is feasible in a non-preemptive context (see [GEO 96]) and reciprocally.

More recently, [DAV 11] have introduced conditions under which the OPA algorithm can be applied with a given schedulability condition $S$ for FP scheduling:

CONDITION 2.1.– The schedulability of a task can depend on higher and lower priority tasks but not on the relative order of their priorities. The value of the priorities does not matter as much, it is sufficient to know whether a task has a higher or lower priority in order to infer on its schedulability under the $S$ FC.

CONDITION 2.2.– For two tasks with adjacent priorities, if we swap their priority, the task which then obtains the higher priority cannot become unschedulable under condition $S$ whereas it was schedulable before the priority swap.

It has to be noted that at a given priority level, OPA allows an arbitrary choice of a task in the set of tasks that respect the FC. [DAV 07] introduces the concept of robust OPA algorithm, allowing us, in the assignment of priorities, to optimize a set of additional interference criteria when several tasks can be selected for a given priority level. For example, a priority assignment can thus be more robust (better maintain the schedulability) during processor speed changes.

### 2.3.2. JFP algorithms

In the state-of-the-art we can mainly find two scheduling algorithms: EDF and FIFO. The priority is implicit for FIFO scheduling which is not necessarily used by the scheduling algorithm but is used to establish the associated FC.

#### 2.3.2.1. EDF Scheduling: [LIU 73]

The priority of a task is its latest absolute termination deadline (see section 2.2.2). If $t_i$ is the activation time of a task $\tau_i$ then its priority is $\forall t \geq t_i, t_i + D_i$. The task with the highest priority is that with the smallest absolute deadline.

*Optimality*:

– EDF is optimal for the preemptive scheduling of sporadic or periodic tasks [DER 74].

– EDF is optimal for the non-preemptive scheduling of non-concrete sporadic or periodic tasks [JEF 91].

– This optimality is no longer valid for non-preemptive, concrete periodic tasks [JEF 91].

This algorithm presents very interesting optimality results. However, it is unstable in case of an overload. An avalanche effect may occur: in case of an overload, a lot of time is spent executing tasks which miss their deadlines. Solutions allowing us to handle overload situations are proposed in [LOC 86, BUT 93, KOR 92]. The principle is, in case of overload, to switch to fixed-priority algorithms and eliminate a subset of tasks to stabilize the system.

### 2.3.2.2. *FIFO scheduling*:

FIFO can be considered a dynamic priority algorithm (the priority of a task is in fact its activation time even though FIFO does not explicitly need this information). The implicit priority of a task $\tau_i$ activated at time $t_i$ is $\forall t \geq t_i, t_i$.

*Optimality*:

– FIFO is not optimal for the scheduling of periodic or sporadic tasks.

– FIFO is optimal for the scheduling of non-concrete tasks when the tasks have the same temporal constraints (deadlines). FIFO behaves exactly as EDF in this case.

– FIFO is optimal for minimizing the maximum response time of a set of tasks of equal importance [JAC 55].

### 2.3.3. *Dynamic priority algorithms*

We will now study two dynamic-priority scheduling algorithms: LLF and RR (and variants thereof).

*LLF scheduling: [MOK 83]*

The highest priority task at a time $t$ is the task with the lowest slackness. For each task $\tau_i$ activated at time $t_i$, slackness is defined at time $t$ by: $t_i + D_i - (t + C_i(t))$ where $C_i(t)$ is the remaining execution time for the task $\tau_i$ at time $t$ (see Figure 2.2). Therefore, the priority of $\tau_i$ is $\forall t \geq t_i, t_i + D_i - (t + C_i(t))$.

This algorithm, when two tasks have the same slackness, has the disadvantage of leading to a large number of context switches (we alternate from one task to another).

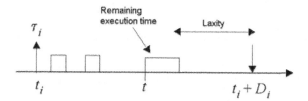

**Figure 2.2.** *The LLF algorithm*

*Optimality*:

– LLF is optimal for the preemptive scheduling of periodic or sporadic tasks [MOK 83].

– LLF is not optimal for the non-preemptive scheduling of tasks [GEO 96].

*RR scheduling: [MIG 03]*

This algorithm is one of the algorithms defined by the 1003.1.b standard. (SCHED_RR is applied to tasks of same priority). Principles:

– Each task is assigned a time quantum for its execution.

– After consumption of its quantum, the task is moved to the end of the queue.

– Therefore, the order of execution is cyclic, the tasks are executed in turns at the rate of their quantum.

*Optimality:*

– This algorithm is not optimal for the scheduling of periodic or sporadic tasks.

– But it is possible to find schedulable configurations with RR even though there are no solutions with FP. An FC for RR can be found in [BRI 04].

In a networking context, variants of RR have been proposed based on Weigthed Fair Queuing (WFQ) which proposes RR scheduling weighted by weights in function of the desired throughput for the stream [PAR 94] and [DEM 90].

## 2.4. Busy periods and worst-case scenarios

### 2.4.1. *Busy periods*

First of all we introduce the concept of *idle time* and of *busy period*, which are at the foundation of most FCs for uniprocessor real-time scheduling:

– *Idle time:*

 - An idle time is a time $t$ such that there are no more active tasks before $t$ which are not terminated at time $t$.

– *Busy period:*

 - A busy period is a time interval $[a, b[$ such that $a$ and $b$ are two idle times and there is no idle time in $]a, b[$.

[KAT 93] show that the first busy period of the synchronous scenario, when the tasks are activated with their highest density (periodic), is the longest busy period possible. Let $L$ be the duration of this busy period.

$L$ is solution of $L = \sum_{i=1}^{n} \left\lceil \dfrac{L}{T_i} \right\rceil C_i.$

This equation can be solved by determining the first fixed point of the series:

$$\begin{cases} Lm + 1 = \sum i = 1n \left\lceil \dfrac{Lm}{Ti} \right\rceil Ci \\ L0 = \sum i = 1nCi \end{cases}$$

The concepts of idle time and busy periods have been extended for a given scheduling policy.

*In the case of* **FP** *scheduling:*

[LEH 90] introduces the concept of a busy period of priority level $P_i$ for a task $\tau_i$.

An idle time of priority level $P_i$ with reference to a task $\tau_i$ scheduled by FP is defined as follows:

– An idle time of priority level $P_i$ is a time $t$ such that there are no more tasks in $\{hp_i \cup \{\tau_i\}\}$ activation before $t$ and not terminated at time $t$.

A busy period of priority level $P_i$ is then defined as follows:

– A busy period of priority level $P_i$ is a time interval $[a, b[$ such that $a$ and $b$ are two idle times of priority level $P_i$ and that there is no idle time with priority level $P_i$ in $]a, b[$.

[GEO 96] and [MAR 05] show that the definition of the busy period of priority level $P_i$ can be extended in a non-preemptive context by taking into account the maximum non-preemptive effect by activating, just before the beginning of the busy period of level $P_i$, a task $\tau_k$ of maximum duration and with period smaller than that of $\tau_i$.

*In the case of* JFP *scheduling:*

The concept of idle time has been generalized [MAR 05] for JFP schedulers and respecting the following property:

PROPERTY 2.2.– The priority of the job of a task $\tau_i$ activated at time $t_i$ is said to be *invariant* if it verifies the following properties: (1) $\forall t \geq t_i$, the priority of the job of $\tau_i$ activated at time $t$ stays the same as that of $\tau_i$ at time $t_i$, and (2) the priority of the job of $\tau_i$ cannot decrease if $t_i$ decreases.

The EDF and FIFO algorithms respect this property. In the following we will consider the EDF and FIFO fixed-job priority algorithms.

DEFINITION 2.1.– *The fixed-job priority $PG_i(t_i)$ of a task $\tau_i$ activated at time $t_i$ is defined by:*

– $PG_i(t_i) = t_i + D_i$ for **EDF** scheduling;

– $PG_i(t_i) = t_i$ for **FIFO** scheduling.

DEFINITION 2.2.– *An idle time $t'$ of priority level $PG_i(t_i)$ is a moment such that every task with a fixed-job priority greater than or equal to $PG_i(t_i)$ and arrived before $t'$ is terminated in $t'$.*

DEFINITION 2.3.– *A busy period of level $PG_i(t_i)$ is a time interval $[t', t''[$ such that $t'$ and $t''$ are two idle times of level $PG_i(t_i)$ and that there is no idle time of priority level $PG_i(t_i)$ in the interval $]t', t''[$.*

The FCs are established by identifying the worst busy periods which lead to the worst FCs of a task.

### 2.4.2. *Worst-case scenarios*

We will now outline the principles of establishing the worst-case scenario for a task $\tau_i$ activated at time $t_i$ allowing us to calculate the response time:

– In a preemptive context we determine the execution end time of the task. If $W_i(t_i)$ is the execution end time of a job of a task $\tau_i$ activated at time $t_i$, then its response time is $W_i(t_i) - t_i$.

– In a non-preemptive context, a task which has started its execution can no longer be interrupted. Therefore, we aim to calculate its starting time. If $\overline{W}_i(t_i)$ is its worst-case starting time then the response time of $\tau_i$ activated at time $t_i$ is: $\overline{W}_i(t_i) + C_i - t_i$.

We give the values of $W_i(t_i)$ and $\overline{W}_i(t)$ in the following section for FP, FIFO and EDF policies in a preemptive and non-preemptive context.

These calculations of the response time use the following property:

PROPERTY 2.3.– The worst-case feasibility conditions are obtained when the tasks are at their maximum density (periodic).

*For FP scheduling:*

– *Worst-case preemptive FP scenario:*

PROPERTY 2.4.– The worst-case response time of a task $\tau_i$ is obtained for FP scheduling in a preemptive context in the first busy period of priority $P_i$ of the worst-case scenario in which every task with priority greater than or equal to $\tau_i$ is synchronous at the beginning of the busy period (see Figure 2.3)

[LEH 90] shows, in a preemptive context, that the largest busy period $L_i$ of priority level $P_i$ is obtained for a task $\tau_i$ in scenario 2.3. Moreover, $L_i$ is the solution to:

$$L_i = \sum_{\tau_j \in hp_i \cup \{\tau_i\}}^{n} \left\lceil \frac{L_i}{T_j} \right\rceil C_j.$$

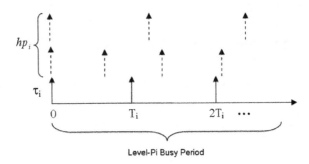

**Figure 2.3.** *Worst-case preemptive FP scenario for a task* $\tau_i$

*– Worst-case non-preemptive FP scenario:*

This property is extended in a non-preemptive context as follows:

PROPERTY 2.5.– The worst-case response time of a task $\tau_i$ is obtained for FP in a non-preemptive context in the first busy period of priority $P_i$ of the scenario in which every task of higher or equal priority to $\tau_i$ is synchronous at the beginning of the busy period and a task with lower priority and of maximum duration is activated one clock tick before (at time $-1$) the beginning of the busy period of level $P_i$ (see Figure 2.4).

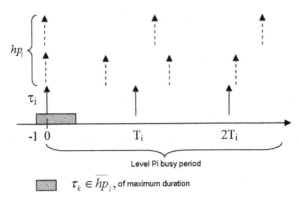

**Figure 2.4.** *Worst-case non-preemptive FP scenario for a task* $\tau_i$

$L_i$ is then solution of:

$$L_i = \sum_{\tau_j \in hp_i \cup \{\tau_i\}}^{n} \left\lceil \frac{L_i}{T_i} \right\rceil C_i + max^*_{\tau_k \in \overline{hp_i}} (C_k - 1).$$

REMARK 2.3.– For the task $\tau_i$ with the lowest priority, in a preemptive or non-preemptive context, $L_i = L$.

*For JFP scheduling:*

In this section, we will look at JFP scheduling algorithms with fixed-job priorities which verify property 2. This property is applied to EDF and FIFO algorithms. Let us note that this property also applies to FP. However, in the case of FP, the worst-case scenarios presented previously are simpler.

Let us consider a busy period of level $PG_i(t_i)$ in which a job of a task $\tau_i$ is activated at time $t_i$.

PROPERTY 2.6.– A job of a task $\tau_j$ is said to have a *potentially higher priority* than a job of a task $\tau_i$ if there exists at least one activation time $t_j$ of $\tau_j$ for which $\tau_j$ has a higher priority than $\tau_i$ activated at time $t_i$ in this busy period.

Following property 2, $\tau_j$ is declared to have potentially higher priority than $\tau_i$ activated at time $t_i$ if the priority of $\tau_j$ activated at time $t_j = 0$, beginning of the busy period of level $PG_i(t_i)$, is greater than that of $\tau_i$ activated at time $t_i$. We formally determine the sets:

– $hp_i(t_i) = \{\tau_j, j \neq i, \ such \ that \ PG_j(0) \leq PG_i(t_i)\}$;

– $\overline{hp_i}(t_i) = \{\tau_j, \ such \ that \ PG_j(0) > PG_i(t_i)\}$.

The tasks $\tau_j \in hp_i(t_i)$ are in the set of tasks with potentially higher priorities than $\tau_i$ activated at time $t_i$, the tasks $\tau_j \in \overline{hp_i}(t_i)$ are of higher priority than $\tau_i$.

– *Worst-case preemptive JFP scenario:*

The following property [GEO 96, MAR 05] determines the scenario leading to the worst-case response time for a job of a task $\tau_i$ activated at time $t_i$ in a busy period of level $PG_i(t_i)$.

PROPERTY 2.7.– The worst-case response time of a job of the task $\tau_i$ scheduled by a JFP scheduling algorithm, with fixed-job priority, activated at time $t_i$ in a busy period of priority $PG_i(t_i)$ is obtained in the worst-case scenario where every task with a potentially higher priority than $\tau_i$ is synchronous at the beginning of the busy period of priority level $PG_i(t_i)$. The first job of $\tau_i$ is activated at time $t_i^0 = t_i$ *mod* $T_i$ such that $0 \leq t_i^0 \leq T_i - 1$ (see Figure 2.5).

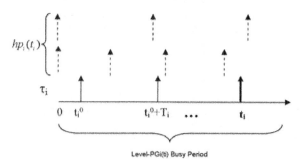

**Figure 2.5.** *Worst-case preemptive scenario for JFP*

In order to find the worst-case response time of a task $\tau_i$, we have to test every time $t_i$ of type $t_i^0 + kT_i, k \in \mathbb{N}$ in $[0, L[$, where $t_i^0$ is an initial activation time of a job of $\tau_i$ in a busy period, such that $0 \leq t_i^0 < T_i$.

The following lemma allows us to reduce the number of points to test and shows a certain analogy with FP scheduling by determining the maximum duration of a busy period of level $PG_i(t_i)$ initiated at time $t_i^0$.

LEMMA 2.1.– The worst-case response time of a task $\tau_i$ is obtained for a task scheduled at time $t_i = t_i^0 + k \cdot T_i$, with $t_i^0 \in [0, T_i - 1]$, $k \in \mathbb{N} \cap [0, K]$ and $K$ is the smallest integer such that $t_i^0 + (K + 1) \cdot T_i \geq \mathcal{B}_i(t_i^0)$, where:

$$\mathcal{B}_i(t_i^0) = \sum_{\tau_j \in hp_i} \left\lceil \frac{\mathcal{B}_i(t_i^0)}{T_j} \right\rceil \cdot C_j + \left\lceil \frac{\mathcal{B}_i(t_i^0) - t_i^0}{T_i} \right\rceil \cdot C_i.$$

We recall the analogy with the busy period of level $P_i$ for FP scheduling, but for a larger set of activation scenarios ($T_i$ activation scenarios for $\tau_i$ which begin at time $t_i^0$, with $t_i^0 \in [0, T_i - 1]$).

– *Worst-case scenario for non-preemptive JFP:*

By analogy, the worst-case scenario to maximize the response time of a task $\tau_i$ activated at time $t_i$ in a busy period of priority $PG_i(t_i)$ with fixed-job priority scheduling in a non-preemptive context is that of the preemptive context by considering a non-preemptive effect at the beginning of the busy period of priority level $PG_i(t_i)$. This non-preemptive effect is maximum when we run at time $-1$ a task with maximum duration in $\overline{hp_i}$.

Thus, determining the worst-case response time of a preemptive or non-preemptive task $\tau_i$ scheduled by a fixed-job priority scheduling algorithm respecting the second property is obtained by calculating the response time of a job of $\tau_i$ activated at time $t_i$ bounded by $L$ in a busy period of level $PG_i(t_i)$. The calculations in Lemma 1 have to be adapted to take into account the non-preemptive effect as follows [MAR 05]:

$$\mathcal{B}_i(t_i^0) = \sum_{\tau_j \in hp_i} \left\lceil \frac{\mathcal{B}_i(t_i^0)}{T_j} \right\rceil \cdot C_j$$

$$+ \left\lceil \frac{\mathcal{B}_i(t_i^0) - t_i^0}{T_i} \right\rceil \cdot C_i + \max_{\tau_k \in \overline{hp_i}}^{*} (C_k - 1).$$

This lemma is applied in section 2.5 for calculating the worst-case response time of a task scheduled by FIFO and EDF.

## 2.5. Feasibility conditions

The FCs established in the state-of-the-art are based on the study of critical periods of activity for the schedulability of the tasks. Let us now recall the concepts of idle and busy period of the processor identifying the useful periods of activity of the processor to bound the interval of arrival times of the tasks to consider in order to establish their schedulability:

– an idle time $t$ is defined on a processor as the moment such that the tasks having an activation request before $t$ be terminated at time $t$;

– a busy period of the processor is defined as a time interval $[a, b[$ such that there is no idle time in $[a, b[$ (the processor is continuously occupied by executing the tasks) and such that $a$ and $b$ are idle times:

- the first synchronous busy period is the first busy period of the synchronous scenario in which all the tasks are activated simultaneously at time 0;

- the duration of the first synchronous busy period is denoted by $L$. Its value is the first solution of the equation $W(t) = t$, with $W(t) = \sum_{j=1}^{n} \lceil \frac{t}{T_i} \rceil C_i$ [BAR 90a]. $W(t)$ is the amount of work corresponding to every activation request of the tasks in the interval $[0, t[$ in the synchronous scenario. If $U \leq 1$ then $L$ is bounded by $U.lcm(T_1, \ldots, T_n)$ (least common multiple (lcm)).

### 2.5.1. *FP feasibility conditions*

If $r_i$ is the worst-case response time of a task $\tau_i$ then a necessary and sufficient condition (NSC) of feasibility is: $\forall i \in \{1, \ldots, n\}, r_i \leq D_i$ and $U \leq 1$. This NSC is valid in preemptive and non-preemptive contexts. We will now recall the various results which allow us to determine whether a set of tasks respects its temporal constraints.

*Preemptive FP scheduling:*

General FC [LEH 90, TIN 95]

This FC consists of calculating, in the first busy period of level $P_i$, the successive completion times $W_i(t)$ of $\tau_i$, activated at times in $0, T_i, 2T_i, \ldots \left\lfloor \frac{L_i}{T_i} \right\rfloor$ (see section 2.4.2).

THEOREM 2.1.– The worst-case response time of a task $\tau_i$ scheduled by FP is the solution of $r_i = max_{t \in S}(W_i(t) - t)$ where $W_i(t)$ is the solution of: $W_i(t) = (1 + \left\lfloor \frac{t}{T_i} \right\rfloor)C_i + \sum_{\tau_j \in hp_i} \left\lceil \frac{W_i(t)}{T_j} \right\rceil C_j$ and $S = \{kT_i, k \in \{0, \ldots, K\}\}$ where $K$ is such that $W_i(KT_i) \leq (K+1)T_i$.

$W_i(t)$ is the completion time of the task $\tau_i$ activated in a busy period of level $P_i$ (see section 2.4.2). The task $\tau_i$ activated at $KT_i$ terminates before its next request activated is at $(K+1)T_i$, it verifies $W_i(KT_i) \leq (K+1)T_i$. Therefore, time $W_i(KT_i)$ is an idle time of level $P_i$, there are no more tasks with priority higher than or equal to $\tau_i$ activated before $W_i(KT_i)$ since if there were, $\tau_i$ activated at $KT_i$ would not be terminated at $W_i(KT_i)$. Thus, we have $W_i(KT_i) = L_i$.

*Special cases:*

– In the special case where the deadlines are constrained ($\forall i, D_i \leq T_i$), we impose that the first job of a task $\tau_i$ activated at time 0 in the worst-case scenario be terminated at the latest at $D_i \leq T_i$. Thus, we have, following theorem 2.1, $K = 0$ and $W_i(t) = C_i + \sum_{\tau_j \in hp_i} \left\lceil \frac{W_i(t)}{T_j} \right\rceil$. The worst-case response time of $\tau_i$ is then the solution of: $r_i = W_i(r_i)$ [JOS 86], calculated in a recursive manner.

[LEH 91] have proposed a non-recursive FC for *Deadline Monotonic (DM)* scheduling, in the case of constrained-deadline tasks. The principle of this theorem is the following.

For a task $\tau_i$, its worst-case response time $r_i$ is the solution of $r_i = W_i(r_i)$. Therefore, it has to exist if $\tau_i$ is schedulable at a time $t$, with $r_i \leq t \leq D_i$, such that $W_i(t) \leq t$ otherwise $\tau_i$ would not be schedulable. This time $t$ necessarily exists for a time in the set $S_i$ of theorem 2.2. For this time, $W_i(t)/t \leq 1$. This test is based on the sensitivity analyses proposed for FP scheduling in section 2.6.1.1.

THEOREM 2.2.– [LEH 91] Let $\tau = \{\tau_1, \ldots, \tau_n\}$ be a set of periodic tasks indexed by relative ascending deadlines, with constrained deadlines scheduled by DM. A task $\tau_i$ is schedulable if and only if:

$$X_i = \min_{t \in S_i} \frac{W_i(t)}{t} \leq 1$$

where $S_i = \{D_i\} \cup \{kT_j : \tau_j \in hp(i), k = 1 \ldots \left\lfloor \frac{T_i}{T_j} \right\rfloor\}$

The set of tasks $\tau$ is schedulable if and only if: $max_{i=1\ldots n}X_i \leq 1$

This test presents the interest of being non-recursive but the number of times to consider can potentially be large. For sets of tasks with arbitrary deadlines, [TIN 95] shows that the worst-case response time of a task $\tau_i$ is not necessarily obtained for the first activation request of $\tau_i$ at time 0. The maximum number of activation requests of $\tau_i$ to consider is $1 + \left\lfloor \frac{L_i}{T_i} \right\rfloor$, where $L_i$ is the length of the first synchronous busy period of level $\tau_i$ [LEH 90]. We have $L_i = \sum_{\tau_j \in hp(i) \cup \tau_i} \left\lceil \frac{L_i}{T_j} \right\rceil C_j$ where $L_i$ is bounded by $(\sum_{\tau_j \in hp(i) \cup \tau_i} \frac{C_j}{T_j}).lcm(T_1, \ldots, T_i)$ leading to an FC of pseudo-polynomial complexity, which is difficult to use for a sensitivity analysis.

– In the special case where $\forall i, D_i = T_i$, with RM scheduling, a sufficient condition of feasibility for a set of sporadic or periodic tasks has been proposed by Liu and Layland in [LIU 73] (proof corrected in [DEV 00]): $U \leq n(2^{1/n} - 1)$. This leads to guaranteeing the feasibility of tasks at least when the processor load is smaller than 69%. [BIN 03] improves this sufficient condition by proposing the following test: $\Pi_{i=1}^{n}(1 + \frac{C_i}{T_i}) \leq 2$. The gain with respect to the bounds set by Liu and Layland [LIU 73] in terms of schedulability tends to $\sqrt{2}$ when $n$ tends to infinity.

*Non-preemptive FP Scheduling:*

A first approach to calculating the worst-case response times is the calculation of the response times in the preemptive context adding the maximum non-preemptive effect. This approach leads to sufficient but not necessary FCs, by potentially taking into account the tasks with higher priority than $\tau_i$ even though $\tau_i$ has begun its execution.

In the following we will be looking at the necessary and sufficient FCs [GEO 96].

This FC consists of calculating, in the first busy period of priority level $P_i$, the successive starting execution times $\overline{W}_i(t)$ of $\tau_i$, activated at times $t$ in $0, T_i, 2T_i, \ldots \left\lfloor \frac{L_i}{T_i} \right\rfloor$ (see section 2.4.2).

THEOREM 2.3.– The worst-case response time of a task $\tau_i$ scheduled by FP is the solution of $r_i = max_{t \in S}(\overline{W}_i(t) + C_i - t)$ where $\overline{W}_i(t)$ is the solution of:

$$\overline{W}_i(t) = \left\lfloor \frac{t}{T_i} \right\rfloor C_i + \sum_{\tau_j \in hp_i} \left(1 + \left\lfloor \frac{W_i(t)}{T_j} \right\rfloor\right) C_j + max^*_{\tau_k \in \overline{hp_i}}(C_k - 1)$$

and $S = \{kT_i, k \in \{0, \ldots, K\}\}$ where $K$ is such that $L_i \leq (K + 1)T_i$.

We can notice that, other than in the preemptive case, we count the higher priority tasks in a closed interval (in $[0, W_i(t)]$) and that only the times of $\tau_i$ activated before $t$ are taken into account.

## 2.5.2. *JFP feasibility conditions*

### 2.5.2.1. *Feasibility conditions for EDF*

There are two ways to solve a feasibility problem of a set of sporadic or periodic tasks scheduled by EDF. The first approach consists of using the demand bound function $dbf(t)$ (see section 2.2.4). The second approach is based on calculating the worst-case response time of a task. The complexity of the test based on $dbf(t)$ is the weakest.

*Feasibility tests of EDF in preemptive context*

*– Test based on* $dbf(t)$

[BAR 90a] proposes an NSC of feasibility based on $dbf(t)$ in a preemptive context. The authors show that an NSC for the feasibility of a set of sporadic or periodic tasks is to verify, in the worst-case synchronous scenario for every task $\tau_i$ such that $D_i \leq t$, that $dbf(t) \leq t$. If by assumption the synchronous scenario is a worst-case scenario for the feasibility of tasks with EDF, then it is necessary to test whether $dbf(t) \leq t$ after $L$ (see section 2.4.1). Indeed, the scenario which restarts at the earliest at $L$ is either synchronous, and therefore already tested, or asynchronous and therefore not the worst-case. By only taking into account the variation times of $dbf(t)$ to the absolute deadlines of the tasks, we obtain the following theorem:

THEOREM 2.4.– An NSC of feasibility for EDF in a preemptive context is: $\forall t \in S, dbf(t) \leq t$, where $S = \cup_{i=1}^{n}\{kTi + D_i, k \in \mathbb{N}\} \cap [0, L[$.

*Special case:*

– When $\forall i \in \{1, \ldots, n\}$, $D_i \geq T_i$, [BAR 90a] then shows that there is a strict equivalence between theorem 3 and the condition $U \leq 1$. In this context, $U \leq 1$ is thus an NSC of feasibility for preemptive EDF. This result has already also been expressed in [LIU 73] in the case $\forall i \in \{1, \ldots, n\}$, $D_i = T_i$.

[BAR 90a] proposes an NSC for the schedulability of a set of periodic tasks valid for sets of tasks with arbitrary deadlines. The principle is to ensure that for every time $t$ in the interval $[0, L[$ corresponding to an absolute deadline, the demand bound function $dbf(t)$ cumulating the amount of work of all the tasks which have reached their deadlines in $[0, t]$ is smaller than or equal to $t$, the maximum amount of work executed by the processor at time $t$. Theorem 2.5 recalls this result.

THEOREM 2.5.– [BAR 90a] A set of periodic tasks with arbitrary deadlines is schedulable by EDF if and only if:

$$\forall t \in \bigcup_{i=1...n} \{kTi + D_i, k \in N\} \bigcap [0, L), dbf(t) \leq t.$$

In the special case where $\forall \tau_i \in \tau, D_i \geq T_i$, theorem 2.5 is equivalent to $U \leq 1$ [BAR 90a].

– *Calculating $r_i$ for preemptive EDF*

Let $t_i$ be the activation time of a task $\tau_i$ in a busy period of level $PG_i(t_i)$. We have $PG_i(t_i) = P_i(t_i, t_i) = t_i + D_i$.

This calculation is based on a worst-case scenario for JFP scheduling determined in section 2.4.1. With EDF, we have $hp_i(t_i) = \{\tau_j, j \neq i / D_j \leq t_i + D_i\}$ and $\overline{hp}_i(t_i) = \{\tau_j, / D_j > t_i + D_i\}$.

The tasks which can impede $\tau_i$ activated at $t_i$ are:

– The tasks $\tau_j$ in $hp_i(t_i)$ with a deadline smaller than or equal to that of $\tau_i$ (with absolute deadline $t_i + D_i$) activated at $t_i$. For a task $\tau_j$ with deadline $D_j$, there are at most $1 + \left\lfloor \frac{t_i + D_i - D_j}{T_j} \right\rfloor$, contrarily to FP scheduling in which a task with higher priority can always delay $\tau_i$ if $\tau_i$ is not terminated.

– The previous activations of $\tau_i$. There are at most $1 + \left\lfloor \frac{t_i}{T_i} \right\rfloor$.

For the calculation of the maximum worst-case preemptive EDF response time, the same calculation concept of the FP fixed point arises, with the difference that more points need to be tested than with FP, where only the activation times of $\tau_i$ in the synchronous scenario have to be tested. With EDF, we have to, in principle, test every time $t_i \in \cup\{\{t_i^0 + kT_i, k \in \mathbb{N}, 0 \leq t_i^0 < T_i\} \cap [0, L[$.

[SPU 96] lies at the origin of this result. The theorem proposes a different, slightly optimized presentation of it.

THEOREM 2.6.– The worst-case response time of a task $\tau_i$ scheduled by EDF is given by: $r_i = \max_{t \in S_i} \{W_i(t) - t\}$ where:

$$W_i(t) = \sum_{\tau_j \in hp_i(t)} min(\left\lceil \frac{W_i(t)}{T_j} \right\rceil, 1 + \left\lfloor \frac{t + D_i - D_j}{T_j} \right\rfloor) \cdot C_j$$

$$+(1 + \left\lfloor \frac{t}{T_i} \right\rfloor) \cdot C_i$$

and $S_i = \quad *{-}.2ex\bigcup_{t_i^0=0}^{T_i-1} \quad *{-}.2ex S_i(t_i^0)$, with $S_i(t_i^0)$ the set of times $t$ such that $t = t_i^0 + k \cdot T_i$ such that:

– $t_i^0 \in [0, T_i - 1[$;

– $k \in \mathbb{N} \cap [0, K]$, with $K$ the smallest integer such that: $t_i^0 + (K+1)T_i \leq B_i(t_i^0)$;

– $t_i^0$ belongs to a busy period with priority level $PG_i(t_i^0)$.

REMARK 2.4.– $B_i(t_i^0)$ is calculated following the formula given in section 2.4.2 for JFP in a non-preemptive context.

*EDF in non-preemptive context – Test based on $dbf(t)$*

[GEO 96] extends the test based on $dbf(t)$ and shows that in this we have to take into account, at a time $t$, every synchronous task having at least one deadline in the interval $[0, t]$ (in $dbf(t)$) as well as the non-preemptive effect of a task with lower priority in the EDF sense which, placed at time 0, would have a deadline $D_k > t$, of maximum duration (by convention, this quantity is nil if there is no lower-priority task).

THEOREM 2.7.– An NSC of feasibility for EDF in the non-preemptive context is: $\forall t \in S, dbf(t) + max^*_{T_k, D_k > t}\{C_k - 1\} \leq t$, where $S = \cup^n_{i=1}\{kTi + D_i, k \in \mathbb{N}\} \cap [0, L[$.

*Special case: [JEF 91]*

In the special case where $\forall i, D_i = T_i$, the test is simplified as follows:

LEMMA 2.2.– An NSC of feasibility for EDF in the non-preemptive context is: $\forall t \in S, dbf(t) + max^*_{T_k, D_k > t}\{C_k - 1\} \leq t$, where $S = \cup^n_{i=1}\{kTi + D_i, k \in \mathbb{N}\} \cap [0, max_{j=1...n}(D_j)[$.

Indeed, beyond $max_{j=1...n}(D_j)$, the non-preemptive effect will disappear and the equivalence $dbf(t) \leq t$ and $U \leq 1$ is verified as in the preemptive case.

*– Calculating $r_i$ for non-preemptive EDF*

Calculating the non-preemptive EDF response time is done with a similar approach as in the preemptive case. However, we have to take into account the non-preemptive effect due to the tasks in $\overline{hp}_i(t)$. Moreover, we calculate the influence of the tasks with higher priority than $\tau_i$ in $[0, \overline{W}_i(t)]$.

THEOREM 2.8.– The worst-case response time of a task $\tau_i$ scheduled by non-preemptive EDF is given by:

$$r_i = \max_{t \in \mathcal{S}_i}\left\{\overline{W}_i(t) - t + C_i\right\}$$

where:

$$\overline{W}_i(t) = \sum_{\tau_j \in hp_i(t)} \left( 1 + \left\lceil \frac{\min(t + D_i - D_j; \overline{W}_i(t))}{T_j} \right\rceil \right) C_j$$

$$+ \left\lfloor \frac{t}{T_i} \right\rfloor C_i + max^*_{\tau_j \in \overline{hp}_i(t)} (C_j - 1)$$

and

$$\mathcal{S}_i = \quad *-.2ex \bigcup_{t_i^0 = 0}^{T_i - 1} \quad *-.2ex \mathcal{S}_i(t_i^0),$$

with $\mathcal{S}_i(t_i^0)$ the set of times $t = t_i^0 + k \cdot T_i$ such that:

$- t_i^0 \in [0, T_i[$ ;

$- k \in \mathbb{N} \cap [0, K]$, with $K$ the smallest integer such that: $t_i^0 + (K+1)T_i \geq B_i(t_i^0)$.

REMARK 2.5.– $B_i(t_i^0)$ is calculated following the formula given in section 2.4.2 for JPJL in a non-preemptive context.

### 2.5.2.2. FIFO feasibility conditions

In this section, we will recall two results related to uniprocessor scheduling. The first result is valid for every scheduler. The second result applies to FIFO scheduling.

With FIFO, the priority of a task is its activation time. Every task activated at the latest at time $t_i$ is, therefore, of higher priority than $\tau_i$. Therefore, we have $PG_i(t_i) = P_i(t, t_i) = t_i$ and $hp_i(t) = \{\tau_j, j \neq i\}$.

LEMMA 2.3.– The response time $r_{i,t}$ of a task $\tau_i$ activated at $t$ in a busy period of level $PG_i(t)$ is:

$$W_{i,t} = (1 + \left\lfloor \frac{t - t_i^0}{T_i} \right\rfloor) C_i + \sum_{\tau_j \in hp_i(t)} (1 + \left\lfloor \frac{t - t_i^0}{T_i} \right\rfloor) C_j.$$

This lemma can be simplified by noticing that $(1 + \lfloor \frac{t-t_i^0}{T_i} \rfloor)C_i = (1 + \lfloor \frac{t}{T_i} \rfloor)C_i$ since $0 \leq t_i^0 < T_i$. But, $t$ is bounded by $L$ (see section 2.4.1).

Therefore, we have the theorem giving the FIFO response time of a task:

THEOREM 2.9.– The worst-case response time $r_i$ of a task $\tau_i$ is the solution of:

$$r_i = max_{t<L} \sum_{\tau_j \in \tau} \left( 1 + \left\lfloor \frac{t}{T_j} \right\rfloor \right) C_j - t.$$

For jitter-free tasks, this theorem is simplified as [GEO 96]:

PROPERTY 2.8.– Necessary and sufficient feasibility conditions for a set $\tau = \{\tau_1, \tau_2, ..., \tau_n\}$ of $n$ sporadic or periodic tasks scheduled using FIFO, are that: (1) $\sum_{j=1..n} C_j \leq min_{j=1..n}(D_j)$ and (2) the utilization factor $U$ verifies $U \leq 1$.

## 2.6. Sensitivity analysis

In traditional FCs, the parameters of a task (WCET, period and relative deadline) are considered constant for every activation request of the task. In the following, we will evoke problems which can be encountered in real systems:

– The WCET can be difficult to obtain. The calculation of the WCET is done either by machine code analysis obtained on a given architecture, or by measuring the execution time of the task on a real architecture (see [COL 00] for a thorough study). In both cases, the precision of the WCET is obtained using analyses which can be complex and often with the price of over-sizing resources. Moreover, the observed online execution time a task depends strongly on the execution conditions of a task (architecture type, memory type, etc) sometimes leading to an observed execution time very distant from the WCET.

Furthermore, the WCET analyses do not take into account the possibility of software-design errors which can lead to an overrun of the WCETs.

– Considering that the task parameters are constant is not necessarily adapted to every application. It could be interesting to adapt the task parameters online (for example, it could be relevant to execute an altitude-measuring task of an aeroplane more frequently when the plane is approaching the ground). Moreover, recent architectures allow us to optimize energy consumption and reduce the dissipated heat, by adapting the speed of the processor. A decrease of speed of the processor allows us to save energy but has the effect of increasing the WCET of the tasks. It could be interesting to study the impact of a speed change of a processor in the FCs. Is it possible to extend the obtained FCs for a given processor speed to another processor speed?

– The FCs allow us to guarantee the compliance with the latest termination deadlines. However, for command and multimedia control applications, the jitter after the execution of a task, defined by its maximum response time minus its minimum response time, strongly determines the quality of the control of the process or the visualization of the multimedia stream. If a scheduling algorithm has the property that the response time of a task is as short as the deadline of a task is small, then reducing the relative deadline of a task can allow us to reduce the jitter after execution of the task. The DM scheduling algorithms for FP as well as EDF have this property.

Therefore, it may be interesting to study the temporal robustness of an RTS in the case of variation of task parameters: WCET, period and deadline:

– in the design phase by a sensitivity analysis. The aim is to characterize the acceptable variations of task parameters (WCET, periods and deadlines) for which an RTS still complies with the temporal constraints of the tasks;

– online, if the parameters of the tasks evolve or no longer comply with the specifications. It is then possible to consider errors related to exceeding the WCETs, which can lead to cascade-like breakdowns of deadlines if not properly processed. An algorithm allowing us to stabilize a system in such situations should be implemented to guarantee its robustness. A mechanism based on the transmission of alarms is for instance considered in the case of exceeding the WCET in the AUTOSAR specification, even though there is no solution proposed to process this overrun in the [HLA 07] specification at the present time.

Various approaches are proposed in the state-of-the-art:

– the first approach consists of calculating the multiplicative factor $\alpha$ applies to the WCET, to the period and the deadline of the tasks, such that the set of tasks is still schedulable. The other two parameters are assumed to be constant. This correction can be applied to a task or a set of tasks;

– another approach introduced by [BIN 06b] consists of describing the parametric equation of the $n$-dimensional feasibility domain associated with a task parameter ($C$-space, $T$-space or $D$-space), such that for every vector $X = \{X_1, \ldots, X_n\}$ in the $X$-space (with $X = C$, $T$ or $D$), the set of tasks is schedulable. Let us note that for FP scheduling, most results assume constrained-deadline sets of tasks ($\forall i \in \{1, \ldots, n\}$, $D_i \leq T_i$) due to the complexity of FCs.

We study the state-of-the-art sensitivity analyses of WCETs, periods and deadlines for FP and EDF scheduling. We characterize, in each section, the feasibility domains and approaches aiming to calculate the variation limits of task parameters guaranteeing the schedulability of tasks.

### 2.6.1. *Sensitivity of WCETs*

2.6.1.1. *Sensitivity of WCETs with FP*

2.6.1.1.1. Determination of the $C$-space with FP scheduling

In the case of DM scheduling, the NSC proposed in [LEH 91], revisited in theorem 2.2 has been improved in a significant way in [MAN 98] through a decrease of $S_i$ in the set $S_i'$ defined as follows: $S_i' = \cup_{j=1}^i Q_j^i$ with

$$\begin{cases} Q_i^i = \{D_i\} \\ Q_j^i = \{\lfloor \frac{t}{T_j} \rfloor T_j\}, t \in Q_k^i (j+1 \leq k \leq i) \end{cases}$$

and

$$t < \lfloor \frac{t}{T_j} \rfloor T_j + D_j, 1 \leq j < i.$$

By definition, $S_i' \subset S_i$. $S_i'$ is composed of $D_i$ and a set of activation request times of the tasks from $\tau_1$ to $\tau_{i-1}$. For the task $\tau_{i-1}$: at $t_{i-1} = kT_i, k \in \mathbb{N}$ such that $t_{i-1} \leq D_i \leq t_{i-1} + D_{i-1}$. For the task $\tau_{i-2}$: at two times $t_{i-2}$ verifying for both previous times at $D_i$ and $t_{i-1}$: $t_{i-2} \leq D_i \leq t_{i-2} + D_{i-2}$ and $t_{i-2} \leq t_{i-1} \leq t_{i-2} + D_{i-2}$ and so forth until $\tau_1$, leading to $2^{i-1}$ times at most instead of $1 + \sum_{\tau_j \in hp(i)} \left\lfloor \frac{D_i}{T_j} \right\rfloor$ times.

This same result has also been proposed in [BIN 04] in a recursive form, to determine the $C$-space. With this improvement, [BIN 04] proposes a characterization of the $C$-space for sets of tasks with constrained deadlines, obtained for a reasonable number of tasks with acceptable complexity. The $C$-space is a feasibility domain of $n$ dimensions such that for every vector $C = \{C_1, \ldots, C_n\}$ of WCET in the $C$-space, the set of corresponding tasks is schedulable. The $C$-space is defined by the following theorem [BIN 04]:

THEOREM 2.10.– [BIN 04] Let $\tau = \{\tau_1, \ldots, \tau_n\}$ be a set of periodic tasks with constrained deadlines, indexed by decreasing priority and scheduled using FP. The $C$-space is a domain such that $\forall C = \{C_1, \ldots, C_n\} \in \mathbb{R}^{+n}$: $\forall i = 1 \ldots n$, $\exists t \in S_i' = \mathcal{P}_{i-1}(D_i), W_i(t) \leq t$ where $\mathcal{P}_i(t)$ is the solution of the recursive equation:

$$\mathcal{P}_i(t) = \mathcal{P}_{i-1}\left(\left\lfloor \frac{t}{T_i} \right\rfloor T_i\right) \cup \mathcal{P}_{i-1}(t)$$

with $\mathcal{P}_0(t) = \{t\}$.

The $C$-space feasibility domain is then defined by:

$$Card(\bigcup_{i=1}^{n}\{\mathcal{P}_{i-1}(D_i)\})$$

inequalities. We will now give the example presented in [BIN 04], for which the algorithm of [MAN 98] gives the same result, in the case of three periodic tasks $\tau = \{\tau_1, \tau_2, \tau_3\}$ defined in Table 2.1.

| | $T_i$ | $D_i$ | $\mathcal{P}_{i-1}(D_i)$ |
|---|---|---|---|
| $\tau_1$ | 3 | 3 | $\{3\}$ |
| $\tau_2$ | 8 | 7 | $\{6, 7\}$ |
| $\tau_3$ | 20 | 19 | $\{15, 16, 18, 19\}$ |

Table 2.1. *Set of tasks and critical times*

By applying theorem 2.10, the $C$-space feasibility domain (see Figure 2.6), is reduced to three groups of inequalities in conjunction corresponding to the times to test for the tasks $\tau_1$, $\tau_2$ and $\tau_3$. In each group, the inequalities are in disjunction (the WCETs have to satisfy at least one of these inequalities).

2.6.1.1.2. Margin on the WCETs with FP scheduling

In the case of a set of periodic tasks with implicit deadlines, [LEH 89] have introduced the concept of critical scaling factor

$\alpha$ applied to the WCETs, such that the WCET of a task $\tau_i$ is $\alpha C_i$. This approach has been extended by [VES 94] who shows how to introduce a margin in the response time of the tasks and study a scaling factor applied to a task or a set of tasks.

In the case of constrained deadlines, [BIN 06b] shows how to calculate the multiplicative factor $\lambda$ applied to the set of tasks, such that for every task $\tau_i$, its WCET becomes $C_i + \lambda C_i$. $\lambda$ is the maximum value for the set of tasks to be schedulable. The scaling factor is given by $\alpha = \lambda + 1$. For a given set of tasks $\lambda < 0$ indicates that the initial set of tasks is not schedulable and that the WCET of $\lambda C_i$ needs to be decreased in order to obtain a set of schedulable tasks. The calculation of $\lambda$ is made explicit in theorem 2.11. The complexity of the calculation of $\lambda$ is acceptable by applying theorem 2.10. The principle of calculating $\lambda$ is the following: if we multiply the WCET of tasks in theorem 2.10 by $\alpha$ then we find, for a task $\tau_i$, that there has to exist a time $t \in \mathcal{P}_{i-1}(D_i)$, such that $\alpha \leq \frac{t}{W_i(t)}$, leading, with $\alpha = \lambda + 1$, to $\lambda \leq \frac{t}{W_i(t)} - 1$. $\lambda$ is then the maximum value satisfying $\lambda \leq \frac{t}{W_i(t)} - 1$, for every time $t \in \mathcal{P}_{i-1}(D_i)$. By applying this calculation to all the tasks, the $\lambda$ to be retained is the minimum of $\lambda$s obtained for the set of tasks.

$$\left\{ \begin{array}{l} C_1 \leq 3 \\ \left. \begin{array}{l} 2C_1 + C_2 \leq 6 \\ 3C_1 + C_2 \leq 7 \end{array} \right\} \\ \left. \begin{array}{l} 5C_1 + 2C_2 + C_3 \leq 15 \\ 6C_1 + 2C_2 + C_3 \leq 16 \\ 6C_1 + 3C_2 + C_3 \leq 18 \\ 7C_1 + 3C_2 + C_3 \leq 19 \end{array} \right\} \end{array} \right.$$

**Figure 2.6.** *Inequalities describing the FP feasibility domain*

THEOREM 2.11.– [BIN 06b] The maximum multiplicative factor $\lambda$ for which the WCET of every task $\tau_i, i \in [i, n]$ becomes $C_i + \lambda C_i$ guaranteeing the schedulability of a set of periodic

tasks with deadlines constrained by FP is the solution to the
following equation [BIN 06b]:

$$\lambda = \min_{i=1\ldots n} \max_{t\in\mathcal{P}_{i-1}(D_i)} \left(\frac{t}{W_i(t)} - 1\right) \qquad [2.1]$$

[BIN 06b]: also shows how to apply $\lambda$ to a subset of tasks.
However, a WCET $\lambda C_i$ gives as much more margin to the task
$\tau_i$ as its $C_i$ is large, a choice which does not necessarily reflect
the importance of the task.

This constraint is lifted by [BOU 07], still in the case of a
set of tasks with constrained deadlines, in which a criterion
of importance $\phi_i$ is assigned to each task $\tau_i$ in order to
calculate the allowable margin on the WCET of a task $\tau_i$. The
margin $A_{i,k}$ (referred to as *allowance*) on the WCETs of a task
$\tau_i$ is the maximum allowable value maintaining the
schedulability of the set of tasks when the execution time of $\tau_i$
is $C_i + A_{i,k}$. $k$ denotes an additional parameter to take into
account temporal faults related to the WCETs being exceeded
(permanent or transient). The considered model of faults is a
sliding window model: at most $k$ faulty tasks in the set
$\tau = \{\tau_1, \ldots, \tau_n\}$ over $n$ on a sliding window $W = \min_{i=1\ldots n}(T_i)$
are taken into account in the calculation of $A_{i,k}$. If we assume
that $\tau_i$ is faulty, how do we distribute the margin given to the
faulty tasks? [BOU 07] proposes a weighted sharing of the
margin between the faulty tasks following an importance
criterion. If $\tau_i$ is faulty then each faulty task $\tau_j$ has a margin
of $\frac{\phi_i}{\phi_j}A_{i,k}$. For a task $\tau_i$, in order to minimize the value $A_{i,k}$,
the $k-1$ faulty tasks minimizing $A_{i,k}$ have to be determined,
assuming that each faulty task $\tau_j$ uses up a margin of $\frac{\phi_i}{\phi_j}A_{i,k}$.
$A_{i,k}$ has to satisfy three constraints expressed in theorem
2.12 from the three inequalities [2.2], [2.3] and [2.4]. $A_{i,k}$ is
calculated independently for each inequality. The final
retained value for $A_{i,k}$ is the minimum of the maximum
values obtained.

– Inequality [2.2] calculates the worst response time of the faulty task $\tau_i$. The response time of the task $\tau_i$ together with margin consumption has to stay smaller than or equal to its deadline $D_i$. The $k - 1$ faulty tasks in competition with $\tau_i$ are chosen in the set $MaxR_{(i,k-1)}(t)$ denoting the set of at most $(k-1)$ tasks $\tau_j$ in $hp(i)$ maximizing the usable margin at a time $t$ (maximizing the function $\left\lceil \frac{t}{T_j} \right\rceil \frac{\phi_i}{\phi_j}$). In the particular case in which $\forall(i,j), \phi_i = \phi_j$, the assignment of the margin is fair for a faulty task $\tau_i$, the set $MaxR_{(i,k-1)}(t)$ is reduced to the choice of tasks in $hp(i)$ of minimum period.

– Inequality [2.3] ensures that the worst response time of tasks with lower priority than $\tau_i$ stays smaller than or equal to their deadline, when the faulty tasks taken into account in the calculation of $r_i$ in inequality [2.2] use up their margin;

– Inequality [2.4] ensures that the utilization factor resulting from the consumption of the margin $\frac{\phi_i}{\phi_j} A_{i,k}$ by the $k$ faulty tasks stays smaller than or equal to 1. We retain in the sum the margin of the task $\tau_i$ as well as that of at most $k - 1$ faulty tasks $\tau_j \neq \tau_i$ maximizing the quantity $\frac{\phi_i}{\phi_j} A_{i,k}$. We denote $MaxU_{(i,k-1)}$ this set.

THEOREM 2.12.– [BOU 07] Let $\tau$ be a set of periodic tasks with constrained deadlines. The maximum weighted margin $A_{i,k}$ of a task $\tau_i$ with WCET $C_i + A_{i,k}$, for a FP scheduling, under the hypothesis of at most $k$ faulty tasks over a sliding window $W = min_{i \in [i,n]}(T_i)$ is the minimum value of the maximum values of $A_{i,k}$ satisfying inequalities [2.2], [2.3] and [2.4] with:

$$r_i = C_i + A_{i,k} + \sum_{\tau_j \in hp(i)} \left\lceil \frac{r_i}{T_j} \right\rceil C_j$$

$$+ \sum_{\tau_j \in MaxR_{(i,k-1)}(r_i)} \left\lceil \frac{r_i}{T_j} \right\rceil \frac{\phi_i}{\phi_j} A_{i,k} \leq D_i \qquad [2.2]$$

$\forall \tau_j \in lp(i),$

$$r_j = C_j + \sum_{\tau_m \in hp(j)} \left\lceil \frac{r_i}{T_m} \right\rceil C_m$$

$$+ \sum_{\tau_m \in MaxR_{(i,k-1)}(r_j) \cup \tau_i} \left\lceil \frac{r_j}{T_m} \right\rceil \frac{\phi_i}{\phi_m} A_{i,k} \leq D_j \qquad [2.3]$$

$$U + \sum_{\tau_j \in \tau_i \cup MaxU_{(i,k-1)}} \frac{\frac{\phi_i}{\phi_j} A_{i,k}}{T_j} \leq 1 \qquad [2.4]$$

An analysis of various margin distribution strategies (fair, weighted) is detailed in [BOU 07].

### 2.6.1.2. Sensitivity of WCETs with EDF

2.6.1.2.1. Determination of the $C$-space with EDF scheduling

In [HER 07a], the authors show that the EDF feasibility domain ($C$-space) on the WCETs, denoted by $\mathcal{D}^{EDF}(\tau)$, is defined by a set of constraints of type $dbf(t) \leq t$, where $t$ is contained in a set of absolute task deadlines in the synchronous scenario. They show that the interval $[0, L[$ proposed to test the schedulability of tasks with EDF is insufficient. The $C$-space needs to be studied in the interval $[D_{min}, P[$ where $D_{min} = min_{i \in [1,n]}(D_i)$ and $P = lcm\{T_1, \ldots, T_n\}$. This number is potentially large. However, the authors show that it is possible to reduce, in a very significant manner, the number of moments to consider for an expression of the constraints in the form of a linear programming problem. They prove that the EDF feasibility domain of the WCETs is convex, which allows us to solve the linear programming problem using the simplex algorithm.

The $C$-space is defined in theorem 2.13 by the set of constraints $dbf(t) \leq t$ for every absolute deadline time $t$ of a task in the interval $[Dmin, P[$, corresponding to the set $\mathcal{M}$, in the synchronous scenario. The necessary constraint on the utilization factors is added to these constraints: $U \leq 1$.

THEOREM 2.13.– [HER 07a] The feasibility domain of WCETs ($C$-space) $\mathcal{D}^{EDF}(\tau)$ for a set of periodic tasks $\tau$ with arbitrary deadlines, scheduled by EDF, is the solution of:

$$\mathcal{D}^{EDF}(\tau) = \left\{ X \in \mathbb{R}^{+n}, \max \left( sup_{t \in \mathcal{M}} \frac{dbf(t)}{t}, U \right) \leq 1 \right\} [2.5]$$

where:

$$\mathcal{M} = \bigcup_{j=1}^{n} \left\{ D_j + k_j \, T_j, \ 0 \leq k_j \leq \left\lceil \frac{P - D_j}{T_j} \right\rceil - 1 \right\}$$

From the expression of the feasibility domain of WCETs, a linear programming formalization of the problem is proposed. The aim is to determine whether a moment $t_i$ in $\mathcal{M}$ enforces a significant constraint on the WCETs of the $C$-space. To solve this problem, the objective function $h(t_i)$ has to be maximized for a moment $t_i$ under the constraint:

$$\bigcup_{\substack{k=1 \\ k \neq i}}^{m} \{ h(t_k) \leq t_k \} \tag{2.6}$$

Let us note that, for a given time $t_i$, the constraint $h(t_i) \leq t_i$ is not considered, which allows us to well determine, when we do not consider this constraint, whether it is possible to find WCETs such that $h(t_i) \geq t_i$, in which case time $t_i$ is significant and has to be conserved. However, if $h(t_i) < t_i$ then $t_i$ can be removed from the set $\mathcal{M}$.

As an example, let us consider a set of three periodic tasks $\tau = \{\tau_1, \tau_2, \tau_3\}$, such that for every task $\tau_i$, $T_i$ and $D_i$ are fixed and $C_i \in \mathbb{R}^+$, the WCET of the task is a parameter.

$$\tau_1 : (C_1, T_1, D_1) = (C_1, 7, 5), \tau_2 : (C_2, T_2, D_2) = (C_2, 11, 7)$$

and

$$\tau_3 : (C_3, T_3, D_3) = (C_3, 13, 10).$$

In this example, $P = 1001$ and $D_{min} = min\{D_1, \ldots, D_n\} = 5$. Following equation [2.6], we have to consider the set of activation request times in $\mathcal{M}$ in the interval $[5, 1001[$ and $\mathcal{M}$ is defined for our example as:

$$\mathcal{M} = \{5 + 7\,k_1, \ k_1 \in \{0, \ldots, 142\}\} \cup$$
$$\{7 + 11\,k_2, \ k_2 \in \{0, \ldots, 90\}\} \cup$$
$$\{10 + 13\,k_3, \ k_3 \in \{0, \ldots, 76\}\}$$

We have $m = Card(\mathcal{M}) = 281$ moments of time in $\mathcal{M}$. Equation [2.6] is a convex subset of the feasibility domain, defined from moments in $\mathcal{M}$. Applying the simplex algorithm on this subset of constraints, for all moments $t_i \in \mathcal{M}$, starting from $t_1$ until $t_m$, we obtain the subset of moments in $\mathcal{M}$ maximizing $dbf(t)$ for every vector of WCET $C = \{C_1, \ldots, C_n\} \in \mathbb{R}^{+n}$. The solution of the linear programming problem leads to only considering moments in $S = \{5, 7, 10, 12, 40\} \subseteq \mathcal{M}$ for expressing the EDF feasibility domain.

Finally, the feasibility domain is obtained from the conjunction of the inequalities of Figure 2.7 (the last condition being $U \leq 1$).

$$\begin{cases} \frac{C_1}{5} \leq 1; \frac{C_1 + C_2}{7} \leq 1 \\[2mm] \frac{C_1 + C_2 + C_3}{10} \leq 1; \frac{2C_1 + C_2 + C_3}{12} \leq 1 \\[2mm] \frac{6C_1 + 4C_2 + 3C_3}{40} \leq 1; \frac{C_1}{7} + \frac{C_2}{11} + \frac{C_3}{13} \leq 1 \end{cases}$$

**Figure 2.7.** *Inequalities describing the EDF feasibility domain*

## 2.6.1.2.2. Margin on the WCETs with EDF scheduling

[BAL 02] shows how to calculate the additional maximum margin on the execution time (WCET) of a single task without undermining the schedulability of the tasks (the WCET of the other tasks remaining unchanged). With EDF, an NSC testing the schedulability of the tasks (see section 2.5.2.1) is: $\forall t \in [0, L), dbf(t) \leq t$. As for FP scheduling in general, increasing the execution time of the tasks up until their maximum values leads to the increase of $U$, and $L$ tends to $P = lcm\{T_1, \ldots, T_n\}$ when $U$ tends to 1. Therefore, in order to determine the maximum margin of a task we need to perform an analysis in the interval $[0, P[$. The maximum margin $A_i$ for a single task $\tau_i$ is obtained by considering, in the test $\forall t \in ]0, P[, dbf(t) \leq t$, that the WCET of $\tau_i$ is $C_i + A_i$. This leads to $\forall t \in ]0, P[, dbf(t) + A_i.\lfloor \frac{t+T_i-D_i}{T_i} \rfloor \leq t$. Hence the expression of $A_i$ in theorem 2.14.

THEOREM 2.14.– [BAL 02] Let $\tau$ be a set of periodic tasks with arbitrary deadlines. The maximum margin $A_i$ on the WCET of a periodic task $\tau_i$ scheduled by EDF is the solution to the following equation:

$$A_i = \max_{0<t<P, D_i \leq t} \left( \frac{t - dbf(t)}{\left\lfloor \frac{t+T_i-D_i}{T_i} \right\rfloor} \right) \qquad [2.7]$$

[BOU 07] shows how to calculate the margin of $k \leq n$ faulty tasks over a sliding window $W = min_{i=1...n}(T_i)$, with a similar approach to that presented for FP scheduling (see section 2.6.1.1). The margin $A_{i,k}$ of a faulty task $\tau_i$ in the case of a fair allocation the margin to the faulty tasks is the minimum value of the maximum values obtained in theorem 2.15, for the two inequalities [2.8] and [2.9] [BOU 07]:

– inequality [2.8] corresponds to a condition on the utilization factor $U^*$ integrating the utilization factor $U$ of the tasks and the utilization of the margins of the $k$ faulty tasks (including $\tau_i$). For $\tau_i$, the worst-case occurs when the $k - 1$ faulty tasks have a minimal period;

– inequality [2.9] is the extension of the EDF FC $dbf(t) \leq t$ to the interval $[D_{min}, U^*.P[$ integrating the utilization of the margin by the $k$ faulty tasks (including task $\tau_i$). $U^*.P$ is a bound on the first busy period of the synchronous scenario [BOU 07]. The $k - 1$ faulty tasks in competition with $\tau_i$ are in the worst-case tasks $\tau_j$ which maximize $(1 + \lfloor \frac{t-D_j}{T_j} \rfloor)$, making inequality [2.9] more constrained.

THEOREM 2.15.– [BOU 07] Let $\tau$ be a set of periodic tasks with arbitrary deadlines in which the tasks are indexed by ascending periods. The maximum fair period $A_{i,k}$ of a task $\tau_i$, with EDF scheduling, under the assumption of at most $k$ faulty tasks over a sliding window $W = min_{i \in [i,n]}(T_i)$, is the minimum value of the maximum values of $A_{i,k}$ satisfying inequalities [2.8] and [2.9] with:

$$U^* = U + \sum_{\tau_j \in lp(i,k-1) \cup \tau_i} \frac{A_{i,k}}{T_j} \leq 1 \qquad [2.8]$$

$$\forall t \in [D_{min}, U^*.P),$$

$$dbf(t) + \left\{ (1 + \lfloor \frac{t-D_i}{T_i} \rfloor) + \sum_{\tau_j \in ld(i,k-1)} (1 + \lfloor \frac{t-D_j}{T_j} \rfloor) \right\} . A_{i,k} \leq t$$

$$[2.9]$$

where:

– $lp(i,k-1)$ represents the set of at most $k-1$ tasks $\tau_j$ except $\tau_i$, with the smallest period;

– $ld(i, k - 1)$ represents the set of at most $k - 1$ tasks $\tau_j$ without $\tau_i$ maximizing the function $(1 + \lfloor \frac{t-D_j}{T_j} \rfloor)$, with $t \geq D_j$.

Finally, [HER 07b] shows how to calculate the critical scaling factor $\alpha$ applied to the set of WCETs, such that the execution time of a task $\tau_i$ becomes $\alpha.C_i$ in the case of EDF scheduling of periodic tasks. This calculation is valid in the case of a set of tasks with arbitrary deadlines.

THEOREM 2.16.– [HER 07b] The scaling factor $\alpha$ for a set of periodic tasks with arbitrary deadlines scheduled by EDF is the solution of the following equation:

$$\alpha = \frac{1}{\max\left\{U, sup_{t\in[\min\{D_1,...,D_n\},P[}\left\{\frac{dbf(t)}{t}\right\}\right\}} \qquad [2.10]$$

If $\alpha < 1$ then the initial set of tasks (without multiplying the WCET by $\alpha$) is not schedulable with EDF; however, multiplying the WCET of the tasks by $\alpha$ leads to a schedulable set of tasks. If $\alpha \geq 1$ then the initial set of tasks is schedulable by EDF and it is possible to increase all the WCETs by a multiplicative factor $\alpha$ while respecting the deadlines of the tasks.

For example, if we consider the following set of tasks $\tau = \{\tau_1, \tau_2, \tau_2\}$ with

$$\tau_i = \{C_i, T_i, D_i\} : \tau_1 = \{40, 70, 50\}, \tau_2 = \{60, 110, 70\}$$

and $\tau_3 = \{100, 130, 100\}$ then: $\alpha = \frac{1}{2}$ with $U = 1.89 > 1$. The set of tasks is, therefore, non-schedulable. However, it becomes schedulable if $C_1 = \frac{1}{2}.40 = 20$, $C_2 = \frac{1}{2}.60 = 30$, and $C_3 = \frac{1}{2}.100 = 50$.

### 2.6.2. *Sensitivity of periods*

The sensitivity analysis of periods is certainly more complex than that of the WCETs or the deadlines. To our knowledge, there are results only for FP scheduling in the state-of-the-art, and none for EDF. For FP, there is no closed formula describing the feasibility domain of periods ($T$-space). $T$-space (or $f$-space, $f = 1/T$) has been studied in [BIN 06b]. They show that the $T$-space is composed of an infinite number of hyperplanes. A sensitivity analysis for a particular direction in the $T$-space is still an open problem.

[BIN 06b] shows how to determine the minimum period $T_i^{min}$ of a task $\tau_i$ such that every period smaller than $T_i^{min}$ leads to a set of non-schedulable tasks. The principle behind the proposed solution is based on lemma 2.4 detailed in [BIN 06a] and [BIN 06b]. It builds on the calculation of the worst-case response time $r_i$ of a task $\tau_i$.

LEMMA 2.4.– [BIN 06a], [BIN 06b] Let $T_i^{min}$ be the minimum period of the task $\tau_i$, we then have either (1) $T_i^{min} = \frac{r_i}{\delta_i}$, where $0 < \delta_i = \frac{D_i}{T_i}$ or (2) there exists a task $\tau_j \in lp(i)$ with priority lower than $\tau_i$ such that the worst-case response time $r_j$ of $\tau_j$ is an integer multiple of $T_i^{min}$.

The first condition comes from the condition $r_i \leq D_i = \delta_i T_i$, the second condition seeks to maximize the impact of the task $\tau_i$ by maximizing the number of activation requests of $\tau_i$ that can be executed before the termination of a task $\tau_j$ with priority lower than $\tau_i$. This number is calculated by successive iterations starting from $n_j^i = 1$ until $n_j^i = N_j^i$ interferences of $\tau_i$ such that for $N_j^i + 1$ interferences, the task $\tau_j$ is not schedulable. For a task $\tau_j$ with priority lower than $\tau_i$, its worst-case response time $r_j(n_j^i)$, taking $n_j^i$ activation requests of $\tau_i$ into account, is:

$$r_j(n_j^i) = C_j + n_j^i C_i + \sum_{\tau_k \in hp(j), k \neq i} \left\lceil \frac{r_j(n_j^i)}{T_k} \right\rceil C_k$$

Finally, the minimum period $T_i^{min}$ of $\tau_i$ can be calculated as follows:

THEOREM 2.17.– [BIN 06a, BIN 06b] Let $\tau$ be a set of $n$ periodic tasks with constrained deadlines. The minimum period of a task $\tau_i$ guaranteeing the schedulability of $\tau$ with an FP scheduling is the solution to the following equation:

$$T_i^{min} = max \left\{ \frac{r_i}{\delta_i}, \max_{j \in lp(i)} \min_{n_j^i = 1 \ldots N_j^i} \frac{r_j(n_j^i)}{n_j^i} \right\} \qquad [2.11]$$

Determination of the optimum scaling factor

[BIN 06a] shows an interesting property related to the $C$-space and $T$-space feasibility domains with an FP scheduling.

THEOREM 2.18.– [BIN 06a] Let $\tau^C$ be a set of tasks with constrained deadlines scheduled by FP where for every task $\tau_i$, the WCET is multiplied by $\alpha$. Let $\tau^T$ be the set of tasks where, for every task $\tau_i$, the period is divided by $\alpha$. The set of tasks $\tau^C$ is schedulable if and only if the set of tasks $\tau^T$ is schedulable.

The maximum scaling factor applied to the set of periods by dividing the periods by $\alpha$ can thus be determined by computing the maximum scaling factor $\alpha$ applied to the WCETs.

## 2.6.3. Sensitivity of deadlines

To the best of our knowledge, there are no state-of-the-art results for FP scheduling. All the results presented in the following are related to EDF scheduling. First of all, we present a recent result of [BIN 07] for the characterization of the deadline feasibility domain ($D$-space). We will then present the various state-of-the-art results that allow the reduction of the deadline of a task while preserving the schedulability of the tasks. The reduction of the deadline of a task results in the reduction of its maximum response time and, therefore, of the jitter after execution of the task defined by its maximum response time minus its WCET. When the task is used to control a feedback loop, the jitter of the task is a fundamental parameter for the stability of the loop.

## 2.6.3.1. *Determination of the D-space with EDF*

[BIN 07] looks at the expression of the deadline feasibility domain called $D$-space for the synchronous scenario. The authors also propose a sufficient deadline feasibility domain and show that it is convex. The principle of $D$-space characterization is to start from a dual expression obtained from the NSC [BAR 90a]: $\forall t \geq 0, dbf(t) \leq t$.

From $dbf(t) = \sum_{i=1}^{n} K_i(t, D_i)C_i$, where $K_i(t, D_i) = \max\left\{0, 1 + \left\lfloor \frac{t - D_i}{T_i} \right\rfloor\right\}$, they express the constraints on every integer $K_i(t, D_i)$ in function of every time $t$:

$$\begin{cases} K_i(t, D_i) = 0 & \text{if } t < D_i \\ \frac{t - D_i}{T_i} < K_i(t, D_i) \leq \frac{t - D_i}{T_i} + 1 & \text{otherwise} \end{cases}$$

Which allows us to express the associated constraint in the domain of deadlines: $\forall t \geq 0, \forall k_i \in K_i(t, D_i)$:

$$\begin{cases} D_i > t & \text{if } k_i = 0 \\ t - k_i.T_i < D_i \leq t - (k_i - 1).T_i & \text{otherwise} \end{cases} \qquad [2.12]$$

Let $K(t, D) = \{K_1(t, D_1), \ldots, K_n(t, D_n)\}$ be a vector of integers. The set of deadlines for a time $t$ and a vector of integers $k = K(t, D)$, satisfying the equation [2.12], is denoted by $dom D(t, k)$ and $dom D^c(t, k)$ is its complement.

[BIN 07] shows that an NSC for the schedulability of a set of tasks with EDF, for a vector $D = \{D_1, \ldots, D_n\}$ of deadlines (with $C = \{C_1, \ldots, C_n\}$), is:

$$\forall k \in \mathbb{N}^n, \forall t \in [0, k.C[, D \in dom D^c(t, k) \qquad [2.13]$$

The $D$-space is then the intersection of the feasibility domains $dom D^c(t, k)$, $\forall k \in \mathbb{N}^n$ and $\forall t \in [0, k.C[$:

$$\bigcap_{t \in [0, k.C[} dom D^c(t, k) \qquad [2.14]$$

From the characterization of the feasibility domain, [BIN 07] shows that it is sufficient to look at the limiting points (vertices) of the feasibility domain. The coordinates of a limiting point, denoted by $D^{vert}(k) = \{D_1^{vert}, \ldots, D_n^{vert}\}$ where $D_i^{vert}(k)$ is equal to:

$$D_i^{vert}(k) = \begin{cases} k.C - (k_i - 1)T_i & \text{if } i \in I \\ +\infty & \text{otherwise} \end{cases} \qquad [2.15]$$

where $I$ is the set of indices of the tasks for which the components of the vector $k = \{k_1, \ldots, k_n\}$ are non-zero.

The feasibility domain corresponds to deadlines above a certain limit:

$$\bigcap_{k \in \mathbb{N}^n} \bigcup_{i:k_i \neq 0} D_i \geq k.C - (k_i - 1)T_i \qquad [2.16]$$

However, [BIN 07] shows that the number of limiting points (vertices) to be tested can be very large. They describe the subset of dominant vectors $k \in \mathbb{N}^n$, denoted by $domK$ and show that $domK$ is defined by:

$$domK = \bigcup_{i=1}^{n} \{k : k_i = 1, k_j = 0, j \neq i\} \cup \bigcap_{i=1}^{n} \{k : k_i(T_i - C_i) $$
$$- \sum_{j \neq i} k_j C_j < T_i - C_i\}$$

$domK$ is bounded when $U < 1$. The $D$-space deadline feasibility domain is finally defined by the following theorem:

THEOREM 2.19.– [BIN 07] Let $\tau$ be a set of periodic tasks with arbitrary deadlines. The $D$-space deadline feasibility domain is defined by the following set of inequalities:

$$\bigcap_{k \in domK} \bigcup_{i:k_i \neq 0} D_i \geq k.C - (k_i - 1)T_i \qquad [2.17]$$

$$\sum_{i=1}^{n} U_i D_i \geq \sum_{i=1}^{n} C_i - D_{min}(1 - \sum_{i=1}^{n} U_i) \qquad [2.18]$$

### 2.6.3.2. *Deadline modification with EDF*

The principle of modifying the deadlines of tasks with precedence relations to study their schedulability was proposed in [CHE 90]. [BAR 99] proposes to modify the deadlines of a set of tasks to minimize the jitter of the tasks, regarded as a second criteria of scheduling. In [CER 04], the deadlines are modified to guarantee the stability of a closed control loop of a real-time system. In [MAR 04a], the problem of distributing a global deadline into local deadlines in a distributed system for multimedia streams is presented. The problem of local assignment of a deadline on a node is formalized using a linear programming problem.

[BAL 06] shows how to calculate the maximum reduction factor $\alpha \leq 1$ applicable to the deadline of a task $\tau_i$, such that its deadline is $\alpha.D_i$, for which the set of obtained tasks is always schedulable by EDF. The context is that of a set of tasks with constrained deadlines.

[BAL 06] first of all considers the case of the reduction of the deadline of a single task $\tau_i$. Let $D_i^{min}$ be the minimum deadline of the task $\tau_i$ such that every deadline smaller than $D_i^{min}$ for the task $\tau_i$ leads to a non-schedulable set of tasks. The principle is to calculate $D_i^{min}$ by considering the successive absolute deadlines of $\tau_i$ in $[0, L[$, in the synchronous scenario. The maximum number $k_i$ of activation requests of $\tau_i$ in $[0, L)$ is given by $k_i = \left\lceil \frac{L}{T_i} \right\rceil$. The final deadline is the maximum of the minimum deadlines obtained for each activation request of $\tau_i$. $s_{i,j}$ ($d_{i,j}$, respectively) representing the $j^{th}$ activation deadline (absolute deadline, respectively) of $\tau_i$ at time $(j-1)T_i$ ($(j-1)T_i + D_i$, respectively). For an absolute deadline of $\tau_i$ at $d_{i,j}$, two situations can occur:

– there is no absolute deadline of the tasks $\tau_k$, $k \neq i$, in the interval

$$[s_{i,j} + C_i, d_{i,j}[$$

or there are only deadlines of $\tau_k$ such that for every absolute deadline of $\tau_k$ at $t$, $t - dbf(t) \geq C_i$, then the minimum absolute deadline of $\tau_i$ can be changed to $s_{i,j} + C_i$, verifying $dbf(s_{i,j} + C_i) = s_{i,j} + C_i$;

– there is at least one absolute deadline of a task $\tau_k$, $k \neq i$, in $[s_{i,j} + C_i, d_{i,j}[$. The algorithm moves to the first deadline of a task $\tau_k$, $k \neq i$, directly smaller than $d_{i,j}$. If at this time $t - dbf(t) \geq C_i$ then there is sufficient margin to reduce the deadline of $\tau_i$. The algorithm decreases $t$ until it finds a time $t$ corresponding to an absolute deadline of a task $\tau_k$, $k \neq i$, such that $t - dbf(t) < C_i$. At this time, the set of tasks would not be schedulable if $\tau_i$ would have this deadline. Indeed, this would lead to having a demand bound function at $t$ equal to $dbf(t) + C_i > t$. The minimum absolute deadline $d'_{i,j}$ for $\tau_i$ corresponds to the time directly bigger at $t$ for which $d'_{i,j} = dbf(t) + C_i$. If $\tau_i$ has an absolute deadline of $d'_{i,j}$ then the demand bound function at $d'_{i,j}$ is equal to $d'_{i,j}$.

Theorem 2.20 summarizes the principles described previously for the calculation of the minimum deadline.

THEOREM 2.20.– [BAL 06] Let $\tau$ be a set of $n$ periodic tasks with constrained deadlines schedulable by EDF. Let $\tau'$ be the modified set of tasks such that the task $\tau_i$ is assigned a relative deadline of $D_i^{min} = max_{j=1}^{k_i}(d'_{i,j} - s_{i,j})$ with: (i) $d'_{i,j} = dbf(t_1) + C_i$ if there exists a time $t_1$ corresponding to the first absolute deadline of a task $\tau_k$ less than $d_{i,j}$ for which $s_{i,j} + C_i \leq t_1 < d_{i,j}$ and $dbf(t_1) > t_1 - C_i$ and (ii) $d'_{i,j} = s_{i,j} + C_i$ otherwise. $D_i^{min}$ is then the minimum deadline such that $\tau'$ is schedulable by EDF.

[GEO 11] revisits an implementation of an algorithm calculating the minimum deadline of a task proposed in [BAL 06]. This implementation solves a few problems identified in the version proposed by [BAL 06].

Algorithm 2 allows us to calculate the minimum deadline $D_i^{min}$ of a task $\tau_i$.

---

$\tau = \{\tau_1, \ldots, \tau_n\}$ : **task set**;
$H \leftarrow$ lcm of the periods of $\tau$ : **integer**;
$D_i^{min} \leftarrow 0$ : **integer**; deadline : **integer**;
$k_i \leftarrow \left\lceil \frac{H}{T_i} \right\rceil$ : **integer**;
*[For each activation request of $\tau_i$ in $[0, H[$]*
**For** $(s = 0; s < k_i; s{+}{+})$ **do**
$\quad t \leftarrow sT_i + D_i$;
$\quad deadline = max(C_i, h(sT_i + C_i) + C_i - sT_i)$;
$\quad$ **If** $(t = dbf(t))$ **then**
$\quad\quad D_i^{min} = D_i$;
$\quad\quad$ exit-for;
$\quad$ **else**
$\quad\quad t = t - 1$;
$\quad\quad$ **While** $(t > sT_i + C_i)$ **do**
$\quad\quad\quad$ *[If t corresponds to an absolute deadline of a task $\tau_j$, $j \neq i$]*
$\quad\quad\quad$ **If** $(t = (\left\lceil \frac{t}{T_j} \right\rceil - 1)T_j + D_j)$ **then**
$\quad\quad\quad\quad$ **If** $(t - dbf(t) < C_i)$ **then**
$\quad\quad\quad\quad\quad deadline = dbf(t) + C_i - sT_i$;
$\quad\quad\quad\quad\quad$ exit-while;
$\quad\quad\quad\quad$ **end If**
$\quad\quad\quad$ **end If**
$\quad\quad\quad t \leftarrow t - 1$;
$\quad\quad$ **done**
$\quad$ **end If**
$\quad D_i^{min} = max(D_i^{min}, deadline)$
**end For**

---

**Algorithm 2:** *Calculation of $D_i^{min}$*

COROLLARY 2.1.– [BAL 06] In the case of a reduction of the deadline applied to a single task $\tau_i$, $D_i^{min}$ is the worst-case response time of the task $\tau_i$.

The maximum factor of reduction $\alpha$ for the task $\tau_i$ is then:
$$\alpha = 1 - \frac{D_i^{min}}{D_i}.$$

In the case of a reduction of the set of deadlines of the tasks by a factor $\alpha$, [BAL 06] shows how to calculate $\alpha$ such that the deadline of each task $\tau_i$ is $\alpha.D_i$ using Algorithm 2. The principle is to calculate the margin $t - dbf(t)$ for each time $t \in [0, L)$ to determine $\alpha$.

---

$\tau = \{\tau_1, \ldots, \tau_n\}$ : **task set**;
L $\leftarrow$ compute-L$(\tau)$ : **integer**; $\alpha \leftarrow 1$ : **real**
$slack = min_{t \in [0,L)}(t - dbf(t))$ : **real**;
**While** $(slack \neq 0)$ **do**
$\quad\left|\begin{array}{l} \alpha = min_{i=1\ldots n}(1 - \frac{slack}{D_i}); \\ \textbf{For } (i = 1; i < n; i + +) \textbf{ do} \\ \quad \left| D_i = \alpha D_i; \right. \\ \textbf{end For} \\ slack = min_{t \in [0,L)}(t - dbf(t)); \end{array}\right.$
**done**
Returns $\alpha$;

---

**Algorithm 3:** *Calculation of* $\alpha$

Let us however note that in the case of a reduction of the deadlines of the set of tasks, the property of Corollary 2.1 is no longer valid.

## 2.7. Conclusion

In this chapter, we have looked at the problems and solutions in real-time scheduling for uniprocessor architectures.

In the first part, we have presented the classical results from the state-of-the-art allowing us to design a real-time system. These results are based on the expression of feasibility conditions which allow us to guarantee the compliance with temporal constraints associated with the execution of the tasks in a system. Firstly, we looked at the characterization of a scheduling problem leading to the definition of the models and tasks, of temporal constraints and of scheduling of a real-time system. We focused on the periodic and sporadic activation models. We then looked at the main state-of-the-art scheduling algorithms by specifying the contexts in which they were optimal. We then studied the worst-case scenarios as well as the feasibility conditions for the compliance with temporal constraints in a preemptive and non-preemptive context, for the scheduling policies based on task-level fixed priority (FP), job-level fixed priority (JFP) and dynamic.

In the second part, we have presented the sensitivity analyses allowing us to determine the acceptable limit deviations of task parameters (worst-case execution time (WCET), periods, deadlines) guaranteeing the schedulability of tasks. In particular we have studied FP and JFP scheduling (case of Earliest Deadline First: EDF).

## 2.8. Bibliography

[AUD 91] AUDSLEY N.C., "Optimal priority assignment and feasibility of static priority tasks with arbitrary start times", *Department of Computer Science Report YCS 164*, University of York, 1991.

[BAL 02] BALBASTRE P., RIPOLL I., "Schedulability analysis of window-constrained execution time tasks for real-time control", *Proceeding of the 14th Euromicro Conference on Real-Time Systems (ECRTS '02)*, 2002.

[BAL 06]  BALBASTRE P., RIPOLL I., CRESPO A., "Optimal deadline assignment for periodic real-time tasks in dynamic priority systems", *Proceedings of the 18th Euromicro Conference on Real-Time Systems (ECRTS '06)*, Dresden, Germany, July 5–7 2006.

[BAR 90a]  BARUAH S., HOWELL R., ROSIER L., "Algorithms and complexity concerning the preemptive scheduling of periodic real-time tasks on one processor", *Real-Time Systems*, vol. 2, pp. 301–324, 1990.

[BAR 90b]  BARUAH S., MOK A.K., ROSIER L., "Preemptively scheduling hard real-time sporadic tasks on one processor", *Proceedings of the 11th Real-Time Systems Symposium*, pp. 182–190, 1990.

[BAR 99]  BARUAH S., BUTTAZO G., GORINSKY S., *et al.*, "Scheduling periodic task systems to minimize output jitter", *In $6^{th}$ Conference on Real-Time Computing Systems and Applications*, pp. 62–69, 1999.

[BER 02]  BERNAT G., COLIN A., PETTERSREAL-TIME S.M., "Wcet analysis of probabilistic hard real-time systems", in *Proceedings of the 23rd Real-Time Systems Symposium RTSS 2002*, pp. 279–288, 2002.

[BIN 03]  BINI E., BUTTAZZO G.C., "Rate monotonic analysis: the hyperbolic bound", *IEEE Transactions on Computers*, vol. 52, pp. 933–942, 2003.

[BIN 04]  BINI E., BUTTAZZO G., "Schedulability analysis of periodic fixed priority systems", *IEEE Transactions on Computers*, vol. 53, no. 11, November 2004.

[BIN 06a]  BINI E., DI NATALE M., "Optimal task rateselection in fixed priority systems", *Proceedings of the 26th IEEE International Real-Time Systems Symposium (RTSS '05)*, 2006.

[BIN 06b]  BINI E., DI NATALE M., BUTTAZZO G., "Sensitivity analysis for fixed-priority real-time systems", *Proceedings of the 18th Euromicro Conference on Real-Time Systems (ECRTS '06)*, Dresden, Germany, July 5–7 2006.

[BIN 07]  BINI E., BUTTAZZO G., "The space of EDF feasible deadlines", *Proceedings of the 19th Euromicro Conference on Real-Time Systems (ECRTS '07)*, Pisa, Italy, July 4–6 2007.

[BOU 07] BOUGUEROUA L., GEORGE L., MIDONNET S., "Dealing with execution-overruns to improve the temporal robustness of real-time systems scheduled FP and EDF", *The 2nd International Conference on Systems (ICONS '07)*, Sainte-Luce, Martinique, France, April 22–28 2007.

[BRI 04] BRITO R., NAVET N., "Low-power round-robin scheduling", *Proceedings of the 12th International Conference on Real-Time Systems, (RTS '04)*, Paris, 30–31 March 2004.

[BUR 95] BURNS A., WELLINGS A., "Engineering a hard real-time system: from theory to practive", *Software Practice and Experience*, vol. 25, no. 7, pp. 705–726, 1995.

[BUT 93] BUTTAZO G., STANKOVIC J., "RED: a robust earliest deadline scheduling", *3rd International Workshop on Responsive Computing*, September 1993.

[CER 04] CERVIN A., LINCOLN B., EKER J., *et al.*, "The jitter margin and its application in the design of real-time control systems", *Proceedings of the IEEE Conference on Real-Time and Embedded Computing Systems and Applications*, 2004.

[CHE 90] CHETTO H., SILLY M., BOUCHENTOUF T., "Dynamic scheduling of real-time tasks under precedence constraints", *Real-Time Systems*, Kluwer Academic Publishers, vol. 2, no. 3, pp. 181–194, 1990.

[COL 00] COLIN A., PUAUT I., "Worst case execution time analysis for a processor with branch prediction", *Journal of Real-Time Systems*, vol. 18, nos. 2–3, pp. 249–274, 2000.

[DAV 07] DAVIS R., BURNS A., "Robust priority assignment for fixed priority real-time systems", *Real-Time Systems Symposium, RTSS 28th IEEE International*, pp. 3–14, 2007.

[DAV 11] DAVIS R., BURNS A., "Improved priority assignment for global fixed priority pre-emptive scheduling in multiprocessor real-time systems", *Real-Time Systems*, vol. 47, no. 1, pp. 1–40, 2011.

[DEM 90] DEMERS A., KESHAV S., SKER S., "Analysis and simulation of a fair queueing algorithm", *Journal of Internetworking Research and Experience*, pp. 3–26, October 1990.

[DER 74]  DERTOUZOS M., "Control robotics: the procedural control of physical processors", *Proceedings of the IFIP congress*, pp. 807–813, 1974.

[DEV 00]  DEVILLERS R., GOOSSENS J., "Liu and Layland's schedulability test revisited", *Information Processing Letters*, pp. 157–161, 2000.

[GEO 96]  GEORGE L., RIVIERRE N., SPURI M., "Preemptive and non-preemptive scheduling real-time uniprocessor scheduling", *INRIA Research Report*, RR no. 2966, September 1996.

[GEO 11]  GEORGE L., COURBIN P., SOREL Y., "Job vs. portioned partitioning for the earliest deadline first semi-partitioned scheduling", *Journal of Systems Architecture*, Special Issue on Multiprocessor Real-time Scheduling, vol. 57, no. 5, pp. 518–535, 2011.

[GOO 97]  GOOSSENS J., DEVILLERS R., "The non-optimality of the monotonic priority assignments for hard real-time offset free systems", *Real-Time Systems*, vol. 13, no. 2, pp. 107–126, 1997.

[GOO 03]  GOOSSENS J., "Scheduling of offset free systems", *Real-Time Systems*, vol. 24, no. 2, pp. 239–258, March 2003.

[HER 07a]  HERMANT J., GEORGE L., "A C-space sensitivity analysis of earliest deadline first scheduling", *ISoLA Workshop on Leveraging Applications of Formal Methods (ISOLA '07)*, ENSMA, Poitiers-Futuroscope, France, pp.12–14 December 2007.

[HER 07b]  HERMANT J., GEORGE L., "An optimal approach to determine the minimum architecture for real-time embedded systems scheduled by EDF", *3rd IEEE International Conference on Self-Organization and Autonomous Systems in Computing and Communications (SOAS'07)*, Leipzig, Germany, pp. 24–27, September 2007.

[HLA 07]  HLADIK P., DEPLANCHE A., FAUCOU S., *et al.*, "Adequacy between AUTOSAR OS specification and real-time scheduling theory", *IEEE 2nd International Symposium on Industrial Embedded Systems – (SIES '2007)*, Lisbon, Portugal, pp. 4–6, July 2007.

[JAC 55]  JACKSON J., "Scheduling a production line to minimize maximum tardiness.", University of California, 1955.

[JEF 91] JEFFAY K., STANAT D.F., MARTEL C.U., "On non-preemptive scheduling of periodic and sporadic tasks", *IEEE Real-Time Systems Symposium*, San Antonio, TX, pp. 129–139, December 1991.

[JOS 82] JOSEPH Y.-T.LEUNG J.W., "On the complexity of fixed-priority scheduling of periodic, real-time tasks", *Performance Evaluation*, vol. 2, pp. 237–250, 1982.

[JOS 86] JOSEPH M., PANDYA P., "Finding response times in a real-time system", *BCS Computer Journal*, vol. 29, no. 5, pp. 390–395, 1986.

[KAT 93] KATCHER D., LEHOCZKY J., STROSNIDER J., Scheduling models of dynamic priority schedulers, Research Report CMUCDS-93-4, Carnegie Mellon University, Pittsburgh, April 1993.

[KOP 03] KOPETZ H., BAUER G., "The time-triggered architecture", *Proceedings of the IEEE*, vol. 91, no. 1, pp. 112–126, 2003.

[KOR 92] KOREN G., SHASHA D., D-over: an optimal on-line scheduling algorithm for over loaded real-time system, INRIA Research Report, vol. 138, February 1992.

[LEB 97] LE BOUDEC J.Y., THIRAN P., A note on time and space methods in network calculus, Technical Report, no. 97/224, Ecole Polytechnique Fédérale de Lausanne, Switzerland, April 1997.

[LEH 89] LEHOCZKY J., SHA L., DING Y., "The rate-monotonic scheduling algorithm: exact characterization and average case behavior", *Proceedings of 10th IEEE Real-Time Systems Symposium*, pp 166–172, 1989.

[LEH 90] LEHOCZKY J., "Fixed priority scheduling of periodic task sets with arbitrary deadlines", *Proceedings 11th IEEE Real-Time Systems Symposium*, Lake Buena Vista, FL, pp 201–209, December 1990.

[LEH 91] LEHOCZKY J., SHA L., STROSNIDER J., *et al.*, "Fixed priority scheduling theory for hard real-time systems", *Foundations of Real-Time Computing: Scheduling and Resource Management*, Kluwer Academic Publishers, pp. 1–30, 1991.

[LEU 80] LEUNG J.Y.T., MERRIL M., "A note on premptive scheduling of periodic, real time tasks", *Information Processing Letters*, vol. 11, no. 3, November 1980.

[LIU 73] LIU L.C., LAYLAND W., "Scheduling algorithms for multi-programming in a hard real time environment", *Journal of ACM*, vol. 20, no 1, pp. 46–61, January 1973.

[LOC 86] LOCKE C., Best effort decision making for real-time scheduling, PhD Thesis, Computer Science Department, Carnegie-Mellon University, 1986.

[MAN 98] MANABE Y., AOYAGI S., "A feasibility decision algorithm for rate monotonic and deadline monotonic scheduling", *Real-Time Syst.*, vol. 14, no. 2, pp. 171–181, 1998.

[MAR 04a] MARINCA D., MINET P., GEORGE L., "Analysis of deadline assignment methods in distributed real-time systems", *Computer Communications*, Elsevier, 2004.

[MAR 04b] MARTIN S., MINET P., GEORGE L., "End-to-end response time with fixed priority scheduling: trajectory approach vs. holistic approach", *International Journal of Communication Systems*, 2004.

[MAR 05] MARTIN S., MINET P., GEORGE L., "Improving non-preemptive fixed priority scheduling with dynamic priority as secondary criterion", *RTS '05*, Paris, France, April 2005.

[MEU 07] MEUMEU YOMSI P., SOREL Y., "Extending rate monotonic analysis with exact cost of preemptions for hard real-time systems", *Proceedings of the 18th Euromicro Conference on Real-Time Systems (ECRTS '07)*, 2007.

[MIG 03] MIGGE J., JEAN-MARIE A., N. N., "Timing analysis of compound scheduling policies : application to Posix1003.1b", *Journal of Scheduling*, vol. 6, no. 5, pp. 457–482, 2003.

[MOK 83] MOK A.K., Fundamental design problems for the hard real-time environments, PhD Thesis, May 1983.

[PAR 94] PAREKH A., GALLAGER R., "A generalized processor sharing approach to flow control in integrated services networks: the multiple node case", *IEEE ACM Transactions on Networking*, vol. 2, no. 2, April 1994.

[PUS 97] PUSCHNER P., SCHEDL A., "Computing maximum task execution Times – a graph-based approach", *Journal of Real-Time Systems*, vol. 13, no. 1, pp. 67–91, July 1997.

[RAC 06] RACU R., HAMANN A., ERNST R., "A formal approach to multi-dimensional sensitivity analysis of embedded real-time systems", *Proceedings of the 18th Euromicro Conference on Real-Time Systems (ECRTS '06)*, 2006.

[RAH 12] RAHNI A., GROLLEAU E., RICHARD M., *et al.*, "Feasibility analysis of real-time transactions", *Real-Time Systems*, vol. 48, no. 3, pp. 320–358, 2012.

[SIL 99] SILLY M., "The EDL server for scheduling periodic and soft aperiodic tasks with resource constraints", *Real-Time Systems*, vol. 17, no. 1, pp. 87–111, 1999.

[SPR 89] SPRUNT B., SHA L., LEHOCZKY P., "Aperiodic task scheduling for hard real-time systems", *Real-Time Systems Journal*, vol. 1, no. 1, pp. 27–60, June 1989.

[SPU 96] SPURI M., Analysis of deadline scheduled real-time systems, INRIA Research Report, vol. no. 2772, January 1996.

[STR 95] STROSNIDER J.K., LEHOCZKY J.P., SHA L., "The deferrable server algorithm for enhanced aperiodic responsiveness in hard real-time environments", *IEEE Transactions on Computers*, vol. 44, p. 1, January 1995.

[TIN 94a] TINDELL K., BURNS A., WELLINGS A.J., "An extendible approach for analysing fixed priority hard real-time tasks", *Real-Time Systems*, vol. 6, no. 2, 1994.

[TIN 94b] TINDELL K., CLARK J., "Holistic schedulability analysis for distributed hard real-time systems", *Microprocessors and Microprogramming, Euromicro Journal*, vol. 40, 1994.

[TIN 95] TINDELL K., BURNS A., WELLINGS A.J., "Analysis of hard real-time communications", *Real-Time Systems*, vol. 9, pp. 147–171, 1995.

[VES 94] VESTAL S., "Fixed-priority sensitivity analysis for linear compute time models", *IEEE Transactions on Software Engineering*, vol. 20, no. 4, April 1994.

# 3

# Multiprocessor Architecture Solutions

Something as simple as adding an extra processor to the platform severely increases the complexity of real-time scheduling problems. As early as 1969, C.L. Liu, founder of real-time scheduling, saw that very few results established in a uniprocessor environment can be directly generalized to multiprocessor systems. This chapter presents the main results for partitioned and global scheduling of multiprocessor systems.

## 3.1. Introduction

In this chapter, we are interested in real-time systems whose proper functioning depends not only on the results of calculations, but also on the moments these results are produced. These systems play an important role in our society, their applications include: air traffic control problems, nuclear power plant control, multimedia communications, robotics, aeronautics, embedded systems...

We will more specifically consider in this chapter *parallel* architectures composed of *several* processors for the execution

Chapter written by Joël GOOSSENS and Pascal RICHARD.

of real-time applications. Indeed, complex real-time applications need several processors to satisfy the time constraints, or very powerful, costly and voluminous uniprocessor architectures such as super-computers. It is acknowledged today that the cost of a multiprocessor architecture (i.e. composed of a collection of less powerful processors) is far less than that of a uniprocessor architecture (for instance, a super-computer) for an equivalent computing power. In this chapter, we will present the main results of multiprocessor system scheduling.

### 3.1.1. *Application modeling*

In this section, we will introduce the calculation model in order to represent the real-time applications. In particular, the *periodic* and *sporadic task* models will be presented. These workload models are the most popular ones in the literature, and most of the scheduling algorithms are based on these models.

Before defining the periodic and sporadic models themselves, we introduce a preliminary model, more general than the latter ones. Indeed, we will first introduce the concepts of *job* and aperiodic tasks.

DEFINITION 3.1 (Job).– *A job $j$ will be described by the triplet $(a, e, d)$. A release time $a$, an execution time $e$ and an absolute deadline $d$. The job $j$ has to receive $e$ execution units in the $[a, d)$ interval. The real-time system is a finite or infinite collection of jobs: $J = \{j_1, j_2, \ldots\}$.*

An *aperiodic* task is a *non-recurring* task that generates a single job in the system.

Usually, real-time applications are composed of calculations (or operations) that are *recurrent* in nature. Furthermore, we distinguish between the periodic and sporadic tasks.

DEFINITION 3.2 (Periodic task).– *A periodic task $\tau_i$ is described by the tuple $(T_i, D_i, C_i)$, where:*

– *the* execution time $C_i$ *that specifies an upper limit to the execution time of each job of the task $\tau_i$ (the WCET – worst-case execution time – in the literature) ;*

– *the* relative deadline $D_i$, *denotes the separation between the release of the job and the deadline (a job arriving at time t has a deadline at time $t + D_i$) ;*

– *a* period $T_i$ *denoting the time that separates two successive job releases for $\tau_i$.*

A sporadic task is defined by the same $(T_i, D_i, C_i)$ tuple, with the difference that $T_i$ denotes the *minimal* time separating two successive job releases for $\tau_i$.

The majority of the results we present correspond to *implicit-deadline* tasks, in other words that $D_i = T_i$ $(\forall i)$, in this case, each task is described by the couple $\tau(C_i, T_i)$.

A periodic (or sporadic) system $\tau$ is composed of a *finite* collection of periodic (or sporadic) tasks $\tau = \{\tau_1, \ldots, \tau_n\}$.

The following quantities will be useful in our presentation: first, the *utilization ratio of a task,* which is the quotient between its execution time and its period, more formally $U_i = C_i/T_i$. This corresponds, at least for uniprocessor systems, to the portion of processor time used by the task, under the hypothesis that the system is schedulable and for sufficiently large amounts of time. By extension, we define *the utilization of the system* as being the sum of the utilizations of each of the tasks, more formally $U_{\mathrm{sum}} = \sum_{\tau_i \in \tau} U_i$. Numerous schedulability constraints are based on this metric, for instance, it is not difficult to admit that $U_{\mathrm{sum}} \leq 1$ is a necessary (and not sufficient) condition of the schedulability of periodic systems on uniprocessor platforms. By extension, the condition $U_{\mathrm{sum}} \leq m$ is a necessary condition for the schedulability of $\tau$ on a platform composed of $m$ processors. Finally, the largest utilization ratio will often characterize the periodic (or sporadic) set, more formally we have: $U_{\max} = \max_{\tau_i \in \tau} U_i$.

### 3.1.2. *Platform modeling*

In this chapter, we consider *identical* multiprocessor platforms, to the extent that the processors are interchangeable and have the same computing power. In the following, $m$ will represent the the size of the platform $\pi$ that will be composed of the processors $\pi_1, \pi_2, \ldots, \pi_m$.

## 3.2. Scheduler classification

The scheduler is the real-time kernel component that handles the allocation of computing resources to jobs generated by the tasks. The schedulers are distinguished by the following characteristics.

### 3.2.1. *Online and offline schedulers*

In the hard real-time context, the scheduling of tasks must lead to the respect of their deadlines, no matter what situations encountered during the lifetime of the real-time system. The scheduling can either be constructed offline, during the design of the system, or online, i.e. when the system is running.

The use of a fully offline scheduler brings a great predictability to the system, since all the behaviors of the tasks are set by a design. Such a scheduling algorithm defines the allocation of tasks or portions of tasks on the processors and their starting dates on each processor. During the construction of the schedule, the respect of the deadlines is checked. The design of an offline schedule is in essence a hard combinatorial problem.

The computed schedule is then stored in a table that will be used by the real-time kernel in order to schedule the tasks on the processors. While running, the scheduler is a simple dispatcher that follows the scheduling table built offline. The schedule is built based on the worst-case parameters of the tasks, if a task $\tau_i$ is not executed during its $C_i$ units of time, then the processor is left idle. These periods of processor inactivity are hardly reusable, mainly for non-critical tasks or those with soft real-time constraints. Real-time systems are reactive systems by nature, and thus have to take into account events whose occurrences are not predictable in time. Online scheduling algorithms, therefore, offer a higher flexibility than offline algorithms.

It is for this reason that the vast majority of works on multiprocessor system scheduling focuses on online scheduling algorithms. The scheduler makes the allocation and scheduling decisions online for tasks that are ready to run. The scheduling decisions, which will be taken by the scheduler, have to be checked using a schedulability test that is generally done during the design of the system, in other words before it is run. The online task acceptance that guarantees their schedulability is of course possible, but results from specific applications will not be discussed in the following. We will furthermore limit ourselves to online schedulers.

### 3.2.2. *Task preemption and migration*

A scheduler is said to be preemptive when it is authorized to interrupt the execution of a task at any moment on a processor. The preempted task will be able to resume its execution at the latest at the point of interrupt on the same processor or on another depending on the migration scheme considered. The online task allocation strategies on the processors require, in practice, a task migration mechanism. The migration of a task instance (of a job) consists of preempting the execution of the task on a processor and transferring its context to another processor in order to resume its execution at the preemption point. In many studies on real-time scheduling, the costs associated with preemptions and migrations are assumed to be negligible and integrated into the WCET of the tasks (WCET, $C_i$ in our model). This hypothesis is of course very much simplified with respect to the complex architecture of multiprocessor systems, but this allows us, in practice, to simplify the formulation of real-time scheduling problems that are intrinsically difficult to solve. Three main families of schedulers are distinguished by the times when the migrations are performed:

– Scheduling *without migration* or *partitioned* scheduling. In a partitioned system, the tasks are not authorized to migrate and are statically allocated on the different processors before starting their execution. They will stay on the same processor for their entire lifetime. Once the allocation step is done, the tasks are scheduled using traditional algorithms known in a uniprocessor environment. For systems of independent tasks, the scheduling on each processor is completely independent from those calculated on the other processors.

– Scheduling with (*RM*): the tasks are authorized to migrate from one processor to another but only between the two instances (jobs of a same task). Thus, a job, which has started its execution on a processor, will continue to execute on this processor until its end. On the other hand, the next job can be executed on another processor. From an offline point of view, restricted-migration scheduling means establishing a partitioning of the jobs of tasks.

– *Global* scheduling or scheduling with *job-level migration* (*JLM*). In this paradigm, no placement strategy (partitioning of tasks of jobs) is *a priori* fixed. All the tasks ready to be executed are placed in a single queue, and the $m$ highest priority tasks are allocated on the $m$ processors of the platform. The migration is called JLM, since it can happen at any time during the execution of the jobs. The scheduler can interrupt a task running on a processor at any time, and then resume its execution on a different processor. We then refer to JLM.

### 3.2.3. *Priorities of tasks*

The schedulers are classified by the nature of the priorities they assign to the tasks: fixed-task priority (FTP), fixed-job priority (FJP) and dynamic priority (DP).

### 3.2.4. *Classification*

3.2.4.1. *Definition*

The class of a scheduler is defined by its priority assignment policy and the authorized types of migration. These algorithms are characterized by a couple: $\langle a, b \rangle$, where the parameter $a$ indicates the priority policy (1) FTP, (2) FJP and (3) DP and $b$ is the migration level (1) partitioned (P), (2) RM and (3) JLM).

By crossing the priority scheme and the migration level, nine classes of multiprocessor scheduling algorithms can be defined [CAR 04]. For instance, the class $\langle 1, 3 \rangle$ denotes the class of schedulers with FJP and JLM authorized.

### 3.3. Properties of schedulers

Schedulers can be analyzed and compared using qualitative and quantitative criteria. The main qualitative and quantitative criteria of schedulers are presented below.

### 3.3.1. *Qualitative properties*

#### 3.3.1.1. *Comparability of algorithms*

The comparison of two scheduling algorithms, $A$ and $B$, for a given multiprocessor platform leads to three possible results:

– Dominance (denoted $\subseteq$): algorithm $A$ dominates algorithm $B$ if all the systems of tasks schedulable by $B$ are also schedulable by $A$. On the other hand, there are systems of tasks schedulable by $A$ but not by $B$.

– Equivalence (denoted $=$): every system of tasks schedulable by algorithm $A$ is also schedulable by $B$, and vice-versa.

– Incomparability (denoted $\otimes$): there is at least one system of tasks non-schedulable by algorithm $A$ but schedulable by $B$, *and* there is at least one system of tasks non-schedulable by $B$ but schedulable by $A$.

| Notation | Semantics | Obligation of proof |
|---|---|---|
| $\langle w,x\rangle = \langle y,z\rangle$ | Equivalence | $\langle w,x\rangle \subseteq \langle y,z\rangle \wedge \langle y,z\rangle \subseteq \langle w,x\rangle$ |
| Example $\langle w,x\rangle \otimes \langle y,z\rangle$ | Incomparable | $\langle w,x\rangle \not\subseteq \langle y,z\rangle \wedge \langle y,z\rangle \not\subseteq \langle w,x\rangle$ |
| $\langle w,x\rangle \subset \langle y,z\rangle$ | $\langle y,z\rangle$ Dominates $\langle w,x\rangle$ | $\langle w,x\rangle \subseteq \langle y,z\rangle \wedge \langle y,z\rangle \not\subseteq \langle w,x\rangle$ |

**Table 3.1.** *Comparison of multiprocessor scheduling algorithms*

The two-by-two comparisons of scheduling classes allow us to decide on one of the three comparison results indicated in Table 3.1. We will give three simple examples below allowing us to show the principle of proof for each possible comparison result.

*Example : Dominance*: $\langle 1,x\rangle \subseteq \langle 2,x\rangle \subseteq \langle 3,x\rangle$, for any migration level $x$. □

*Example : Equivalence*: $\langle 2,1\rangle = \langle 3,1\rangle$. In the class of partitioned systems, each processor is scheduled independently of the others. Consequently, since EDF is optimal in this context (FJP), it allows the scheduling of any system of tasks that is schedulable with DPs.    □

*Example : Incomparability*: $\langle 1,1 \rangle \otimes \langle 1,3 \rangle$.

– $\langle 1,3 \rangle \not\subseteq \langle 1,1 \rangle$: let us consider the system of tasks $\tau_i(C_i, T_i)$: $\tau_1(1,2)$, $\tau_2(1.1,3)$, $\tau_3(2.1,3)$, $\tau_4(0.8,4)$ to schedule on 2 identical processors. The total utilization is 1.76. No partitioning into two groups will lead to a feasible scheduling. Given the utilization factors of the tasks, each processor has to imperatively schedule the two tasks. It is easy to verify that the only partitioning leading to utilizations smaller than or equal to 1 on each of the processors is $\{\tau_1, \tau_2\}, \{\tau_3, \tau_4\}$, leading, respectively, to a total utilization of 0.86 and 0.9 on the processors. However, on the processor which $\tau_1$ and $\tau_2$ are assigned to, $\tau_1$ has to have a higher priority than $\tau_2$, $\tau_2$ will not be able to comply with its first deadline, since $\tau_1$ will be completely executed two times before $\tau_2$ terminates (at time 3.1). This system of tasks is, therefore, not schedulable with FTP in a partitioned system. Figure 3.1 gives a feasible scheduling with the following task priority migration $\tau_1 \prec \tau_3 \prec \tau_2 \prec \tau_4$.

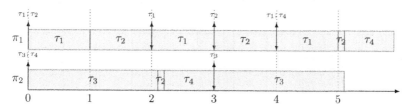

**Figure 3.1.** *Global scheduling with feasible fixed priority*

– $\langle 1,1 \rangle \not\subseteq \langle 1,3 \rangle$. Let us consider the system of tasks $\tau_1(1,2)$, $\tau_2(2,4)$, $\tau_3(2,3)$, $\tau_4(2,6)$. The partitioning of the tasks is such that $\tau_1$ and $\tau_2$ are placed on processor $\pi_1$ and the other two tasks on processor $\pi_2$ that leads to a feasible scheduling. In global scheduling, a thorough study of assignment of priorities to tasks shows that no feasible scheduling exists [LEU 82]. □

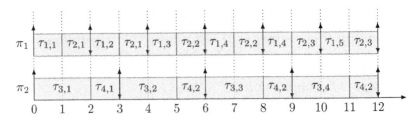

**Figure 3.2.** *Partitioned scheduling with feasible fixed priority*

Table 3.2 summarizes all the known results in multiprocessor scheduling of periodic, independent tasks with implicit deadlines [CAR 04]. In this table, the symbol "✗" represents the open problems.

| Classes of algorithms | Partitioned (P) | | | Restricted migration (RM) | | | Job-level migration (JLM) | | |
|---|---|---|---|---|---|---|---|---|---|
| | FTP $\langle 1,1 \rangle$ | FJP $\langle 2,1 \rangle$ | DP $\langle 3,1 \rangle$ | FTP $\langle 1,2 \rangle$ | FJP $\langle 2,2 \rangle$ | DP $\langle 3,2 \rangle$ | FTP $\langle 1,3 \rangle$ | FJP $\langle 2,3 \rangle$ | DP $\langle 3,3 \rangle$ |
| (P)  FTP $\langle 1,1 \rangle$ | = | ⊂ | ⊂ | ⊗ | ⊗ | ⊗ | ⊗ | ⊗ | ⊂ |
| (P)  FJP $\langle 2,1 \rangle$ | ⊃ | = | = | ⊗ | ⊗ | ⊗ | ⊗ | ⊗ | ⊂ |
| (P)  DP $\langle 3,1 \rangle$ | ⊃ | = | = | ⊗ | ⊗ | ⊗ | ⊗ | ⊗ | ⊂ |
| (RM)  FTP $\langle 1,2 \rangle$ | ⊗ | ⊗ | ⊗ | = | ⊂ | ⊂ | ⊗ | ✗ | ⊂ |
| (RM)  FJP $\langle 2,2 \rangle$ | ⊗ | ⊗ | ⊗ | ⊃ | = | ⊆ | ⊗ | ✗ | ⊂ |
| (RM)  DP $\langle 3,2 \rangle$ | ⊗ | ⊗ | ⊗ | ⊃ | ⊇ | = | ⊗ | ⊗ | ⊂ |
| (JLM)  FTP $\langle 1,3 \rangle$ | ⊗ | ⊗ | ⊗ | ⊗ | ⊗ | ⊗ | = | ⊂ | ⊂ |
| (JLM)  FJP $\langle 2,3 \rangle$ | ⊗ | ⊗ | ⊗ | ✗ | ✗ | ⊗ | ⊃ | = | ⊂ |
| (JLM)  DP $\langle 3,3 \rangle$ | ⊃ | ⊃ | ⊃ | ⊃ | ⊃ | ⊃ | ⊃ | ⊃ | = |

**Table 3.2.** *Comparison of multiprocessor scheduling algorithm classes. FTP: fixed-task priority, FJP: fixed-job priority and DP: dynamic priority*

### 3.3.1.2. *Optimality and existence of online algorithms*

Studies on the existence of optimal algorithms have been led on two task models: on the one hand, aperiodic and on the other, periodic or sporadic. A set of aperiodic tasks will be called from now on a set of jobs subject to deadlines.

In offline scheduling, the arrival times, durations and deadlines are completely known beforehand. The duration of the tasks is assumed to be constant. In this context, it is possible to define a feasible scheduling on a feasibility interval using techniques based on operations research [HOR 74] (maximum-flow search in a graph). The algorithmic complexity of this test is in $\mathcal{O}(n^3)$.

In an online multiprocessor scheduling, Hong and Leung have shown that there is no optimal online algorithm to schedule a set of tasks with no common deadlines [HON 92]. More precisely, these authors have shown that an optimal algorithm is necessarily clairvoyant, in other words it has to know in advance the arrival times of the jobs as well as their execution times [DER 89].

A scheduling algorithm is optimal for a class of algorithms if it allows us to build a feasible scheduling if there is one. For multiprocessor systems, there are optimal online algorithms for the systems of periodic or sporadic tasks with implicit deadlines. The first algorithm of a long list of algorithms was the PF algorithm (Pfair: fair progression) [BAR 93] that uses JLM and DPs for all the tasks. Optimal algorithms are also known for sporadic tasks with implicit deadlines such as a variant of PF called PD$^2$ [SRI 05]. Outside of these special cases, it has been shown that there is no optimal online algorithm [HON 92, FIS 10]. Such an algorithm is thus required to be clairvoyant, in other words know the characteristics of future tasks to be activated in the system.

*3.3.1.3. Predictability, sustainability and scheduling anomalies*

In multiprocessor systems, the anomalies are present in numerous situations [HA 94], as illustrated in the following example. This example defines a case of period anomaly for the global scheduling algorithm with FTP in which all the tasks will comply with their deadlines with the indicated parameters, whereas the increase of the period of a task with one time unit will lead to a scheduling that will not comply with all the deadlines. The considered tasks are described by their WCET and their period [AND 03]: $\tau_1 = (2,3)$, $\tau_2 = (2,4)$ and $\tau_3 = (7,12)$; $\tau_1$ has a higher priority than $\tau_2$, and $\tau_2$ has a higher priority than $\tau_3$. If the period of $\tau_1$ is increased by one time unit, then $\tau_1$ and $\tau_2$ have the same period and are activated at the same time. Since these two tasks have higher priorities than $\tau_3$, so they always occupy the two processors on the intervals $[2k, 2k+2)$, $k \geq 0$. The first instance of $\tau_3$, which cannot be parallelized on 2 processors, can in consequence only be executed 6 time units in the interval $[0,12)$ and cannot, therefore, comply with its deadline. Figure 3.3 presents the GANTT diagrams corresponding to the cases $T_1 = 3$ (upper part) and $T_1 = 4$ (lower part).

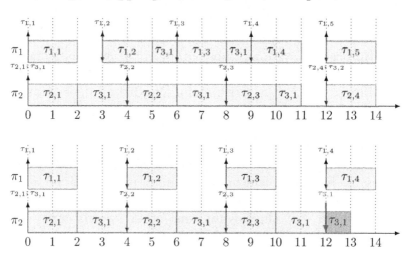

**Figure 3.3.** *Scheduling anomaly for fixed-priority multiprocessor algorithms*

Knowing whether a scheduling algorithm is subject to anomalies or not is a problem analyzed through predictability and sustainability properties. A scheduling algorithm is *predictive* if the decrease of execution times of the jobs does not undermine the schedulability of the system. This concept has been extended to the other characteristics of the jobs/tasks (periods and deadlines) under the name of *sustainability*.

Ha and Liu [HA 94] have shown that all preemptive multiprocessor schedulers (global or partitioned) and with fixed priority (fixed-task or fixed-job) are predictive. However, predictability has to be studied specifically for preemptive algorithms with DPs. When the sustainability property is considered, such positive results cannot be achieved. For instance, scheduling anomalies are being brought to light for global algorithms based on EDF where the FTPs are not viable [BAK 09].

### 3.3.2. *Quantitative properties*

The schedulability conditions are often defined over indicators of performance that represent the quantitative measures of processor activity. In the following, the main quantitative metrics used, on the one hand to define schedulability conditions, and on the other hand to characterize the performance of scheduling algorithms, are: utilization bounds, resource augmentation ratios and speedup factors, as well as empirical measures.

#### 3.3.2.1. *Utilization bounds*

The utilization bound $U$ of a scheduler guarantees that every system of tasks whose total utilization of smaller than or equal to $U$ will be correctly scheduled. Beyond this utilization limit, and if the bound is said to be tight, then there exists systems of tasks that are not schedulable. If the bound is not tight, then there may exist non-schedulable systems but neither have been seen in practice. An algorithm is optimal when its utilization bound is equal to the capacity of the platform. In uniprocessor systems, FJP or DP algorithms allow us to reach the maximum utilization of the platform (for example, EDF or LLF).

Only the class of schedulers authorizing JLMs and DPs allows us to define optimal algorithms for the most simple of task models: implicit deadline. The PF algorithm [BAR 93] goes into this class. In every other case, the maximum utilization, which can be guaranteed by a class of schedulers, is $(m + 1)/2$, where $m$ is the number of processors [CAR 04]. This, therefore, leads to only exploiting 50% of the computing capacities of the platform in the worst case. The limit of 50% of the usable processor capacity can be illustrated using a simple example in partitioned scheduling. It is sufficient for this to consider $(m + 1)$ identical tasks with an execution time of $(1 + \epsilon)$ with periods of 2, where $\epsilon$ is an arbitrarily small number. These tasks have to be scheduled by partitioning on $m$ identical processors. Regardless of the partitioning considered for these $(m + 1)$ tasks on $m$ processors, there will necessarily be two tasks that will have to be allocated on the same processor. On this processor, the two tasks cannot be scheduled, since the utilization of this processor is then equal to $1 + \epsilon > 1$. By choosing $\epsilon$ close to zero, the maximum total utilization of the platform approaches $(m + 1)/2$.

### 3.3.2.2. *Resource augmentation ratio*

For numerous problems, there is no optimal online algorithm. Despite the poor performances with respect to optimal offline methods, online algorithms can reach a behavior equivalent to an optimal algorithm as soon as the resources given to the online algorithm are moderately superior to those exploited by the optimal offline algorithm.

The resource augmentation technique allows us to quantify in the worst case what increase in resources has to be necessarily given to the online algorithm for it to be comparable to the optimal algorithm (which of course does not benefit from this increase in resources). In multiprocessor scheduling, the increase in resources consists of giving faster processors to the online algorithm, and this ratio is called the speedup factor in the literature. This quantitative measure, therefore, indicates the utilization cost of a scheduling heuristic in terms of quantity of resources that would not have been necessary if an optimal method would have been chosen [KAL 95, KAL 00].

We illustrate the point of this technique by considering the EDF algorithm with preemption and JLM in a system composed of identical processors. The following example shows that EDF, used as a global scheduler has, for the systems of tasks with implicit deadlines, a utilization bound equal to 1 and this, no matter the number of processors of the platform. This means that if the schedulability test is based only on the utilization factor of the platform, then it is equal to: $U_{\text{sum}} \leq 1$. This test directly comes from the optimality of EDF in a uniprocessor environment. In order to show that this test is precise no matter what the number of processors, we have to prove the existence of non-schedulable systems of tasks under EDF with a total utilization factor of: $U_{\text{sum}} = 1 + \epsilon$, where $\epsilon$ is an arbitrarily small number. This phenomenon is often called the DHALL effect [DHA 78]. It is proved in the following way: let $n$ be periodic tasks with implicit deadlines, there exists a feasible (online) scheduling with EDF on $m$ identical processors if and only if $U_{\text{sum}} \leq 1$. The sufficient condition comes from the fact that the EDF algorithm is optimal for one processor [LIU 73]. We show the necessary condition by proving the converse property: there exists systems of tasks with a total utilization of $1 + \epsilon$ non-schedulable on $m$ processors with EDF. Let us consider $n$ tasks, $m < n$, defined by $\tau_i(C_i, T_i)$ in the following manner: $\tau_k(2\epsilon, 1)$ for $1 \leq k \leq n - 1$ and $\tau_n(1, 1 + \epsilon)$. The maximum utilization is obtained by the task $\tau_n$ with a utilization of 1. Clearly, a processor has to be dedicated to this task in every feasible scheduling. However, the utilization of EDF leads to starting at time 0 the tasks $\tau_1, \ldots, \tau_{n-1}$, each on a separate processor, since their deadlines are smaller than that of $\tau_n$. The $m$ processors are simultaneously ready at time $t = 2\epsilon$ and consequently, $\tau_n$ will not be able to terminate its execution before its deadline. Yet, the total utilization of this system of tasks is given by:

$$\lim_{\epsilon \to 0} U_{\text{sum}} = \lim_{\epsilon \to 0} \left( 2(n-1)\epsilon + \frac{1}{1+\epsilon} \right) = 1$$

This counter-example also holds for the rate monotonic algorithm (RM) when FTP tasks are being considered [DHA 78]. However, this poor behavior of EDF can be made relative if the capacity of the processors it uses is moderately superior to that exploited by the optimal algorithm. We illustrate this problem through an example. A processor of speed $\alpha$ will be denoted in the following by an $\alpha-$processor. Let us consider three jobs $J_i(C_i, D_i)$, ready at time 0: $J_1(2,2)$, $J_2(2,3)$, $J_3(4,4)$. On a system with two processors, EDF scheduling leads to starting $J_1$ and $J_2$ at time 0 and starting $J_3$ after the end of execution of one of the two first tasks, on of the two processors that are simultaneously ready at time 2. Consequently, $J_3$ does not comply with its deadline under EDF. The optimal scheduling of these jobs consists of course in scheduling $J_1$, $J_2$ on one processor and $J_3$ on the second processor. All the tasks are terminated before their deadlines. As illustrated in Figure 3.4, if EDF uses $(3/2)-$processors (in other words, processors of capacity $3/2$), then the execution time of $J_1$ and $J_2$ is $4/3$ and that of $J_3$ is $8/3$. The total duration of the scheduling will be 4 time units, and all the tasks comply with their deadlines. In [PHI 97, PHI 02], it was shown that the resource augmentation ratio of EDF is bounded by 2. Thus, the price to pay for using EDF instead of an optimal algorithm is to use processors which are 2 times faster.

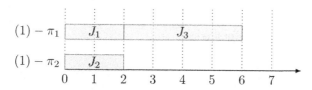

(a) EDF with unitary-capacity processors

(b) Optimal scheduling with unitary-capacity processors

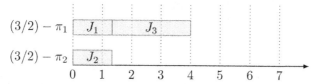

(c)EDF scheduling with processors of capacity $3/2$

**Figure 3.4.** *Example of resource augmentation: the optimal algorithm on two processors of speed 1 and* EDF *on two processors of speed 3/2. The speedup factor is 3/2*

## 3.4. Partitioned scheduling

### 3.4.1. *Partitioning algorithms*

In a partitioned scheduling, the tasks are not authorized to migrate and are statically allocated on the different processors before starting their execution. They will stay on the same processor for their entire lifetime. Once the allocation step is done, the tasks are scheduled using traditional algorithms known in uniprocessor scheduling (for example, RM or EDF). For systems of independent tasks, the scheduling on each processor is completely independent of those calculated on the other processors. The results for periodic tasks are, therefore, generalized, as for uniprocessor systems, to sporadic tasks.

The calculation of the scheduling of the tasks in order to allocate them on the processors is a variant of the famous bin-packing optimization problem [COF 96]) that has been intensely studied since the early 1970s and is used as a canonical problem for the implementation of new algorithmic techniques such as the techniques of approximation and resource increasing. The partitioning problem of the tasks is nondeterministic polynomial time (NP)-complete in the strong sense [GAR 79], and in consequence there is no polynomial or pseudo-polynomial algorithm to calculate a partitioning using a minimum number of processors.

The real-time task partitioning algorithms are based on heuristics or on variations of algorithms solving the bin-packing problem [OH 95]. Most allocation heuristics are greedy algorithms (which never change an already performed allocation) and are based on two decisions:

– *Step 1* – sorting: preprocessing to calculate a permutation of the tasks: $L$;

– *Step 2* – distribution: take the tasks of $L$ in this order, and place them one by one on the processors following a distribution rule. Update the utilization factor $\text{Level}(j)$ of processor $j$ chosen by the rule after allocation of the current task. If the number of processors is not fixed beforehand, the algorithm can decide to add one if the rule is not able to place the current task on the previously created processors.

In a real-time scheduling framework, step 2 of distribution of tasks must be associated with a uniprocessor schedulability test aiming to guarantee that the current task as well as the tasks already allocated on the current processor will be schedulable together. In the framework of EDF or LLF scheduling (optimal uniprocessor schedulings), the schedulability test corresponds to the test of accepting an element in a box in the bin-packing problem: the capacity, of the processor or of the box, has to be smaller than or equal to 1. However, this will not be the case for fixed-priority schedulers that do not have a guarantee of utilization equal to the capacity of the processor (for instance, the guarantee of RM is equal to 69%). A schedulability test then has to be executed before any allocation of task that can take place on a processor.

In its online version, bin-packing algorithm considers that the sequence $L$ of tasks to place is not known (or arbitrary). The tasks are, therefore, placed one after the other in the order of the list $L$ without any preprocessing (in other words, step 1 of the heuristic is not used). In its offline version, a rule is associated with every step. The main rule of step 1 consists of sorting the tasks of $L$ in a non-ascending way according to their utilization factors. The heuristic names often end with the term $D$ as in decreasing, indicating that the list of tasks $L$ has been sorted. Numerous different rules have been created in step 2 to perform the distribution of tasks on the different processors. We consider that the current task is $\tau_i$. The most widespread rules are:

– First-fit (FF): assign the task $\tau_i$ on the first processor able to contain it, in the order of their indices.

– Best-fit (BF): assign the task $\tau_i$ on the first processor with the highest utilization factor able to receive it (i.e. Level($j$) $\leq$ $1 - U_i$).

– Worst-fit (WF): assign the task $\tau_i$ on the processor with the lowest utilization factor able to receive it (i.e. Level($j$) $\leq 1 - U_i$).

– Almost worst-fit (AWF): is a variant of WF in which the chosen processor has the second smallest utilization factor.

– Next-fit (NF): only the last processor created can receive tasks. When it is not possible to place the task $\tau_i$, the current processor is closed (it will no longer be able to receive new tasks). The next processor then becomes the new current processor.

These heuristics correspond to algorithms close the ones solving the bin-packing problem and combine in practice the two steps of sorting and distribution (in other words, FFD, BFD, WFD and so forth). We refer the readers to [COF 96] for a detailed review of the results of worst case and average analyses of these heuristics.

An allocation algorithm is said to be reasonable [LÓP 04] if it can always allocate a task on a processor if there is one able to accept the allocation. For instance, FF, BF and WF are reasonable while NF is not.

We illustrate these algorithms with an example of 7 tasks $\{\tau_1, \ldots, \tau_7\}$ with respective utilizations of $\{0.8, 0.7, 0.6, 0.5, 0.4, 0.2, 0.1\}$. The tasks are sorted according to their decreasing utilization factors. The platform is composed of 4 identical processors $\{\pi_1, \pi_2, \pi_3, \pi_4\}$. Each processor is scheduled by EDF. The tasks being periodic and with implicit deadlines, placed on a same processor will be schedulable if and only if their total utilization is smaller than or equal to 1. This necessary and sufficient condition of the schedulability of tasks on a processor constitutes a test of acceptance. If a task cannot be allocated, the heuristics fail to build a feasible partitioning. The allocations performed by the present heuristics are given in Figure 3.5 and are detailed below:

– Next-fit decreasing (NDF): the NF allocation places $\tau_1$ on the first processor $\pi_1$; $\tau_2$ that cannot be placed on $\pi_1$ will be placed on $\pi_2$. Likewise, $\tau_3$, which cannot be placed on $\pi_2$, will be placed on $\pi_3$ and $\tau_4$ that cannot be placed on $\pi_3$ will be placed on $pi_4$. $\tau_5$ is placed on $\pi_4$. However, the placement of $\tau_6$ whose utilization is 0.2 will not be done on processor $\pi_4$. NF, no longer able to consider new processors, fails to build a feasible scheduling of the tasks.

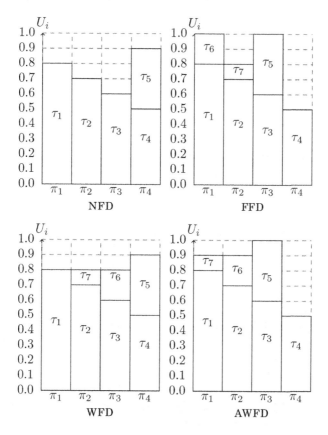

**Figure 3.5.** *Examples of allocations performed by the main bin-packing heuristics*

– First-fit decreasing (FFD): the first 4 tasks are placed in the same way as with NFD. Task $\tau_5$ is then placed on the first processor able to receive it ($\pi_3$). After this allocation, $\pi_3$ is 100% loaded. $\tau_6$ whose utilization is 0.2 will then be placed on the first processor $\pi_1$, which will then be 100% loaded. $\tau_7$ is finally placed on processor $\pi_2$.

– Best-fit decreasing (BFD): the first 4 tasks are placed in the same way as with NFD. Task $\tau_5$ is then placed on processor $\pi_3$, since it is the highest loaded processor able to receive it. After this allocation, $\pi_3$ is 100% loaded. $\tau_6$ whose utilization is $0.2$ will then be placed on processor $\pi_1$, which is the highest loaded one able to receive it, and finally $\tau_7$ is placed on processor $\tau_2$. The corresponding allocation is identical to the FF allocation. It is consequently not represented in Figure 3.5.

– Worst-fit decreasing (WFD): here again, the first 4 tasks are placed in the same way as with NFD. At each step, the chosen processor is the one with the least load. Thus, $\tau_5$ is placed on processor $\pi_4$; then, $\tau_6$ is placed on processor $\tau_3$, and finally $\tau_7$ is placed on processor $\tau_2$.

– Almost worst-fit decreasing (AWFD): works the same way as WF but chooses, at each step, the second processor with the least load. Here again, the first 4 tasks are placed in the same manner as with NFD. $\tau_5$ is placed on processor $\pi_3$, which is the second-lowest charged processor. $\tau_6$ is then placed on processor $\pi_1$, which is the second-lowest charged processor. And finally, $\tau_7$ is placed on processor $\pi_1$, which is the second-lowest charged processor.

### 3.4.2. *Evaluation of partitioning algorithms*

Before illustrating some algorithms, let us not forget that they are generally built in order to optimize a particular evaluation criterion. The three main criteria studied in the literature are:

– The asymptotic ratio of the number of processors necessary to schedule a system of tasks using a heuristic with an optimal placement algorithm.

– The utilization bound guaranteed by the heuristic: every system of tasks with total utilization over the guaranteed utilization bound will be schedulable.

– The resource augmentation ratio.

3.4.2.1. *Asymptotic ratio of the number of processor*

The asymptotic ratio of the number of processors has mainly been studied for FTP tasks. Indeed, for tasks with FJPs (for instance, EDF) and DP tasks, the problem of allocation of the tasks corresponds exactly to a bin-packing problem. The heuristics are looking to determine the approximation ratio defined as the number of processors necessary for the heuristic over the optimal number of processors to partition a system of tasks. Let $N_0$ be the number of processors necessary to schedule a system of tasks using an optimal partitioning, and $N$ the number of processors necessary for an approached algorithm, the ratio is defined by $N/N_0$. Unfortunately, this ratio can only be calculated when the number of processors used by the optimal algorithm approaches infinity. It is for this reason that the ratio is said to be asymptotic. For instance, for the EDF scheduling algorithm and an allocation of tasks performed by FFD, the asymptotic ratio is directly derived from results known for the bin-packing problem and is equal to $3/2$ [COF 96]. In the case of tasks with FTP, it is necessary to take into account the task acceptance schedulability test on each processor. It has, for example, been shown in [DHA 78] that RMNF (RM scheduling coupled with an NFallocation) has an asymptotic ratio between 2 and 2.67. The best possible ratio for a fixed-priority algorithm, with value of $3/2$ for EDF, has been defined in [KAR 11], after more than 30 years of research on the subject.

The asymptotic ratio of the number of processors is of limited interest in practice, since the schedulability tests that can be derived from it (in other words, utilization bounds) are pessimistic [OH 98]. The utilization bounds of the platforms allow us to establish schedulability test that is at the same time more efficient and simpler to verify. In the context of periodic tasks with implicit deadlines, the utilization bounds are known for RM and EDF scheduling policies. We will detail the case of EDF later on.

### 3.4.2.2. *Utilization bounds*

For the EDF algorithm, the utilization bound varies depending on the allocation strategy used. The condition over the maximum utilization bound is based on the number of processors and the task with the highest utilization among all the tasks to schedule: $U_{\max} = \max_{\tau_i \in \tau} U_i$. The number of tasks, which can be scheduled on a processor and respecting the condition that the total utilization is smaller than or equal to 1, is at least equal to:

$$\beta = \left\lfloor \frac{1}{U_{\max}} \right\rfloor$$

This indicates that a processor can schedule with EDF at least $\beta$ tasks, or equivalently, $m$ tasks can be scheduled regardless of the reasonable allocation algorithm used. The utilization bounds of EDF for the main reasonable allocation algorithms are defined in the interval $[L_{\mathrm{EDF}}, H_{\mathrm{EDF}}]$. $L_{\mathrm{EDF}}$ is the utilization bound guaranteed by every reasonable algorithm. Thus, any configuration of tasks with a utilization smaller than $L_{\mathrm{EDF}}$ will be scheduled by EDF if a reasonable allocation algorithm is used. The upper utilization bound $H_{\mathrm{EDF}}$ is the maximum bound that can be reached by a reasonable allocation algorithm with EDF. In other words, beyond this limit, there exists systems of tasks non-schedulable by a reasonable allocation algorithm with EDF. The values of these bounds are given by the following formulas [LÓP 04]:

$$L_{\mathrm{EDF}} \geq m - (m-1)U_{\max}$$
$$H_{\mathrm{EDF}} \leq \frac{\beta m + 1}{\beta + 1}$$

In other words:

– Every reasonable algorithm has an upper utilization bound equal to $m - (m-1)U_{\max}$.

– Every algorithm (reasonable or not) cannot admit a utilization bound higher than $\frac{\beta m+1}{\beta+1}$.

For the most widespread reasonable algorithms, we distinguish between two cases [LÓP 04]:

– Online algorithms: WF guarantees a utilization corresponding to the minimum bound $L_{\mathrm{EDF}}$, whereas FF and BF guarantee the upper bound $H_{\mathrm{EDF}}$. This constitutes an interesting result, since an optimal online algorithm exists with respect to the maximum utilization criterion.

– Offline algorithms: if the tasks are sorted in decreasing order of their utilization, then the WFD, FFD and BFD algorithms guarantee the upper bound $H_{\mathrm{EDF}}$.

The utilization bounds have been defined for a similar approach when the RM algorithm is used on each processor to schedule the tasks. We refer the readers to [LÓP 03] for more details.

### 3.4.2.3. *Resource augmentation ratio*

The maximum utilization of the platform being bounded by $(m+1)/2$ and a large number of algorithms being subject to the DHALL effect, the previous criterion, based on the worst-case analysis of the utilization factor, can be considered restrictive in order to allow a relevant comparison of partitioning algorithms. The resource augmentation ratio allows us to establish other forms of comparing partitioning algorithms. Few studies have been performed so far in this direction, but it is nevertheless possible to link the problem of determination of the resource augmentation ratio to a dual problem, that of bin packing: the minimization of the duration of multiprocessor scheduling without preemption (multiprocessor makespan scheduling) [BAR 13].

Before illustrating the link between the problem of the worst-case resource augmentation ratio and the problem of

minimization of the duration of the scheduling, we recall its
definition. Given $n$ aperiodic jobs of known durations $C_i$, a
non-preemptive scheduling must be built on $m$ processors.
The absence of preemption of the $n$ jobs imposes that
migrations are not authorized. Consequently, does the
scheduling algorithm necessarily partitions the jobs on the
different processors? The aim is to find the partitioning that
would lead to terminating the scheduling at the earliest time
(minimal makespan scheduling problem - MSP) — minimizing
the completion time of the last terminated job in the
scheduling. If the aperiodic jobs of this scheduling problem
are defined as the utilization factors of the tasks of the
real-time scheduling problem, then every schedule with a
maximum duration of 1 leads to a feasible partitioning (under
the hypothesis that EDF is used locally on each processor).
The longest processing time heuristic (LPT) which, as soon as
a processor is free, allocates the longest non-allocated job,
leads to the same partitioning as that defined by WFD.

The approximation ratio of the duration of the scheduling
of the MSP problem allows us to establish the resource
augmentation ratio. For this, we recall the definition of the
approximation ratio of a list of algorithm [GRA 69]: let $w_0$ be
the duration obtained by an optimal scheduling algorithm,
and $w_L$ that is obtained by a list of algorithm, which places
the tasks of $L$, in that order, on the first ready processor. The
approximation ratio gives the worst ratio $w_L/w_0$ that can be
obtained by any list $L$ of tasks. GRAHAM, in 1969 [GRA 69],
has shown for the MSP problem that the approximation ratio
is bounded by:

$$w_L \leq \left( \frac{4}{3} - \frac{1}{3m} \right) w_0$$

In order to link this result to the real-time scheduling
problem, $w_0$ is the utilization necessary for an optimal
algorithm exploiting processors with unitary capacities, and

the approximation ratio guarantees that if the list of algorithm exploits faster processors, with a factor equal to the approximation ratio, then it is building a feasible partitioning. The approximation ratio of MSP, therefore, corresponds exactly to the rate of increase of the desired resource.

## 3.5. Global scheduling

In this paradigm, no placement strategy (partitioning of tasks or of jobs of tasks) is *a priori* fixed. All the tasks ready to be executed are placed in a single queue, and the $m$ highest priority tasks are allocated on the $m$ processors of the platform. The migration is unrestricted and called JLM, since it can occur at any time during the execution of the jobs. The scheduler can interrupt a task executing on a processor at any time, and then resume its execution on a different processor. We then refer to global scheduling.

Contrarily to the case of partitioned systems which consider, after the allocation of the tasks, as many uniprocessor scheduling problems as there are processors, the global scheduling only uses a single queue of tasks ready to execute. The $m$ highest priority tasks are, therefore, always running. The possibility to migrate tasks allows us, in general, to reach a better usage of the platform, and in some cases to reach a 100% maximum usage on each processor. However, global scheduling is more complex to understand in principle, since the results known for uniprocessors, which could easily be re-used in the case of partitioned multiprocessors, no longer hold in the case of a global scheduler. For example:

– The analysis of sporadic tasks is not reduced to the analysis of periodic tasks with the same period. The tasks are subject to period anomalies. Thus, increasing the period of a task can make the system unschedulable. Moreover, there is no optimal scheduling algorithm for sporadic tasks, as soon as they are not implicit-deadline.

– It is not possible to easily define a feasibility interval to verify the compliance with the deadlines of the periodic tasks. Contrarily to uniprocessor systems, it is not sufficient to look for a temporal fault in a time interval that starts with a critical instant. The following example comes from [GOO 03] and considers a global scheduling with EDF on 2 identical processors of the system of tasks with synchronous releases $\{(3,6),(2,7),(5,5)\}$. EDF leads to a temporal fault at time 85 while the interval started by a critical instant terminates at time 5.

Two main approaches have been proposed to define the schedulers with total migration authorized: guarantee the fairness of the distribution time of the processor capacities between the tasks and the extension of uniprocessor techniques. These two approaches are discussed below.

### 3.5.1. *Proportionate fair algorithms*

The proportionate fair algorithms define a class of optimal schedulers for real-time systems with the following properties: $m$ identical processors; periodic tasks with implicit deadlines, ready at time 0 and defined by $\tau_i(C_i, T_i)$, $1 \leq i \leq n$; a task can be preempted and migrate at 0 cost (the corresponding costs are assumed negligible). Let us note that the existence of such optimal algorithms has been an open problem for over 20 years, since the first algorithm was defined in 1993 [BAR 93]. Afterward, numerous variations of algorithms have been defined in the literature, and we will limit ourselves to presenting the main common principles of this family of schedulers.

In the following, we define the concept of fluid scheduling that guarantees a fully fair distribution of the capacities of the platform to the tasks. However, this simple and ideal approach is not possible in practice. Numerous algorithms have been proposed in order to comply with this fairness property while preserving the optimality of the algorithms. Then, with the advances in knowledge, this fairness property was progressively relaxed until the recent definition of optimal algorithms that does not exploit this property. The following sections present the main corresponding results.

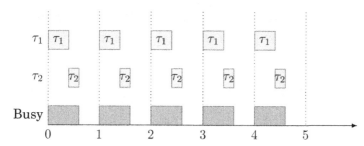

**Figure 3.6.** *Fair (fluid) scheduling in continuous time*

For the sake of brevity, the following presentation will be limited to systems of independent tasks with implicit deadlines, having to execute on identical processors.

### 3.5.1.1. *Fair and fluid scheduling*

The idea of a fluid scheduling is to fairly progress the execution of each task at every time unit in such a way as to comply with all the temporal constraints. In continuous time, this means attributing the processor to each task $\tau_i$ for a time interval equal to its utilization factor $U_i = C_i/T_i$ in every time unit of the scheduling. The corresponding scheduling is then said to be "fluid". Figure 3.6 presents the beginning of a fair, fluid scheduling for two tasks $\tau_1(2,5)$, $\tau_2(2,10)$. At each time unit, $\tau_1$ receives $U_1 = 2/5 = 0.4$ and $U_2 = 2/10 = 0.2$. Therefore, at each time unit 0.4 time units are not used.

Under these hypotheses of fluid scheduling, illustrated in the previous example, there always exists a fluid scheduling that complies with the deadlines for any system of period tasks such that $U_{\mathrm{sum}} \leq m$ and $U_{\mathrm{max}} \leq 1$. This ideal approach is, therefore, optimal, but of course it is not realistic, since all the tasks are executed within each time unit.

Two "fair" scheduling classes have been proposed in the literature, depending on whether the decision times of the scheduler follow a discrete or continuous time interval. The concept of discrete time assumes that the scheduler is activated at the kernel clock ticks. Without loss in generality, these times are represented in the set of integers. In the continuous case, the scheduler can be activated at any time. Historically, the first optimal algorithm is a discrete-time scheduler.

### 3.5.1.2. Discrete-time fair algorithms

The fair algorithms will allow us to relax the hypothesis of fluidity of the scheduling. The scheduling is decomposed into time intervals, called blocks. The schedule will be progressively built block by block. The scheduler is invoked at every beginning of a block in order to build the scheduling of the tasks within the current block. The PF algorithm (proportionate fairness) [BAR 93] is historically the first optimal online algorithm for tasks with implicit deadlines having to execute on $m$ identical processors. This type of algorithm basically decomposes each task into subtasks of unitary duration. Each subtask will be given a pseudo-release time and a pseudo-deadline defining the temporal window in which it will have to be executed in order to be the closest possible to a fluid scheduling. The scheduling decisions are made at each time unit. Every block, therefore, has a unitary duration. In order to distinguish this special case, a block of duration 1 will be designated as the slot from now on. Contrarily to the fluid scheduling case, no tasks will be preempted within a slot. The Pfair approach, therefore, corresponds to a discrete passage of time and to the decomposition of each task into subtasks of one time unit (therefore, equivalent to a processor quantum).

The hypothesis of the continuous progression of each task within each slot is not realistic in practice. The idea of the family of *Pfair* algorithms [BAR 93, BAR 96] is to only authorize context switches (in other words, preemption and migration of tasks) at the boundaries of each slot while remaining the fairest possible. Without loss of generality, each time slot is identified by an integer $t$. $t = 0$ corresponds to the first slot, and therefore to the time interval $[t, t + 1)$. The lag or the gap between the discrete scheduling and continuous scheduling of a task $\tau_i$, in slot $t$, will be measured using the function $\text{LAG}(\tau_i, t)$.

DEFINITION 3.3.– *A scheduling of a task $\tau_i$ is a function of $S(\tau_i, t) : \mathbb{N} \to \{0, 1\}$, with $S(\tau_i, t) = 1$ if $\tau_i$ is executed in slot $t$, and 0 otherwise.*

DEFINITION 3.4.– *For a task $\tau_i$ in an interval $[0, t)$, the lag between the quantity executed in the fluid scheduling and discrete scheduling $S$ is defined as:*

$$\text{LAG}(\tau_i, t) = t \cdot U_i - \sum_{k=1}^{t} S(\tau_i, k)$$

*where $t \cdot U_i$ gives the quantity of $\tau_i$ executed in the fluid scheduling and $\sum_{k=1}^{t} S(\tau_i, k)$ is the quantity executed in the discrete scheduling, in the interval $[0, t)$.*

Thus, when task $\tau_i$ is executed $\text{LAG}(\tau_i, t)$ is decreased by $1 - U_i$, otherwise it would increase by $U_i$. The formulation of the function $\text{LAG}(\tau_i, t)$ can, therefore, be done in the following manner:

$$\text{LAG}(\tau_i, t + 1) = \begin{cases} \text{LAG}(\tau_i, t) + U_i & \text{if } S(\tau_i, t) = 0 \\ \text{LAG}(\tau_i, t) - (1 - U_i) & \text{if } S(\tau_i, t) = 1 \end{cases}$$

*The question now for every task $\tau_i$ is: how much can the function* $\mathrm{LAG}(\tau_i, t)$ *move away from* 0 *while complying with its deadline?* Since the system is discrete, the task parameters are integers. Thus, if a task which does not meet its deadline, will exceed its deadline by at least one time unit. Consequently for this task, there is a lag of at least one time unit between the discrete scheduling and fluid scheduling (in other words, $\mathrm{LAG}(\tau_i, t) \geq 1$). Compliance with the condition $\mathrm{LAG}(\tau_i, t) < 1$, for every time $t$, and therefore including the deadline, necessarily leads to a feasible scheduling. The following example will illustrate that a discrete scheduling verifying $-1 < \mathrm{LAG}(\tau_i, t) < 1$ is a feasible scheduling.

*Example :* Let us consider a uniprocessor system with $k \in \mathbb{N}$ tasks of duration 1 and of period $k$ ($\tau_i(1, k), 1 \leq i \leq k$). In order to comply with the deadlines, every feasible scheduling has to execute the tasks in consecutive intervals of length $k$. In this interval of length $k$ (for example, $[0, k)$):

– If the task is served in the first slot, in other words $t = 1$ and $S_i(1) = 1$: $\mathrm{LAG}(\tau_i, 1) = \frac{1}{k} - 1$. When $k$ is large, then $\mathrm{LAG}(\tau_i, 1)$ approaches $-1$.

– If the task is served in the last slot, then at $t = k - 1$: $\sum_{j=1}^{k-1} S_i(k) = 0$, and therefore $\mathrm{LAG}(\tau_i, k - 1) = (k - 1)\frac{1}{k} - 0$. When $k$ is large, then $= \mathrm{LAG}(\tau_i, k - 1)$ approaches 1.

Clearly, for this system of tasks, every feasible scheduling verifies: $-1 < \mathrm{LAG}_i(t) < 1$.    □

The condition on the function $\mathrm{LAG}$ defines the notion of fairness in a scheduling.

DEFINITION 3.5 ([BAR 93, BAR 96]).– *A scheduling is Pfair if and only if for every task* $\tau_i$: $-1 < \mathrm{LAG}(\tau_i, t) < 1$.

The following result shows that every Pfair scheduling complies with the deadlines of periodic tasks. The fairness property is, therefore, a sufficient condition of feasibility.

THEOREM 3.1.– Every Pfair scheduling is feasible.

The PF algorithm is based on a priority rule that takes into account the upcoming tasks. These tasks are known, since they follow strict activation periods. The recursive definition of certain priority rules makes the practical implementation of PF complex. Simpler implementations have been proposed to facilitate the calculations while preserving optimality mainly by decomposing the tasks into subtasks and assigning them pseudo-release times and pseudo-deadlines (see for example [SRI 05]). We will not go into algorithmic details will limit ourselves to one example.

Let us consider an example with 5 tasks: $\tau_1(1,3), \tau_2(2,5)$, $\tau_3(2,5), \tau_4(2,3), \tau_5(1,5)$ to execute on 2 identical processors. Fluid scheduling would consist, within each time unit, of scheduling each task with a duration equal to its utilization factor. The PF scheduling will build a schedule in which each task receives a time quantum. Figure 3.7 presents the corresponding scheduling. Each task $\tau_i$ is ensured by the PF algorithm to receive $C_i$ time units between its release and its deadline (in other words, every $T_i$ time unit interval starting from the initial time). We refer the readers to the article [BAR 93] for the precise definition of the PF algorithm.

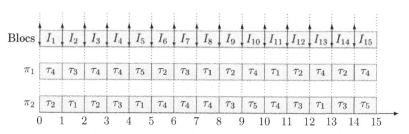

**Figure 3.7.** *Discrete-time* PF *scheduling*

Numerous variants and extensions of PF have been proposed in the literature. These fair scheduling algorithms are differentiated by:

– The definition of blocks: quantum of time (slot of length of one processor time unit) or an interval delimited by two consecutive task deadlines. An algorithm is said to be proportionate fair ([BAR 96]) if each block is exactly one quantum. It is said to be boundary fair ([ZHU 11, ZHU 03]) if the size of the block can be larger than one quantum. The blocks are then delimited by consecutive deadlines.

– The portion of each task that has to be executed in a block. This step is often called allocation.

– The sequencing of the tasks within the block in order to ensure that a task is not executed at the same time on two different processors. This step is often called distribution.

The quantum-by-quantum construction of the scheduling is not necessary in order to define an optimal algorithm [ZHU 03]. BF (Boundary fair) is the first algorithm that does not decompose the tasks into single-time unit subtasks. The construction of the scheduling is done over time intervals delimited by two consecutive deadlines. Thus, these scheduling blocks are delimited by boundaries defined by the consecutive deadlines of the tasks. The BF algorithm only guarantees the fairness property at the boundaries. The fairness condition $-1 < \text{LAG}(\tau_i, t) < 1$ is respected for each time $t$ corresponding to a deadline. However, it is not necessarily respected within the blocks.

In the example in Figure 3.7, the two task periods used are 3 and 5 time units. Thus, the blocks delimited by successive deadlines are: $[0, 3), [3, 5), [5, 6), [6, 9), [9, 10), [10, 12), [12, 15)$. Where PF invoked the scheduler 15 times over the 15 units of time corresponding to the hyperperiod of the system, BF will invoke it 7 times. Without going into the algorithmic details of BF (see [ZHU 11]), Figure 3.8 gives the boundary fair scheduling built by BF on the same system of tasks as that in Figure 3.7.

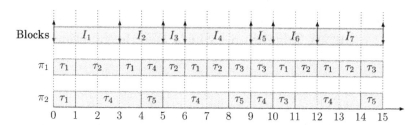

**Figure 3.8.** *Deadline fair scheduling built with the* BF *algorithm*

### 3.5.1.3. *Continuous-time fair algorithms*

The previous algorithms assume that time is by its nature discrete: the times at which the scheduler can be activated are integers (in other words, correspond to the clock ticks of the real-time operating system). Discrete time is by its nature a source of complexity in multiprocessor scheduling and for this reason, algorithms that exploit the continuous nature of time have been defined. We will now detail the simplest algorithm in this category: the DP-WRAP algorithm.

The DP-WRAP algorithm is a very simple deadline fair algorithm that is optimal for tasks with implicit deadlines [FUN 11]. Contrarily to the previous algorithms, DP-WRAP considers that the time is continuous. The scheduling is broken down into blocks delimited by deadlines/periods. These time intervals correspond to those defined by HORN's method, defined in 1974, to analyze the feasibility of a set of task instances subject to deadlines [HOR 74]. The slicing of the time following the intervals is called *DP-fair* (deadline partitioning fair) by the designers of DP-WRAP. The distribution of the tasks into each interval is equal to the length of the interval multiplied by the utilization of the task. Thus, in the interval $[s_j, s_{j+1})$, each task $\tau_i$ is given $U_i \times (s_{j+1} - s_j)$. Consequently, at each deadline, the tasks have received an execution time equivalent to that which they would have received in a fluid scheduling. The fairness property is, therefore, strictly ensured for each task at every deadline $t$: LAG$(\tau_i, t) = 0$. The scheduling (distribution) in each block is done by the McNAUGHTON algorithm, which has been proposed in 1959 [MCN 59].

After allocating the jobs to the blocks, the quantity $C_i(j)$ is the portion of the task $\tau_i$ (subtask) that has to be executed in scheduling block $j$. The construction of the schedule is totally independent of the scheduling in other blocks, we will limit ourselves in the following, without loss of generality, to a block $j$. The McNAUGHTON algorithm allows us to build a schedule in a block with a number of migrations bounded by $m - 1$. The length of the scheduling in block $j$ (in other words, the makespan in traditional scheduling, denoted $C_{max}$) on $m$ identical processors is given by [MCN 59]:

$$C_{\max} = \max \left( \frac{1}{m} \sum_{i=1}^{n} C_i(j); \max_{1 \leq i \leq n} C_i(j) \right)$$

Each subtask can be scheduled at any time in the interval. The only constraint to comply with is not to simultaneously schedule a subtask on more than one processor. A simple way to build multiprocessor scheduling is to consider a uniprocessor problem [PIN 08]:

– *Step 1*: schedule all the subtasks in any order without preemption on a single processor. The length of this scheduling is necessarily smaller than or equal to $m \times C_{\max}$.

– *Step 2*: slice this uniprocessor scheduling into intervals of length $C_{\max}$: $[0, C_{\max}), [C_{\max}, 2C_{\max}), [2C_{\max}, 3C_{\max})$, etc. There are at most $m$ intervals.

– *Step 3*: the interval $k$, $1 \leq k \leq m$ defines the scheduling of processor $\pi_k$. A task sliced at the end of the interval will be found at the beginning of the next interval, thus avoiding that a task is simultaneously executed on two processors at the same time.

Let us look once again at the example of the scheduling performed in order to illustrate fair algorithms (see Figure 3.7 and Figure 3.8). The durations of the subtasks in each scheduling block are presented in Table 3.3. The MCNAUGHTON scheduling is built within each block. The corresponding scheduling is presented in Figure 3.9. Let us note that the MCNAUGHTON algorithm always leads to the same allocation of the tasks on the processors, no matter what the length of the block is. The number of preemptions can easily be reduced if the sequence of tasks is reversed between two consecutive blocks, by the mirror effect [FUN 11].

| Block | | Distribution $C_i(j) = U_i(s_j - s_{j-1})$ | | | | |
|---|---|---|---|---|---|---|
| $j$ | $[s_{j-1}, s_j)$ | $\tau_1$ | $\tau_2$ | $\tau_3$ | $\tau_4$ | $\tau_5$ |
| 1 | [0    3) | 1 | 1.2 | 1.2 | 2 | 0.6 |
| 2 | [3    5) | 0.66 | 0.8 | 0.8 | 1.33 | 0.4 |
| 3 | [5    6) | 0.33 | 0.4 | 0.4 | 0.66 | 0.2 |
| 4 | [6    9) | 1 | 1.2 | 1.2 | 2 | 0.6 |
| 5 | [9    10) | 0.33 | 0.4 | 0.4 | 0.66 | 0.2 |
| 6 | [10   12) | 0.66 | 0.8 | 0.8 | 1.33 | 0.4 |
| 7 | [12   15) | 1 | 1.2 | 1.2 | 2 | 0.6 |

**Table 3.3.** *Distribution of the subtasks in each scheduling block* DP-WRAP

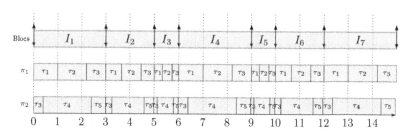

**Figure 3.9.** *Continuous-time* DP-WRAP *scheduling*

*3.5.1.4. Relaxation of the property of fairness and sporadic tasks*

Two optimal algorithms for periodic/sporadic tasks with implicit deadlines have been proposed in the literature: RUN [REI 11] (periodic) and U-EDF [NEL 12] (sporadic). Thus, these sophisticated algorithmsbring to light the existence of optimal algorithms that do not respect the property of fairness which is exploited by the algorithms presented previously.

The extension of the algorithms presented to systems of sporadic tasks has only been studied for implicit deadline tasks. We have already highlighted that there is no optimal online algorithm for sporadic tasks with constrained or arbitrary deadlines.

### 3.5.2. *Generalization of uniprocessor scheduling algorithms*

The generalization of uniprocessor scheduling techniques, such as RM or EDF, to multiprocessor systems has been intensely studied in the literature. The results show that these algorithms lead to greatly under-using the platform and illustrate once again the difficulty of efficiently solving multiprocessor scheduling problems. We will illustrate this problem with the EDF scheduling as global scheduling to schedule tasks with implicit deadlines on $m$ identical processors: at any time, EDF schedules the $m$ tasks having the closest deadlines; the assignment of the tasks on the processors is arbitrary. Goossens *et al.* [GOO 03] have shown that the maximum utilization bound of EDF is in practice equal to: $m - (m - 1)U_{\max}$ and that this bound is tight (in other words, it cannot be improved), whereas in a uniprocessor context we have a maximum bound of: $U_{\text{sum}} \leq 1$. Furthermore, Andersson *et al.* [AND 03] have shown that the best possible total utilization for every FJP scheduler is: $(m + 1)/2$. Variants of EDF have, therefore, been proposed in order to guarantee this maximum utilization bound, and thus improve the guarantees of performance that EDF cannot reach on a multiprocessor platform.

One of the variants of EDF, denoted EDF-US[$\lambda$] consists of assigning the highest priority to the tasks whose utilization is greater than the value $\lambda$, the arbitration in the case of equality being done randomly [SRI 02]. Srivinasan and Baruah have shown that the total utilization guaranteed by this algorithm is equal to $m^2/(2m-1)$ when $\lambda = m/(2m-1)$. Baker [BAK 05] has then shown that if $\lambda = 1/2$ then the best possible guarantee of utilization is reached, in other words $(m+1)/2$. We also refer to [BAK 05] for the definition of a second variant of EDF that dominates EDF-US[1/2] in practice while guaranteeing the same maximum utilization bound.

## 3.6. Conclusion

In this chapter, we have introduced the problems (and sometimes the solutions) of *multiprocessor* real-time scheduling. We have presented the theoretical foundations of this discipline. We have shown that the solutions to multiprocessor scheduling problems are not merely extensions of uniprocessor solutions, as is illustrated for instance by the scheduling anomaly phenomenon, or the non-existence of optimal (online) algorithms.

## 3.7. Bibliography

[AND 03] ANDERSSON B., JONSSON J., "The utilization bounds of partitioned and pfair static-priority scheduling on multiprocessors are 50%", *Proceedings of 15th Euromicro Conference on Real-Time Systems*, pp. 33–40, 2003.

[BAK 05] BAKER T., "An analysis of EDF scheduling on a multiprocessor", *IEEE Transactions on Parallel and Distributed Systems*, vol. 15, no. 18, pp. 760–768, 2005.

[BAK 09] BAKER T., BARUAH S., "Sustainable multiprocessor scheduling for sporadic task systems", *Euromicro Conference on Real-Time Systems, ECRTS*, pp. 141–150, 2009.

[BAR 13] BARUAH S.K., "Partitioned EDF scheduling: a closer look", *Real-Time Systems*, vol. 49, pp. 715–729, 2013.

[BAR 93] BARUAH S.K., COHEN N.K., PLAXTON C.G., *et al.*, "Proportionate progress: a notion of fairness in resource allocation", *Proceedings of the 25th Annual ACM Symposium on Theory of Computing*, (STOC'93), pp. 345–354, 1993.

[BAR 96] BARUAH S.K., COHEN N.K., PLAXTON C.G., *et al.*, "Proportionate progress: a notion of fairness in resource allocation", *Algorithmica*, Springer New York, vol. 15, pp. 600–625, 1996.

[CAR 04] CARPENTER J., FUNK S., HOLMAN P., *et al.*, A categorization of real-time multiprocessor scheduling problems and algorithms", in LEUNG J.Y.-T. (ed.), *Handbook of Scheduling: Algorithms, Models, and Performance Analysis*, Chapman Hall/CRC Press, 2004.

[COF 96] COFFMAN E.G., JR., D. S.JOHNSON M. R.G., "Approximation algorithms for bin packing: a survey", in HOCHBAUM D. (ed.), *Approximation Algorithms for NP-Hard Problems*, PWS Publishing, 1996.

[DER 89] DERTOUZOS M., MOK A., "Multiprocessor online scheduling of hard-real-time tasks", *IEEE Transactions on Software Engineering*, vol. 15, pp. 1497–1506, 1989.

[DHA 78] DHALL S.K., LIU C.L., "On a real-time scheduling problem", *Operations Research*, vol. 26, no. 1, pp. 127–140, JSTOR, 1978.

[FIS 10] FISHER N., GOOSSENS J., BARUAH S., "Optimal online multiprocessor scheduling of sporadic real-time tasks is impossible", *Real-Time Systems*, vol. 45, no. 11, pp. 26–71, 2010.

[FUN 11] FUNK S., LEVIN G., SADOWSKI C., *et al.*, "DP-fair: a unifying theory for optimal hard real-time multiprocessor scheduling", *Real-Time Systems*, vol. 47, no. 5, pp. 389–429, 2011.

[GAR 79] GAREY M.R., JOHNSON D.S., *Computers and Intractability: A Guide to the Theory of NP-Completeness*, W. H. Freeman, 1979.

[GOO 03] GOOSSENS J., FUNK S., BARUAH S., "Priority-driven scheduling of periodic task systems on multiprocessors", *Real-Time Systems*, vol. 25, no. 12, pp. 187–205, 2003.

[GRA 69] GRAHAM R.L., "Bounds on multiprocessing timing anomalies", *SIAM Journal on Applied Mathematics*, vol. 17, no. 2, pp. 416–429, 1969.

[HA 94] HA R., LIU J., "Validating timing constraints in multiprocessor and distributed real-time systems", *Proceedings of the 14th International Conference on Distributed Computing Systems*, pp. 162–171, June 1994.

[HON 92] HONG K., LEUNG J.Y.-T., "On-line scheduling of real-time tasks", *IEEE Transactions on Computers*, vol. 41, no. 10, pp. 1326–1331, October 1992.

[HOR 74] HORN W., "Some simple scheduling algorithms", *Naval Research Logistics Quaterly*, vol. 21, pp. 177–185, 1974.

[LEU 82] LEUNG J.Y.-T., WHITEHEAD J., "On the comlpexity of fixed-priority scheduling of periodic, real-time tasks", *Performance Evaluation*, vol. 2, pp. 237–250, February 1982.

[KAL 95] KALYANASUNDARAM B., PRUHS K., "Speed is as powerful as clairvoyance", *36th Annual Symposium on Foundations of Computer Science (FOCS'95)*, pp. 214–221, 1995.

[KAL 00] KALYANASUNDARAM B., PRUHS K., "Speed is as powerful as clairvoyance", *Journal of the ACM*, vol. 47, pp. 617–643, July 2000.

[KAR 11] KARRENBAUER A., ROTHVO T., "A 3/2-approximation algorithm for rate-monotonic multiprocessor scheduling of implicit-deadline tasks", in JANSEN K., SOLIS-OBA R., (eds.), *Approximation and Online Algorithms*, vol. 6534 of *Lecture Notes in Computer Science*, pp. 166–177, Springer Berlin / Heidelberg, 2011.

[LIU 73] LIU J.C., LAYLAND J.W., "Scheduling algorithms for multiprogramming in hard real-time environment", *Journal of the ACM*, vol. 20, no. 1, pp. 46–61, 1973.

[LÓP 03] LÓPEZ J.M., GARCIA M., DIAZ J.L., et al., "Utilization bounds for multiprocessor rate-monotonic scheduling", *Real-Time Systems*, Springer Netherlands, vol. 24, pp. 5–28, 2003.

[LÓP 04] LÓPEZ J.M., DIAZ J.L., GARCÍA D.F., "Minimum and maximum utilization bounds for multiprocessor rate monotonic scheduling", *IEEE Transactions on Parallel and Distributed Systems*, vol. 15, pp. 642–653, July 2004.

[MCN 59] McNAUGHTON R., "Scheduling with deadlines and loss functions", *Management Science*, vol. 6, no. 1, pp. 1–12, 1959.

[NEL 12] NELISSEN G., BERTEN V., NELIS V., *et al.*, "U-EDF: an unfair but optimal mutliprocessor scheduling algorithm for sporadic tasks", *22nd Euromicro Conference on Real-Time Systems (ECRTS'12)*, pp. 13–23, 2012.

[OH 95] OH Y., SON S.H., "Allocating fixed-priority periodic tasks on multiprocessor systems", *Real-Time Systems*, vol. 9, pp. 207–239, Springer Netherlands, 1995.

[OH 98] OH D.-I., BAKER T., "Utilization bounds for N-processor rate monotone scheduling with static processor assignment", *Real-Time Systems*, Springer Netherlands, vol. 15, pp. 183–192, 1998.

[PHI 97] PHILLIPS C.A., STEIN C., TORNG E., *et al.*, "Optimal time-critical scheduling via resource augmentation (extended abstract)", *Proceedings of the 29th Annual ACM Symposium on Theory of Computing*, STOC '97, ACM, pp. 140–149, 1997.

[PHI 02] PHILLIPS C.A., STEIN C., TORNG E., *et al.*, "Optimal time-critical scheduling via resource augmentation", *Algorithmica*, vol. 32, no. 2, pp. 163–200, 2002.

[PIN 08] PINEDO M.L., "Parallel machine models (deterministic)", *Scheduling*, Springer New York, pp. 111–149, 2008.

[REI 11] REIGNER P., LIMA G., MASSA E., *et al.*, "RUN: optimal multiprocessor real-time scheduling via reduction to uniprocessor", *32th IEEE Real-Time Systems Sympposium (RTSS'11)*, pp. 104–115, 2011.

[SRI 02] SRIVINASAN A., BARUAH S., "Deadline-based scheduling of periodic task systems on multiprocessors", *Information Processing Letters*, vol. 84, no. 2, pp. 93–98, 2002.

[SRI 05] SRIVINASAN A., ANDERSON J., "Fair scheduling of dynamic tasks systems on multiprocessors", *Journal of Systems and Software*, vol. 77, no. 11, pp. 67–80, 2005.

[ZHU 03] ZHU D., MOSSÉ D., MELHEM R.G., "Multiple-resource periodic scheduling problem: how much fairness is necessary?", *Proceedings of the 24th IEEE Real-Time Systems Symposium (RTSS 2003),* Cancun, Mexico, pp. 142–151, 3–5 December 2003.

[ZHU 11] ZHU D., QI X., MOSSÉ D., *et al.,* "An optimal boundary fair scheduling algorithm for multiprocessor real-time systems", *Journal Parallel Distributed Computing,* vol. 71, no. 10, pp. 1411–1425, 2011.

# 4

# Synchronizations: Shared Resource Access Protocols

The aim of this chapter is to provide the reader with an understanding of the different concepts related to the synchronization of processes rather than to give an exhaustive description of the existing protocols. We will present the main protocols in detail and we will give references for those which the reader might be interested in consulting. We will focus more specifically on fixed-priority scheduled systems and, in the case of multiprocessor architectures, we only consider the case of partitioned scheduling.

This chapter is organized in the following way: in section 4.2, we lay out the terminology, as well as the notations used. In section 4.2.2, we describe the essential (major) protocols as much in the case of uniprocessor systems as in the case of multiprocessor systems. In section 4.3, we show the undesirable consequences of synchronizations in the scheduling of systems. We show how to avoid these. In section 4.4, we look at the consequences of various blocks on the analysis of systems and we show how to estimate the

Chapter written by Serge MIDONNET and Frédéric FAUBERTEAU.

blocking factor of the tasks. We finish this chapter in section 4.5 by concluding the various aspects addressed.

## 4.1. Introduction

*Hard real-time* systems are systems in which the processes are parametrized by strict deadlines. The analysis of these systems therefore consists of guaranteeing that every process of a given application can be performed by complying with its deadline. This analysis depends on the process parameters, but also on the way they are scheduled on the processor(s). The *scheduling algorithm* then specifies the order in which the processes are executed. In order to be able to propose an analysis for a given scheduling algorithm, the hypothesis that the processes are independent is often considered.

As soon as we consider several processes competitively sharing resources, it has to be guaranteed that this data remain in a coherent state for each applied process. A solution to this problem consists of establishing a shared data access protocol, or *synchronization protocol*.

The impact of the synchronization protocol employed has to be taken into account during the schedulability test of the system. Indeed, processes can be put to wait when they cannot access data currently in use. This waiting time will have an effect on the termination time (the response time) of the processes. Including these in the analysis of the system will complexify it. The challenge is then to design a synchronization protocol with good properties, but whose analysis does not introduce too much pessimism into the general analysis of the system.

## 4.2. Terminology and notations

We consider a system as being composed of a set $\tau = \{\tau_i, \ldots, \tau_n\}$ of $n$ tasks. The priority of the task $\tau_i$ is given by $p(\tau_i)$. We consider that the tasks are sorted by decreasing order of priority ($\tau_1$ having the highest priority). A shared resource $\mathcal{R}_l$ is an element of the system (shared memory, device, communication bus, etc.) which can be used by several tasks. The set of shared resources accessible by a task $\tau_i$ is given by $\mathcal{R}(\tau_i)$. Likewise, the set of tasks having access to a resource $\mathcal{R}_l$ is given by $\tau(\mathcal{R}_l)$. We consider that the access of competitive processes to a shared resource $\mathcal{R}_l$ is exclusive, in other words two tasks cannot access $\mathcal{R}_l$ at the same time. This constraint is necessary in order to guarantee the coherence of $\mathcal{R}_l$. Thus, a task needing access to $\mathcal{R}_l$ when it is already in use by another task will be refused access to it. In order to allow the design of this mutual exclusion mechanism, the code corresponding to the utilization of a resource is executed inside a critical section.

DEFINITION 4.1.– Critical section. *Let $\tau_i$ be a task and $\mathcal{R}_l$ a shared resource. A critical section $\sigma_i\,(\mathcal{R}_l)$ of $\tau_i$ is a subset of the execution of $\tau_i$ in which it accesses $\mathcal{R}_l$.*

When a task $\tau_i$ can execute several critical sections associated with a resource $\mathcal{R}_k$, we denote by $\sigma_{i,k}\,(\mathcal{R}_l)$ the $k$-th one. When a task executes a critical section associated with a shared resource, no other task can execute a critical section associated with this same resource. This constraint is necessary in order to guarantee the coherence of the resource. We distinguish the case where a task accesses a resource without having freed the resource, we then refer to nested critical sections.

DEFINITION 4.2.– Nested critical section. *Let $\tau_i$ be a task and $\mathcal{R}_{l_1}$ and $\mathcal{R}_{l_2}$ two shared resources. The critical sections $\sigma_i\,(\mathcal{R}_{l_1})$ and $\sigma_i\,(\mathcal{R}_{l_2})$ of $\tau_i$ are nested if $[d(\sigma_i\,(\mathcal{R}_{l_1})), f(\sigma_i\,(\mathcal{R}_{l_2}))] \bigcap [d(\sigma_i\,(\mathcal{R}_{l_1}),\ f(\sigma_i\,(\mathcal{R}_{l_2})] \neq \emptyset$ where $d(\sigma_i\,(\mathcal{R}_{l_2}))$ (respectively $f(\sigma_i\,(\mathcal{R}_{l_1}))$) is the start time (respectively the end time) of the execution of the critical section $\sigma_i\,(\mathcal{R}_{l_1k})$.*

A task which attempts to access a resource already in use will incur a blocking.

DEFINITION 4.3.– Blocking. *Let $\mathcal{R}_l$ be a shared resource. Let $\sigma_i(\mathcal{R}_l)$ be a critical section of $\tau_i$ associated with $\mathcal{R}_l$ and $\sigma_{i'}(\mathcal{R}_l)$ a critical section of $\tau_i'$ associated with $\mathcal{R}_l$. A task $\tau_i$ incurs a blocking at time t when it attempts to execute $\sigma_i(\mathcal{R}_l)$ when $\tau_i'$ is already executing $\sigma_{i'}(\mathcal{R}_l)$ at t.*

We distinguish between two types of blocking:

– *direct blocking* when a task with high priority attempts to use a resource already in use by a lower priority task;

– *indirect blocking* when a task with intermediate priority is blocked by a lower priority task which has inherited the priority of a high priority task. This phenomenon is described a bit further in section 4.2.2.1.1.

DEFINITION 4.4.– Blocking factor. *Let $\tau_i$ be a task. The blocking factor $B_i$ is the term associated with $\tau_i$ which represents the duration of the blockings incurred by $\tau_i$ in the worst case.*

The determination of the blocking factor is necessary in order to perform the schedulability analysis of a system of resource sharing tasks.

In the case of a multiprocessor architecture, it is necessary to distinguish between two types of resources, the local resources denoted as $\mathcal{R}^L$ and the global resources denoted as $\mathcal{R}^G$. A local resource is only used by the tasks running on the same processor. In contrast, a global resource will only be executed by tasks running on different processors.

### 4.2.1. *Diagrams*

The sections of this chapter are illustrated by a set of execution diagrams. We represent with dashed rectangles the non-critical sections and with colored rectangles the critical sections of the tasks. An arrow pointing upwards on the execution diagram of a task represents its activation time and an arrow pointing downwards its deadline. An arrow pointing downwards on the task with reference to a resource indicates the request time for the use of this resource. In the same manner, an arrow pointing upwards on the task with reference to a resource indicates the time when this resource is freed by the task. The sections represented by a rectangle with smaller height than that of the tasks corresponds to the blocking of the task which we are considering in the example. In the table describing the system, $\tau$ represents the set of tasks, $\pi$ the set of processors (for multiprocessor architectures), $r$ the set of activation times of the various instance(s) of the tasks, $d$ the set of deadlines of the various instance(s) of the task and $\sigma$ the critical sections of the task.

### 4.2.2. Synchronization protocols

In this section we present the main resource access protocols in the case of uni- and multiprocessor architectures.

#### 4.2.2.1. The case of uniprocessor architectures

#### 4.2.2.1.1. Priority Inheritance Protocol

The *Priority Inheritance Protocol* (PIP) was proposed by Sha, Rajkumar and Lehoczky [SHA 87, SHA 90] in order to avoid the unbounded priority inversion problem in uniprocessor systems. We discuss this problem in more detail in section 4.3.1.

The functioning of PIP can be described in the following ways:

– if, during an access to a resource $\mathcal{R}_l$, a task $\tau_i$ is blocked by another task $\tau_j$ of lower priority, then $\tau_j$ inherits the priority of $\tau_i$. We say that the task which is blocked gives its priority to the task which blocks it;

– when a task $\tau_j$ frees the resource $\mathcal{R}_l$, it continues its execution with its nominal priority and the highest priority task blocked waiting for the liberation of $\mathcal{R}_l$ is notified;

– priority inheritance has to be transitive, in other words if $\tau_h$ blocks $\tau_j$ and $\tau_j$ blocks $\tau_i$, then $\tau_h$ inherits the priority of $\tau_i$ via $\tau_j$.

Transitive inheritance is necessary to avoid unbounded priority inversions.

### 4.2.2.1.2. Priority Ceiling Protocol

The *Priority Ceiling Protocol* (PCP) was proposed by Sha, Rajkumar and Lehoczky [SHA 87, SHA 90] in order to avoid unbounded priority inversion problems, multiple blocking and deadlocks. For this, the concept of priority ceiling was introduced. It is defined in the following manner:

DEFINITION 4.5.– Priority ceiling of a resource. *The priority ceiling $\bar{p}(\mathcal{R}_l)$ of a resource $\mathcal{R}_l$ is given by the priority of the highest priority task using $\mathcal{R}_l$:*

$$\bar{p}(\mathcal{R}_l) = \max_{\tau_i \in \tau(\mathcal{R}_l)} (p(\tau_i))$$

DEFINITION 4.6.– Priority ceiling of the system. *The priority ceiling $\bar{p}$ of the system is given by the highest priority ceiling of the resource being used. By definition, when no resource is being used $\bar{p}$ is lower than the lowest priority of the system.*

The functioning of PCP can be described in the following ways:

– in order for a task $\tau_i$ to execute the critical section $\sigma_i (\mathcal{R}_l)$ associated with the resource $\mathcal{R}_l$, its priority has to be strictly higher than the priority $\bar{p}$ of the system;

– when a task $\tau_i$ is blocked by the task $\tau_j$ executing its critical section $\sigma_j (\mathcal{R}_l)$, $\tau_j$ inherits the priority of $\tau_i$;

– when a task $\tau_j$ frees the resource $\mathcal{R}_l$, it continues its execution with its nominal priority and the highest priority task blocked waiting for the liberation of $\mathcal{R}_l$ is notified;

– priority inheritance has to be transitive, in other words if $\tau_h$ blocks $\tau_j$ and $\tau_j$ blocks $\tau_i$, then $\tau_h$ inherits the priority of $\tau_i$ via $\tau_j$.

As for PIP, the transitivity of priority inheritance allows to avoid deadlocks.

The version of PCP which we have just presented is the original version as presented by Sha, Rajkumar and Lehoczky [SHA 87, SHA 90]. However there is a variant which is simpler to implement, Immediate Ceiling Priority Protocol (*ICPP*). With ICPP, when a task $\tau_i$ enters a critical section $\sigma_i\,(\mathcal{R}_l)$, it inherits the priority ceiling of the latter. In contrast to the original PCP, a task with higher priority than $p(\tau_i)$ cannot preempt $\tau_i$, even if it doesnot use any shared resource. This simplicity in design has made that OCPP is implemented in various languages and application programming interfaces (APIs). It can be found under the name *Priority Ceiling Locking* in *ADA*, *Priority Protect Protocol* in the *POSIX* API and *Priority Ceiling Emulation* (PCE) in Java *RTSJ*.

### 4.2.2.1.3. Other protocols

The *Stack Resource Policy* (SRP) protocol was proposed by Baker [BAK 90, BAK 91]. It allows us to handle tasks scheduled with EDF. It also allows to handle the case in which the tasks are synchronized using a read/write lock mechanism (several readers can access the resource at the same time if there is no writer to modify it). Finally, it allows us to share a same execution stack between different tasks.

The *BandWidth Inheritance* (BWI) protocol was proposed by Lamastra, Lipari and Abeni [LAM 01]. It was developed for open-environment systems, in which the number of applications to execute is not known beforehand (*flexible real-time systems*). The different applications are executed by servers having each a *budget*. To avoid that a task using a resource does not incur a blocking by lack of budget, BWI provides migration between servers. The task can thus use up the budget of another task waiting for the liberation of the resource.

### 4.2.2.2. *The case of multiprocessor architectures*

#### 4.2.2.2.1. Multiprocessor Priority Ceiling Protocol

The *Multiprocessor Priority Ceiling Protocol* (MPCP) was proposed by Rajkumar [RAJ 90] as an extension for the shared memory architectures of the *Distributed Priority Ceiling Protocol* [RAJ 88]. It extends the PCP protocol to multiprocessor architectures by adopting the concept of priority ceiling to global resources. This protocol can be used in the case of a partitioned scheduling.

The priority ceiling $\bar{p}(\mathcal{R}_l^L)$ of a local resource $\mathcal{R}_l^L$ is defined by the algorithm used in PCP. In the case of a global resource $\mathcal{R}_{l'}^G$, its priority ceiling $\bar{p}(\mathcal{R}_{l'}^G)$ is defined in the following way:

DEFINITION 4.7.– Priority ceiling of a global resource. *Let $p^H$ be the highest priority of the tasks of the system. The priority ceiling $\bar{p}(\mathcal{R}_l^G)$ of a global resource $\mathcal{R}_l^G$ is given by the sum of $P^H$ and the priority of the highest priority task which shares $\mathcal{R}_l^G$.*

$$\bar{p}(\mathcal{R}_l^G) = p^H + \max_{\tau_i \in \tau(\mathcal{R}_l^G)} (p(\tau_i))$$

The functioning of MPCP is described in the following ways:

– when a task $\tau_i$ is blocked at the moment of entering a critical section $\sigma_i(\mathcal{R}_l^L)$ associated with a local resource $\mathcal{R}_l^L$, the PCP protocol is applied;

– when a task $\tau_i$ is blocked at the moment of entering a critical section $\sigma_i(\mathcal{R}_l^G)$ associated with a global resource $\mathcal{R}_l^G$, it is placed into a queue associated with $\mathcal{R}_{l'}^G$ then suspended. The tasks in the queue are sorted by priority, the highest priority task being the one which will be able to execute its critical section when $\mathcal{R}_l^G$ is freed;

– when a task $\tau_i$ executes a critical section $\sigma_i(\mathcal{R}_l^G)$ associated with a global resource $\mathcal{R}_l^G$ at time $t$, it inherits the priority ceiling $\bar{p}(\mathcal{R}_l^G)$ from $\mathcal{R}_l^G$ to $t$;

– when a task $\tau_i$ executes a critical section associated with a global resource $\mathcal{R}_{l_1}^G$, it is executed with the priority ceiling $\bar{p}(\mathcal{R}_{l_1}^G)$ and can only be preempted by a task $\tau_j$ executing a critical section $\sigma_i(\mathcal{R}_{l_2}^G)$ associated with a global resource $\mathcal{R}_{l_2}^G$ with the priority ceiling $\bar{p}(\mathcal{R}_{l_2}^G)$ higher than $\bar{p}(\mathcal{R}_{l_1}^G)$. This case can only occur if $\tau_j$ is suspended waiting for the liberation of $\mathcal{R}_{l_2}^G$ on the same processor than $\tau_i$. When $\mathcal{R}_{l_2}^G$ is freed, $\tau_j$ can execute $\sigma_j(\mathcal{R}_{l_2}^G)$ and therefore preempts $\tau_i$.

### 4.2.2.2.2. Flexible Multiprocessor Locking Protocol

The *Flexible Multiprocessor Locking Protocol* (FMLP) was proposed by Block *et al.* [BLO 07]. This protocol is flexible in the sense that it allows us to synchronize the access to shared resources, as much in the case of a partitioned scheduling as in the case of a global scheduling. One study has shown that the schedulability of systems with shared resources was improved when the blocked tasks were put into an active waiting state [BRA 08a, BRA 08b]. When these resources are used for a long time by the tasks, this approach can however have the disadvantage of under-utilizing the processors. This is why, with FMLP, we distinguish between short resources and long resources. Short resources are blocked in an active waiting state whereas long resources are suspended when facing a blocking. The maximum duration of a short resource (or the minimum duration of a long resource) is left up to the developer. In order to avoid deadlocks, the nested resources are grouped together. A task $\tau_i$ must therefore acquire the lock over a group containing the resource $\mathcal{R}_l$ in order to execute its critical section $\sigma_i(\mathcal{R}_l)$ associated with $\mathcal{R}_l$.

The functioning of FMLP is described in the following ways:

– when a task $\tau_i$ is blocked at the moment of entering a critical section $\sigma_i\,(\mathcal{R}_l)$ associated with a short (local or global) resource, it is placed into an active wait for the liberation of $\mathcal{R}_l$. It therefore continues to occupy the processor and this, in a non-preemptive way;

– when a task $\tau_i$ is blocked at the moment of entering a critical section $\sigma_i\,(\mathcal{R}_l)$ associated with a long (local or global) resource, it is suspended. It is placed into a queue associated with $\mathcal{R}_l$. The tasks in the queue are sorted by order of arrival;

– when the short resource $\mathcal{R}_l$ is freed, the task $\tau_i$ executes its critical section $\sigma_i\,(\mathcal{R}_l)$ in a non-preemptive way;

– when the long resource $\mathcal{R}_l$ is freed, the task $\tau_i$ executes its critical section $\sigma_i\,(\mathcal{R}_l)$ in a preemptive way. Let $\mathcal{G}(\mathcal{R}_l)$ be the group containing the resource $\mathcal{R}_l$. The task $\tau_i$ inherits the priority of the highest priority task blocked and waiting for a resource of $\mathcal{G}(\mathcal{R}_l)$.

### 4.2.2.2.3. Other protocols

For the sake of readability and due to a lack of space, we are unable to give an in-depth description of every protocol proposed in the literature on real-time systems. Nevertheless, we will mention and briefly present the most important ones in this section.

The *Spinning Processor Executes for Preempted Processor* protocol (SPEPP) was proposed by Takada and Sakamura [TAK 97]. It allows a blocked task in active waiting for a resource to execute the critical section of another task which has been preempted before being able to access its resource.

The *Multiprocessor Stack Resource Policy* protocol (MSRP) was proposed by Gai *et al.* [GAI 01]. It is an extension of the SRP protocol (section 4.2.2.1.3) for uniprocessor architectures.

The *Parallel Priority Ceiling Protocol* (PPCP) was proposed by Easwaran and Andersson [EAS 09] with the aim of providing a schedulability analysis to systems of sporadic tasks, scheduled globally, with fixed priorities.

The *Multiprocessor BandWidth Inheritance* (M-BWI) protocol was proposed by Faggili, Lipari and Cucinotta [FAG 10]. It is an extension of the BWI protocol (section 4.2.2.1.3) for multiprocessor architectures.

The *O(m) Locking Protocol* (OMLP) was proposed by Brandenburg and Anderson [BRA 10, BRA 12a] and Brandenburg [BRA 11]. It is an optimal protocol in terms of the number of blocks induced by priority inversions.

The *Real-time Nested Locking Protocol* (RNLP) was proposed by Ward and Anderson [WAR 12] in order to handle nested resources with a finer granularity than with FMLP. In other words, RNLP allows to use nested resources without using resource groups.

The *Multiprocessor resource sharing Protocol* (MrsP) was proposed by Burns and Wellings [BUR 13]. The aim of this work is to propose a protocol with an efficient schedulability analysis. In order to minimize the impact of blocking times on this analysis, the authors took inspiration from principles used in SPEPP and M-BWI. A task can thus execute the critical section of another blocked task.

The *O(m) Independence-preserving Protocol* (OMIP) was proposed by Brandenburg [BRA 13] in order to reduce the latency of tasks blocked by resources which they are not using on different processors. The mechanism used is that of *migratory priority inheritance*, introduced in [BRA 12b]. The principle is to migrate a task using a resource on a processor where another task is blocked waiting for the liberation of the same resource.

## 4.3. Synchronization problems

### 4.3.1. *Unbounded priority inversion*

In a real-time system, a high priority task is always executed before a low priority task. When this rule is not respected, we refer to priority inversion. Synchronization can lead to this situation when the higher priority task is waiting for the liberation of a resource used by a low priority task. The interference of a lower priority task blocking a higher priority task is called the blocking factor. This interference must be estimated and integrated into the analysis of the task which incurs it.

When referring to the unbounded priority inversion problem, we imply that there are no bounds on the interference incurred by a task following a priority inversion. In practice, since the set of tasks is known and specified, it is possible to calculate a bound. However, this is so pessimistic that the schedulability analysis is very likely to fail, even for reasonable small systems.

#### 4.3.1.1. *The case of uniprocessor architectures*

The problem of unbounded priority inversion has been identified for a long time since it induces a huge pessimism in the calculation of the blocking factor, and therefore in the schedulability analysis.

In Figure 4.1, we represent an example of an unbounded priority inversion taking place in a uniprocessor context. The obtained scheduling is presented in Figure 4.1(a) and the task parameters are given in Figure 4.1(b). We assume that no synchronization protocol is used in order to underline the phenomenon. The only constraint is that a task cannot execute its critical section if the associated resource is already used by another task. The progression of the scheduling is described by the following events:

– at time $t = 0$, $\tau_3$ begins its execution since it is the only active task on this processor;

– at time $t = 1$, $\tau_3$ begins the execution of its critical section $\sigma_3 (\mathcal{R}_1)$ since the resource $\mathcal{R}_1$ is free;

– at time $t = 2$, $\tau_1$ is activated and preempts $\tau_3$ since it has a higher priority;

– at time $t = 3$, $\tau_1$ attempts to execute its critical section $\sigma_1 (\mathcal{R}_1)$ but is blocked by $\tau_3$;

– at time $t = 4$, $\tau_2$ is activated and preempts $\tau_3$ since it has a higher priority and is executed until $t = 9$;

– at time $t = 10$, $\tau_3$ frees $\mathcal{R}_1$ and $\tau_1$ may begin the execution of $\sigma_1 (\mathcal{R}_1)$.

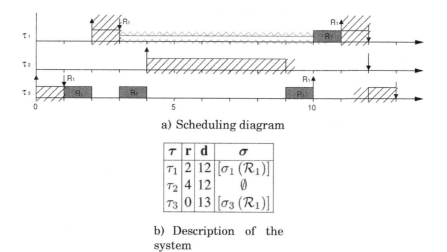

a) Scheduling diagram

| $\tau$ | r | d | $\sigma$ |
|---|---|---|---|
| $\tau_1$ | 2 | 12 | $[\sigma_1 (\mathcal{R}_1)]$ |
| $\tau_2$ | 4 | 12 | $\emptyset$ |
| $\tau_3$ | 0 | 13 | $[\sigma_3 (\mathcal{R}_1)]$ |

b) Description of the system

**Figure 4.1.** *Unbounded priority inversion in a uniprocessor context*

Let us note that the task $\tau_1$ has been subjected to the interference of the task $\tau_2$ with which it does not share any resources. This implies that, in order to calculate the blocking factor of $\tau_1$, we have to take into account the execution time of all the tasks with lower priority than $\tau_3$. In a more general case, we have to consider the interference of all the tasks with higher priority than the lowest priority task with which $\tau_1$ shares a resource. This interference can be very large, which leads to a very pessimistic schedulability analysis.

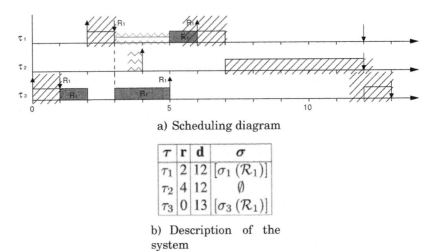

a) Scheduling diagram

| $\tau$ | r | d | $\sigma$ |
|---|---|---|---|
| $\tau_1$ | 2 | 12 | $[\sigma_1(\mathcal{R}_1)]$ |
| $\tau_2$ | 4 | 12 | $\emptyset$ |
| $\tau_3$ | 0 | 13 | $[\sigma_3(\mathcal{R}_1)]$ |

b) Description of the system

**Figure 4.2.** *Absence of unbounded priority inversion with priority inheritance*

That is why the concept of priority inheritance was introduced. In Figure 4.2, we represent an example of an unbounded priority inversion taking place in a uniprocessor context. The obtained scheduling is presented in Figure 4.2(a) and the task parameters are given in Figure 4.2(b). The scenario described on this figure is obtained by synchronizing the system represented in Figure 4.1, either with PIP or with PCP. The progression of the scheduling is described by the following events:

– from $t = 0$ to $t = 3$, the system behaves the same way as in the scenario of Figure 4.1;

– at time $t = 3$, $\tau_1$ is blocked waiting for the liberation of $\mathcal{R}_1$ by $\tau_3$. The task $\tau_3$ therefore inherits the priority $p(\tau_1)$ and may continue the execution of its critical section $\sigma_3(\mathcal{R}_1)$ until $t = 5$;

– at time $t = 5$, $\tau_3$ frees $\mathcal{R}_1$ and is preempted by $\tau_1$ which can begin the execution of its critical section $\sigma_1 (\mathcal{R}_1)$ until $t = 6$;

– at time $t = 7$, $\tau_3$ terminates its execution and $\tau_2$ can then be executed until $t = 12$.

### 4.3.1.2. *The case of multiprocessor architectures*

Systems scheduled on several processors are subject to the same unbounded priority inversion problems as uniprocessor systems. These problems can be avoided in the same manner. This phenomenon is sometimes aggravated on multiprocessor architectures.

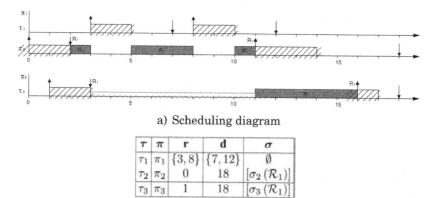

a) Scheduling diagram

| $\tau$ | $\pi$ | r | d | $\sigma$ |
|---|---|---|---|---|
| $\tau_1$ | $\pi_1$ | $\{3, 8\}$ | $\{7, 12\}$ | $\emptyset$ |
| $\tau_2$ | $\pi_2$ | 0 | 18 | $[\sigma_2 (\mathcal{R}_1)]$ |
| $\tau_3$ | $\pi_3$ | 1 | 18 | $[\sigma_3 (\mathcal{R}_1)]$ |

b) Description of the system

**Figure 4.3.** *Unbounded priority inversion with FMLP*

In Figure 4.3, we represent an example in which an unbounded priority inversion takes place when FMLP is used. The obtained scheduling is presented in Figure 4.3(a) and the task parameters are given in Figure 4.3(b). The protocol used to synchronize this resource is FMLP. The progression of the scheduling is described by the following events:

– at time $t = 0$, $\tau_3$ is activated on the processor $\pi_1$ and begins its execution since it is the only active task on this processor;

– at time $t = 1$, $\tau_1$ is activated on the processor $\pi_2$ and begins its execution since it is the only active task on this processor;

– at time $t = 2$, $\tau_3$ begins the execution of its critical section $\sigma_3(\mathcal{R}_1^G)$ associated with $\mathcal{R}_1^G$;

– at time $t = 3$, $\tau_2$ is activated in the processor $\pi_1$ and preempts $\tau_3$. On the processor $\pi_2$, $\tau_1$ attempts to execute its critical section $\sigma_1(\mathcal{R}_1^G)$ but is blocked by $\tau_3$. The task $\tau_1$ is therefore subjected to the interference of $\tau_2$ with which it does not share any resources and which is executed on a different processor;

– at time $t = 5$, $\tau_2$ terminates its execution and $\tau_3$ may resume the execution of $\sigma_3(\mathcal{R}_1^G)$ until $t = 8$;

– at time $t = 8$, $\tau_2$ is reactivated and preempts $\tau_3$ again. The task $\tau_1$ is then subjected a second time to the interference of $\tau_2$;

– at time $t = 10$, $\tau_2$ terminates its execution and $\tau_3$ may resume the execution of $\sigma_3(\mathcal{R}_1^G)$ until $t = 11$;

– at time $t = 11$, $\tau_3$ continues its execution until $t = 14$ and $\tau_1$ may continue executing its critical section $\sigma_1(\mathcal{R}_1^G)$ until its execution at $t = 17$.

It is perfectly legitimate, in the uniprocessor case, that the execution of a critical section $\sigma_j(\mathcal{R}_l^G)$ of the task $\tau_j$ is delayed by the execution of a higher priority task $\tau_i$ which does not use $\mathcal{R}_j^G$. However, it is more difficult to admit that the execution of $\sigma_j(\mathcal{R}_k^G)$ is delayed by a lesser priority task which does not use $\mathcal{R}_k^G$ and which is executed on a different processor. We may consider that $\tau_j$ is subjected to an unbounded priority inversion. The MPCP protocol allows us to avoid this problem by executing the critical sections associated with the global resources at their priority ceiling (always higher then the priority of the highest priority task of the system).

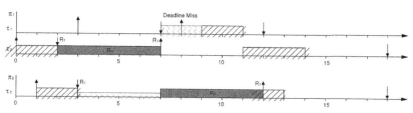

a) Scheduling diagram

| $T$ | $\pi$ | r | d | $\sigma$ |
|---|---|---|---|---|
| $\tau_1$ | $\pi_1$ | $\{3,8\}$ | $\{7,12\}$ | $\emptyset$ |
| $\tau_2$ | $\pi_2$ | 0 | 18 | $[\sigma_2(\mathcal{R}_1)]$ |
| $\tau_3$ | $\pi_3$ | 1 | 18 | $[\sigma_3(\mathcal{R}_1)]$ |

b) Description of the system

**Figure 4.4.** *Absence of unbounded priority inversion with MPCP,*
*but deadline is exceeded*

In Figure 4.4, we represent the same scenario as before but this time using the MPCP protocol to synchronize $\mathcal{R}_1^G$. The obtained scheduling is presented in Figure 4.4(a) and the task parameters are given in Figure 4.4(b). The progression of the scheduling is described by the following events:

– at time $t = 0$, $\tau_3$ starts its execution on $\pi_1$ since it is the only active task on this processor;

– at time $t = 1$, $\tau_1$ starts its execution on $\pi_2$ since it is the only active task on this processor;

– at time $t = 2$, $\tau_3$ begins the execution of its critical section $\sigma_3(\mathcal{R}_1^G)$ associated with the global resource $\mathcal{R}_1^G$ since $\mathcal{R}_1^G$ is free;

– at time $t = 3$, $\tau_2$ is activated on $\pi_1$ but is unable to begin its execution since $\tau_3$ is executed with the priority ceiling $\bar{p}(\mathcal{R}_1^G)$ which is higher than the priority $p(\tau_2)$ of $\tau_2$ by definition. $\tau_1$ cannot begin the execution of its critical section $\sigma_1(\mathcal{R}_1^G)$ on $\pi_2$ since $\mathcal{R}_1^G$ is already is use by $\tau_2$ on $\pi_1$;

– at time $t = 6$, $\tau_2$ is still unable to begin its execution and will therefore exceed its deadline at $t = 8$;

– at time $t = 7$, $\tau_2$ terminates the execution of $\sigma_2(\mathcal{R}_1^G)$ and is preempted by $\tau_2$ which has higher priority. $\tau_1$ can begin the execution of $\sigma_1(\mathcal{R}_1^G)$ on $\pi_2$.

This time, the unbounded priority inversion problem has been resolved by using the MPCP protocol. However the task $\tau_2$ has exceeded its deadline at $t = 8$.

In the scenario of Figure 4.4, the consequence of using a high priority resource by a task ($\tau_3$) is that another task ($\tau_2$) which is not using this resource exceeds its deadline. If $\tau_3$ does not execute its critical section with a high priority, $\tau_1$ will be subject to an unbounded priority inversion. This problem is linked to the use of global resources. It would not occur if the two tasks sharing the resource would be assigned to the same processor. The unbounded priority inversion can therefore be avoided here by adopting a placement which limits the use of global resources. This approach has been studied by Lakshmanan, de Niz and Rajkumar [LAK 09]. They propose a partitioning algorithm which minimizes the use of global resources in order to improve the scheduling of the system. In Figure 4.5, we represent the same scenario as before, but this time, the tasks $\tau_1$ and $\tau_3$ are assigned to the same processor $\pi_2$. There is no unbounded priority inversion problem any more, as well as missed deadlines. But the problem remains for the global resources which were not assigned after the partitioning.

### 4.3.2. *Deadlock*

In a system where the tasks call nested critical sections, it is necessary to verify the absence of deadlocks.

DEFINITION 4.8.– Deadlock. *Let us consider two tasks $\tau_i$ and $\tau_j$ and two resources $\mathcal{R}_{l_1}$ and $\mathcal{R}_{l_2}$ shared by $\tau_i$ and $\tau_j$. A deadlock occurs at time $t$ when $\tau_i$ is blocked waiting for the* *liberation of $\mathcal{R}_{l_1}$ (or of $\mathcal{R}_{l_2}$, respectively) and $\tau_j$ is blocked waiting for the liberation of $\mathcal{R}_{l_2}$ (or of $\mathcal{R}_{l_1}$, respectively).*

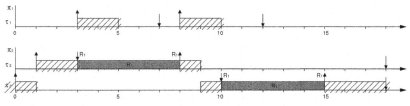

a) Scheduling diagram

| $\tau$ | $\pi$ | r | d | $\sigma$ |
|---|---|---|---|---|
| $\tau_1$ | $\pi_1$ | $\{3,8\}$ | $\{7,12\}$ | $\emptyset$ |
| $\tau_2$ | $\pi_2$ | 1 | 18 | $[\sigma_2\,(\mathcal{R}_1)]$ |
| $\tau_3$ | $\pi_2$ | 0 | 18 | $[\sigma_3\,(\mathcal{R}_1)]$ |

b) Description of the system

**Figure 4.5.** *Absence of unbounded priority inversion with MPCP without missed deadlines*

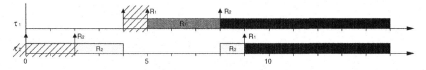

a) Scheduling diagram

| $\tau$ | r | d | $\sigma$ |
|---|---|---|---|
| $\tau_1$ | 4 | 15 | $[\sigma_{1,1}\,(\mathcal{R}_1)\,,\,[\sigma_{1,1}\,(\mathcal{R}_2)],\sigma_{1,2}\,(\mathcal{R}_1)]$ |
| $\tau_2$ | 0 | 15 | $[\sigma_{2,1}\,(\mathcal{R}_2)\,,\,[\sigma_{2,1}\,(\mathcal{R}_1)],\sigma_{2,2}\,(\mathcal{R}_2)]$ |

b) Description of the system

**Figure 4.6.** *Deadlock in uniprocessor context*

### 4.3.2.1. *Uniprocessor deadlock*

In Figure 4.6, we represent an example of interblocking in a uniprocessor context. The obtained scheduling is presented in Figure 4.6(a) and the task parameters are given in Figure 4.6(b). The progression of the scheduling is described by the following events:

– at time $t = 0$, $\tau_2$ is activated and begins its execution since it is the only active task on the processor;

– at time $t = 2$, is begins the execution of its critical section $\sigma_{2,1} (\mathcal{R}_2)$ since $\mathcal{R}_2$ is free;

– at time $t = 4$, $\tau_1$ is activated and preempts $\tau_2$ since its priority $p(\tau_1)$ is higher to the priority $p(\tau_2)$ of $\tau_2$;

– at time $t = 5$, $\tau_1$ begins the execution of its critical section $\sigma_{1,1} (\mathcal{R}_1)$ since $\mathcal{R}_1$ is free,

– at time $t = 8$, $\tau_1$ attempts to use $\mathcal{R}_2$ but is blocked since $\mathcal{R}_2$ is already is use by $\tau_2$. The task $\tau_1$ is suspended and $\tau_2$ continues the execution of $\sigma_{2,1} (\mathcal{R}_2)$;

– at time $t = 9$, $\tau_2$ attempts to use $\mathcal{R}_1$ but is blocked since $\mathcal{R}_1$ is already is use by $\tau_1$. The two tasks are therefore blocked waiting for a resource which will never be freed.

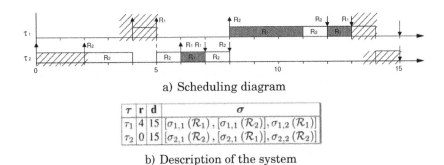

a) Scheduling diagram

| $\tau$ | r | d | $\sigma$ |
|---|---|---|---|
| $\tau_1$ | 4 | 15 | $[\sigma_{1,1} (\mathcal{R}_1), [\sigma_{1,1} (\mathcal{R}_2)], \sigma_{1,2} (\mathcal{R}_1)]$ |
| $\tau_2$ | 0 | 15 | $[\sigma_{2,1} (\mathcal{R}_2), [\sigma_{2,1} (\mathcal{R}_1)], \sigma_{2,2} (\mathcal{R}_2)]$ |

b) Description of the system

**Figure 4.7.** *Absence of deadlock in uniprocessor context with PCP*

In a uniprocessor context, deadlocks can be avoided by using a PCP. In Figure 4.7, we reuse the previous scenario but this this PCP is used to synchronize the resources. The obtained scheduling is presented in Figure 4.7(a) and the task parameters are given in Figure 4.7(b). The progression of the scheduling is described by the following events:

– at time $t = 0$, $\tau_2$ is activated and begins its execution since it is the only active task on this processor;

– at time $t = 2$, it begins the execution of its critical section $\sigma_{2,1}$ ($\mathcal{R}_2$) since $\mathcal{R}_2$ is free;

– at time $t = 4$, $\tau_1$ is activated and preempts $\tau_2$ since its priority $p(\tau_1)$ is higher than the priority $p(\tau_2)$ of $\tau_2$;

– at time $t = 5$, $\tau_2$ attempts to use $\mathcal{R}_1$, but its priority $p(\tau_2)$ is not strictly higher than the priority ceiling $\bar{p}(\mathcal{R}_1)$. The task $\tau_1$ is then suspended and $\tau_2$ may continue the execution of $\sigma_{2,1}$ ($\mathcal{R}_2$);

– at time $t = 6$, $\tau_2$ executes $\sigma_{2,1}$ ($\mathcal{R}_1$) since the resource is free;

– at time $t = 7$, $\tau_2$ terminates $\sigma_{2,1}$ ($\mathcal{R}_1$) and resumes the execution of $\sigma_{2,1}$ ($\mathcal{R}_1$);

– at time $t = 8$, $\tau_2$ terminates $\sigma_{2,1}$ ($\mathcal{R}_2$) and is reassigned its nominal priority, lower than that of $\tau_1$, which therefore preempts it. The task $\tau_1$ can now execute its critical sections.

PIP does not prevent deadlocks, only PCP has this capacity.

### 4.3.2.2. *Multiprocessor deadlock*

If, in a uniprocessor context, it is possible to prevent deadlocks by using PCPs, this will not be the case in a multiprocessor context since here the priorities are managed locally on each processor.

In Figure 4.8, we represent an example which brings into light a deadlock when MPCP is used. The obtained scheduling is presented in Figure 4.8(a) and the task parameters are given in Figure 4.8(b). The progression of the scheduling is described by the following events:

– at time $t = 0$, $\tau_1$ (respectively $\tau_2$) is activated in the processor $\pi_1$ (respectively $\pi_2$) since it is the only active task on this processor;

– at time $t = 1$, $\tau_2$ begins the execution of its critical section $\sigma_2(\mathcal{R}_2^G)$ on $\pi_2$ since $\mathcal{R}_2^G$ is free;

– at time $t = 2$, $\tau_1$ begins the execution of its critical section $\sigma_1(\mathcal{R}_1^G)$ on $\pi_1$ since $\mathcal{R}_1^G$ is free;

– at time $t = 3$, $\tau_2$ is blocked waiting for the liberation of $\mathcal{R}_1^G$;

– at time $t = 5$, $\tau_1$ is blocked waiting for the liberation of $\mathcal{R}_2^G$.

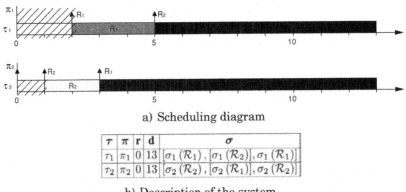

a) Scheduling diagram

| $\tau$ | $\pi$ | $r$ | $d$ | $\sigma$ |
|---|---|---|---|---|
| $\tau_1$ | $\pi_1$ | 0 | 13 | $[\sigma_1(\mathcal{R}_1), [\sigma_1(\mathcal{R}_2)], \sigma_1(\mathcal{R}_1)]$ |
| $\tau_2$ | $\pi_2$ | 0 | 13 | $[\sigma_2(\mathcal{R}_2), [\sigma_2(\mathcal{R}_1)], \sigma_2(\mathcal{R}_2)]$ |

b) Description of the system

**Figure 4.8.** *Deadlock in multiprocessor context with MPCP*

We are in the presence of a deadlock since the tasks $\tau_1$ and $\tau_2$ are mutually waiting for the liberation of a resource used by the other task. One solution to this problem is to impose an order on the utilization of the resources. This solution is not very satisfactory since it implies that the application developer has knowledge of this order or that the synchronization protocol performs a verification of the respect of this order.

A solution other than the one using the order in which the resources are taken consists of using resource groups. This approach is used with FMLP and consists of grouping the nested resources. The access to a resource of the group implies that all resources of the group have to be free. In Figure 4.9, we present the same scenario as before but this time with the FMLP protocol. The resources $\mathcal{R}_1^G$ and $\mathcal{R}_2^G$ therefore belong to the same group. The obtained scheduling is presented in Figure 4.9(a) and the task parameters are given in Figure 4.9(b). The progression of the scheduling is described by the following events:

– at time $t = 0$, $\tau_1$ (respectively $\tau_2$) is activated on processor $\pi_1$ (respectively $\pi_2$) since it is the only active task on the processor;

– at time $t = 1$, $\tau_2$ begins the execution of its critical section $\sigma_2(\mathcal{R}_2^G)$ on $\pi_2$ since $\mathcal{R}_1^G$ and $\mathcal{R}_2^G$ are free;

– at time $t = 2$, $\tau_1$ attempts to use $\mathcal{R}_1^G$ but one of its resources associated with the group containing $\mathcal{R}_1^G$ is used (in this case, $\mathcal{R}_2^G$). The task $\tau_1$ is therefore blocked waiting for the group to be free;

– at time $t = 3$, $\tau_2$ begins the execution of its critical section $\sigma_2(\mathcal{R}_1^G)$ since it holds the lock on this group of resources;

– at time $t = 5$, $\tau_2$ terminates the execution of $\sigma_2(\mathcal{R}_2^G)$ and frees the two resources $\mathcal{R}_1^G$ and $\mathcal{R}_2^G$. The task $\tau_1$ can then begin the execution of $\sigma_1(\mathcal{R}_1^G)$.

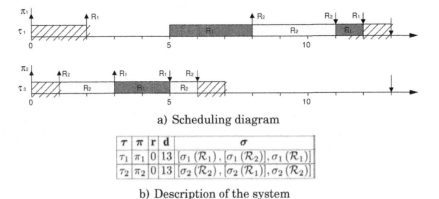

a) Scheduling diagram

| $\tau$ | $\pi$ | r | d | $\sigma$ |
|---|---|---|---|---|
| $\tau_1$ | $\pi_1$ | 0 | 13 | $[\sigma_1(\mathcal{R}_1), [\sigma_1(\mathcal{R}_2)], \sigma_1(\mathcal{R}_1)]$ |
| $\tau_2$ | $\pi_2$ | 0 | 13 | $[\sigma_2(\mathcal{R}_2), [\sigma_2(\mathcal{R}_1)], \sigma_2(\mathcal{R}_2)]$ |

b) Description of the system

**Figure 4.9.** *Absence of deadlock with FLMP*

With the resource grouping mechanism, deadlocks are avoided. But the parallelism of the system is impacted. Indeed, the task $\tau_1$ has to wait for $\tau_2$ to have executed all of its critical sections in order to be able to progress with the execution of its own critical sections.

### 4.3.3. *Chained blocking*

In order to analyze the feasibility of a resource-sharing task, it is necessary to determine the blocking factor due to the synchronizations. This factor is directly linked to the number of blocks that the task can be subject to in the worst case. A good property of a synchronization protocol will be to limit the number of blocks that a task $\tau_i$ can be subject to during its execution.

DEFINITION 4.9.– Chained blocking. *Let us consider a task $\tau_i$ and let $\mathcal{R}(\tau_i)$ be the set of shared resources used by $\tau_i$. A chained blocking occurs for $\tau_i$ when it is subjected to a blockage for several critical sections associated with resources of $\mathcal{R}(\tau_i)$.*

4.3.3.1. *Uniprocessor chained blocking*

In Figure 4.10, we represent an example using the PIP protocol and producing a chained blocking. The obtained scheduling is presented in Figure 4.10(a) and the task parameters are given in Figure 4.10(b). The progression of the scheduling is described by the following events:

– at time $t = 0$, $\tau_4$ is activated and begins its execution since it is the only active task of the system;

– at time $t = 1$, the resource $\mathcal{R}_1$ is free and $\tau_4$ can begin its critical section $\sigma_4\,(\mathcal{R}_1)$;

– at time $t = 2$, $\tau_3$ is activated and preempts $\tau_4$ since $p(\tau_3) > p(\tau_4)$. It is therefore executed until $t = 3$ at which time it begins the execution of its critical section $\sigma_3\,(\mathcal{R}_2)$ associated with the free resource $\mathcal{R}_2$;

– at time $t = 4$, $\tau_2$ is activated and preempts $\tau_3$ in order to be executed until $t = 5$. It executes its critical section $\sigma_2 (\mathcal{R}_3)$ until being preempted by $\tau_1$ at time $t = 6$. The task $\tau_1$ is executed until $t = 7$ at which time it needs to access the resource $\mathcal{R}_1$. This resource being already in use by $\tau_4$, $\tau_1$ is blocked and the PIP protocol implies that $\tau_4$ inherits the priority of $\tau_1$;

– at time $t = 9$, $\tau_4$ terminates the execution of its critical section $\sigma_4 (\mathcal{R}_1)$ and returns to its initial priority. It is then preempted by the highest priority active task of the system, $\tau_1$, which can execute its critical section $\sigma_1 (\mathcal{R}_1)$ until $t = 10$;

– at time $t = 11$, $\tau_1$ is again subjected to a block and the task $\tau_2$ inherits its priority $p(\tau_1)$. The same phenomenon occurs at time $t = 15$ when $\tau_1$ is blocked by $\tau_3$.

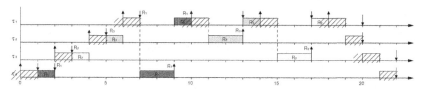

a) Scheduling diagram

| $\tau$ | r | d | $\sigma$ |
|---|---|---|---|
| $\tau_1$ | 6 | 20 | $[\sigma_1 (\mathcal{R}_1)], [\sigma_1 (\mathcal{R}_2)], [\sigma_1 (\mathcal{R}_3)]$ |
| $\tau_2$ | 4 | 20 | $[\sigma_2 (\mathcal{R}_3)]$ |
| $\tau_3$ | 2 | 22 | $[\sigma_3 (\mathcal{R}_2)]$ |
| $\tau_4$ | 0 | 22 | $[\sigma_4 (\mathcal{R}_1)]$ |

b) Description of the system

**Figure 4.10.** *Chained blocking with PIP*

The task $\tau_1$ will therefore be blocked three times by three lesser priority tasks with which it shares resources. The PCP allows us to address this issue.

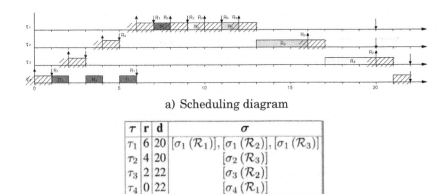

a) Scheduling diagram

| $\tau$ | r | d | $\sigma$ |
|---|---|---|---|
| $\tau_1$ | 6 | 20 | $[\sigma_1 (\mathcal{R}_1)], [\sigma_1 (\mathcal{R}_2)], [\sigma_1 (\mathcal{R}_3)]$ |
| $\tau_2$ | 4 | 20 | $[\sigma_2 (\mathcal{R}_3)]$ |
| $\tau_3$ | 2 | 22 | $[\sigma_3 (\mathcal{R}_2)]$ |
| $\tau_4$ | 0 | 22 | $[\sigma_4 (\mathcal{R}_1)]$ |

b) Description of the system

**Figure 4.11.** *Absence of chained blocking with PCP*

In Figure 4.11, we represent the same system of tasks, but this time using the PCP protocol. As in the case of PIP, at time $t = 0$, $\tau_4$ is activated and begins its execution since it is the only active task of the system. The obtained scheduling is presented in Figure 4.11(a) and the task parameters are given in Figure 4.11(b). The progression of the scheduling is described by the following events:

– at time $t = 1$, the resource $\mathcal{R}_1$ is free and $\tau_4$ can begin its critical section $\sigma_4 (\mathcal{R}_1)$;

– at time $t = 2$, $\tau_3$ is activated and preempts $\tau_4$ since $p(\tau_3) > p(\tau_4)$. It is executed until $t = 3$ when its attempts to execute its critical section $\sigma_3 (\mathcal{R}_2)$. The entrance into $\sigma_3 (\mathcal{R}_2)$ is refused since $\tau_4$ is executing its critical section $\sigma_4 (\mathcal{R}_1)$ whose priority ceiling is $\bar{p}(\mathcal{R}_1) = p(\tau_1)$. The task $\tau_4$ therefore inherits the priority of $\tau_3$ and continue its execution until the point when it is preempted by $\tau_2$ at time $t = 4$;

– at time $t = 5$, a priority inheritance of $\tau_2$ to $\tau_1$ occurs for the same reason as before. At time $t = 6$, $\tau_4$ terminates the execution of $\sigma_4 (\mathcal{R}_1)$ and $\tau_1$ is activated. The task $\tau_1$ therefore preempts $\tau_4$ and executes until $t = 6$ when it attempts to execute its critical section $\sigma_1$ ($\mathcal{R}_1$). The resource $\mathcal{R}_1$ being free, $\tau_1$ can use it and enter into its associated critical section;

– at time $t = 9$, the resource $\mathcal{R}_3$ is also free since $\tau_2$ was not able to enter into critical section $\sigma_2$ ($\mathcal{R}_3$). The task $\tau_1$ can then execute its critical section $\sigma_1$ ($\mathcal{R}_3$) until $t = 10$, as well as its critical section $\sigma_1$ ($\mathcal{R}_2$) until $t = 12$;

– at time $t = 13$ (respectively $t = 17$), $\tau_2$ (respectively $\tau_3$) may execute its critical section $\sigma_2$ ($\mathcal{R}_3$) (respectively $\sigma_3$ ($\mathcal{R}_2$)).

We note that $\tau_1$ has not been subjected to chained blocking since the priority ceiling mechanism prevents the intermediary-priority tasks $\tau_2$ and $\tau_3$ from entering into their critical sections. The PCP protocol (as well as the PCPs such as PCE or SRP) is therefore a solution to avoid this undesirable chained blocking phenomenon.

### 4.3.3.2. *Multiprocessor chained blocking*

We will now be looking at the case of multiprocessor architectures. To our knowledge, this problem has not been raised in the study of multiprocessor synchronization protocols.

In Figure 4.12, we represent a scenario in which a chained blocking occurs, whether the protocol used is MPCP or FMLP. The obtained scheduling is presented in Figure 4.12(a) and the task parameters are given in Figure 4.12(b). The progression of the scheduling is described by the following events:

We consider as a first step the case in which the protocol used is MPCP. At time $t = 0$, the task $\tau_1$ (respectively $\tau_2$) is activated on processor $\pi_1$ (respectively $\pi_2$) and begins its execution since it is the only active task on its processor. At time $t = 1$, $\tau_2$ executes its critical section $\sigma_2(\mathcal{R}_1^G)$ associated with the resource $\mathcal{R}_1^G$ since it is free. The task $\tau_1$ inherits the priority ceiling $\bar{p}(\mathcal{R}_1^G)$. At time $t = 2$, $\tau_1$ attempts to execute its critical section $\sigma_1(\mathcal{R}_1^G)$ associated with $\mathcal{R}_1^G$ but its priority $p(\tau_1)$ is smaller than $\bar{p}(\mathcal{R}_1^G)$ by definition. It is therefore suspended waiting for the release of $\mathcal{R}_1^G$. On processor $\pi_3$, $\tau_3$ begins its execution since it is the only active task on its processor. At time $t = 3$, $\tau_2$ terminates the execution of its critical section $\sigma_2(\mathcal{R}_1^G)$ and frees its resource $\mathcal{R}_1^G$. The task $\tau_1$ is then notified and can begin the execution of its critical section $\sigma_1(\mathcal{R}_1^G)$. At time $t = 4$, $\tau_3$ begins the execution of its critical section $\sigma_3(\mathcal{R}_2^G)$ since the resource $\mathcal{R}_2^G$ is free. At time $t = 5$, $\tau_1$ terminates the execution of its critical section $\sigma_1(\mathcal{R}_1^G)$ and continues its execution until $t = 6$, at which time it is suspended for a second time, and this while waiting for the release of the resource $\mathcal{R}_2^G$. Indeed, the priority of $\tau_1$ is smaller than $\bar{p}(\mathcal{R}_2^G)$ by definition. At time $t = 7$, $\tau_1$ is notified of the liberation of $\mathcal{R}_2^G$ and begins the execution of its critical section $\sigma_3(\mathcal{R}_2^G)$ until $t = 9$ at which time it frees $\mathcal{R}_2^G$ and continues its execution until $t = 11$.

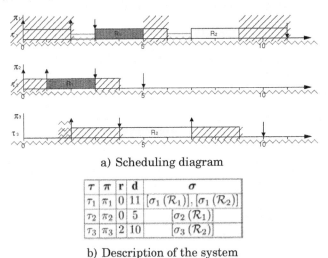

a) Scheduling diagram

| $\tau$ | $\pi$ | r | d | $\sigma$ |
|---|---|---|---|---|
| $\tau_1$ | $\pi_1$ | 0 | 11 | $[\sigma_1(\mathcal{R}_1)], [\sigma_1(\mathcal{R}_2)]$ |
| $\tau_2$ | $\pi_2$ | 0 | 5 | $[\sigma_2(\mathcal{R}_1)]$ |
| $\tau_3$ | $\pi_3$ | 2 | 10 | $[\sigma_3(\mathcal{R}_2)]$ |

b) Description of the system

**Figure 4.12.** *Chained blocking with MPCP and FMLP*

We now consider the protocol used is FMLP. If the resources $\mathcal{R}_1^G$ and $\mathcal{R}_2^G$ are considered to be long, the obtained scenario will be exactly the same as with MPCP. If however these resources are considered to be short, $\tau_1$ will not be suspended but moved to an active waiting state until the resources are released. Which will produce the exact same phenomenon of chained blocking.

This undesirable phenomenon remains unsolved in the case of multiprocessor architectures.

## 4.4. Calculating the blocking factor

We have seen that when tasks share resources, they can be subjected to blockings, in addition to preemptions induced by the fixed-priority scheduling. In order to perform a schedulability analysis, the worst-case blocking times have to be taken into account. We explain how to calculate these blocking times in the case of uniprocessor architectures (section 4.4.1), as well as in the case of multiprocessor architectures (section 4.4.2).

### 4.4.1. *The case of uniprocessor architectures*

In this section, we introduce additional notations in order to simplify the equation which calculates the blocking factor. We denote by $\sigma_{j,k}(\mathcal{R}_l)$ the $k$-th critical section of the task $\tau_j$ associated with the resource $\mathcal{R}_l$. Moreover we denote by $\delta_{j,k}(\mathcal{R}_l)$ the duration of this critical section. The set of resources shared by the tasks $\tau_i$ and $\tau_j$ is denoted as $\beta_{i,j}$ and is defined by $\beta_{i,j} = \{\mathcal{R}(\tau_i) \cap \mathcal{R}(\tau_j)\}$.

#### 4.4.1.1. *PIP*

When the PIP synchronization protocol is used, a task $\tau_i$ can be blocked for every lesser priority task with which it shares a resource.

In order to illustrate this case, we show in Figure 4.13 an example of a system synchronized with PIP. The obtained scheduling is presented in Figure 4.13(a) and the task parameters are given in Figure 4.13(b). We will be looking at task $\tau_1$, the highest priority one. This case is pathological since all tasks with lower priorities than $\tau_1$ and sharing a resource with $\tau_1$ are activated and start the execution of their critical sections right before the activation of $\tau_1$. Let us note that $\tau_1$ shares 3 resources with 2 lesser priority tasks. However, it is only subject to 2 direct blockings since $\tau_3$ can only benefit from a priority inversion once. Indeed, when $\tau_3$ terminates the execution of its critical section $\sigma_3 (\mathcal{R}_1)$, it does not take back control before $\tau_1$ has terminated the execution of its critical section. Thus, the blocking factor $B_i$ subjected to the task $\tau_i$ with PIP is given by the relation:

$$B_i = \sum_{p(\tau_j) < p(\tau_i)} \left( \max_{k} \left( \delta_{j,k} \left( \mathcal{R}_l \right) - 1 \mid \mathcal{R}_l \in \beta_{i,j} \right) \right)$$

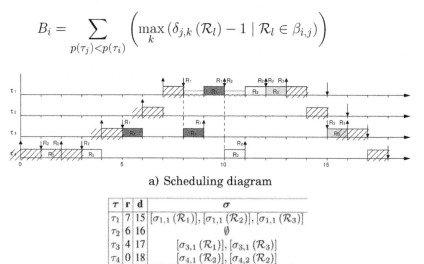

a) Scheduling diagram

| $\tau$ | r | d | $\sigma$ |
|---|---|---|---|
| $\tau_1$ | 7 | 15 | $[\sigma_{1,1} (\mathcal{R}_1)], [\sigma_{1,1} (\mathcal{R}_2)], [\sigma_{1,1} (\mathcal{R}_3)]$ |
| $\tau_2$ | 6 | 16 | $\emptyset$ |
| $\tau_3$ | 4 | 17 | $[\sigma_{3,1} (\mathcal{R}_1)], [\sigma_{3,1} (\mathcal{R}_3)]$ |
| $\tau_4$ | 0 | 18 | $[\sigma_{4,1} (\mathcal{R}_2)], [\sigma_{4,2} (\mathcal{R}_2)]$ |

b) Description of the system

**Figure 4.13.** *Blocking with PIP*

The blocking factor $B_i$ is given by the sum, for each task $\tau_j$ with lower priority than $\tau_i$, of the duration of the largest critical section of $\tau_j$ associated to a resource shared with $\tau_i$. The subtraction of a time unit from the duration of the critical section is explained by the fact that a lower priority task has to have started the execution of its critical section (for at least one time unit) in order to be able to block $\tau_i$. For more details concerning the calculation of the blocking factor with PIP, the interested reader is referred to the works of Sha, Rajkumar and Lehoczky [SHA 90] as well as Buttazzo's book [BUT 11].

### 4.4.1.2. PCP

When the PCP synchronization protocol is used, a task $\tau_i$ can only be subject, in the worst case, to a single blocking.

We show in Figure 4.14 an example similar to the previous one, but this time the system is synchronized with PCP. The obtained scheduling is presented in Figure 4.14(a) and the task parameters are given in Figure 4.14(b). It has to be noted that the duration of the critical section $\sigma_{3,1}$ ($\mathcal{R}_1$) of this example is smaller than that of the same section in the example of Figure 4.13. By contrast, the duration of the critical section $\sigma_{4,2}$ ($\mathcal{R}_2$) is higher. Moreover, the order of utilization of the resources $\mathcal{R}_1$ and $\mathcal{R}_2$ by $\tau_1$ is reversed.

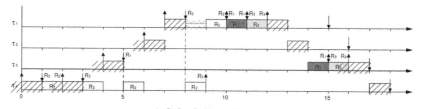

a) Scheduling diagram

| $\tau$ | r | d | $\sigma$ |
|---|---|---|---|
| $\tau_1$ | 7 | 15 | $[\sigma_{1,1}\,(\mathcal{R}_1)],\,[\sigma_{1,1}\,(\mathcal{R}_2)],\,[\sigma_{1,1}\,(\mathcal{R}_3)]$ |
| $\tau_2$ | 6 | 16 | $\emptyset$ |
| $\tau_3$ | 4 | 17 | $[\sigma_{3,1}\,(\mathcal{R}_1)],\,[\sigma_{3,1}\,(\mathcal{R}_3)]$ |
| $\tau_4$ | 0 | 18 | $[\sigma_{4,1}\,(\mathcal{R}_2)],\,[\sigma_{4,2}\,(\mathcal{R}_2)]$ |

b) Description of the system

**Figure 4.14.** *Blocking with PCP*

At time $t = 5$, when the task $\tau_3$ could begin the execution of its critical section $\sigma_{3,1}$ ($\mathcal{R}_1$) with PIP, it is blocked with PCP since its priority $p(\tau_3)$ is not strictly higher than the priority ceiling $\bar{p}(\mathcal{R}_2)$ of the resource $\mathcal{R}_2$ being used by $\tau_4$. The blocking factor $B_i$ subjected to the task $\tau_i$ with PCP is given by the relation:

$$B_i = \max_{p(\tau_j)<p(\tau_i)} \left( \max_k \left( \delta_{j,k}\left(\mathcal{R}_l\right) - 1 \mid \mathcal{R}_l \in \beta_{i,j} \right) \right)$$

$B_i$ corresponds to the duration of the largest critical section related to a resource shared with one of the lower priority tasks. In order to guarantee that a task $\tau_i$ complies with its deadline with a fixed-priority scheduling, one approach consists of calculating its worst-case response time $W_i$. This response time is calculated recursively in the following manner:

$$\begin{cases} W_i^0 = C_i + B_i \\ W_i^n = C_i + B_i + \displaystyle\sum_{p(\tau_h)>p(\tau_i)} \left\lceil \frac{W^{n-1}}{T_h} \right\rceil C_h \end{cases}$$

as well as $W_i^n \leq D_i$ and $W^n \neq W^{n-1}$. This approach to calculating to response time is also applied to the blocking factor of PIP.

For more details concerning the calculation of the blocking factor with PCP, the interested reader is referred to the works of Sha, Rajkumar and Lehoczky [SHA 90] as well as to Buttazzo's book [BUT 11].

### 4.4.2. *The case of multiprocessor architectures*

The tasks scheduled on multiprocessor architectures can be subject to distant blockings due to the global resources. We present in this section the various types of blockings which must be taken into account during the calculation of the blocking factor of tasks sharing global resources.

### 4.4.2.1. *MPCP*

With MPCP, a task $\tau_i$ can be subject to blockings due to the utilization of global resources. The utilization of global resources can provoke various types of blockings, which are (1) blockings due to transitive interferences, (2) blockings due to consecutive executions of a task and (3) blockings due to multiple priority inversions. We present, in the form of examples, these three types of blocking. We also give the details of calculating the worst-case response time of a task by taking into account the impact of these blockings.

The first type of blocking that a task $\tau_i$ can be subject to is the blocking due to transitive interferences. We represent in Figure 4.15 an example scenario in which such a blockage occurs. The obtained scheduling is presented in Figure 4.15(a) and the task parameters are given in Figure 4.15(b). The task $\tau_2$ needs to use resource $\mathcal{R}_2$. When it attempts to execute its critical section $\sigma_2\left(\mathcal{R}_2\right)$ ($t = 5$), the resource is already taken by $\tau_4$ which is then executed at the priority ceiling $\bar{p}(\mathcal{R}_2)$, higher than the priority of $\tau_2$. At time $t = 6$, $\tau_5$ terminates the execution of its critical section $\sigma_5\left(\mathcal{R}_1\right)$. The task $\tau_3$ is then notified and can begin the execution of its critical section $\sigma_3\left(\mathcal{R}_1\right)$. Indeed, the priority ceiling $\bar{p}(\mathcal{R}_1)$ of $\mathcal{R}_1$ is higher than the priority ceiling $\bar{p}(\mathcal{R}_2)$ of $\mathcal{R}_2$. This is due to the fact that the priority $p(\tau_1)$ of the highest priority task which shares $\mathcal{R}_1$ is superior to the priority $p(\tau_2)$ of the highest priority task which shares $\mathcal{R}_2$. The task $\tau_3$ thus preempts $\tau_4$ and the execution time of $\sigma_3\left(\mathcal{R}_1\right)$ contributes to increasing the blocking time of $\tau_2$.

Another type of blocking which a task $\tau_i$ can be subject to is the blocking due to the multiple executions of a task. We represent in Figure 4.16 an example scenario in which this kind of blocking occurs. The obtained scheduling is presented in Figure 4.16(a) and the task parameters are given in Figure 4.16(b). The task $\tau_1$ is blocked at time $t = 2$ by $\tau_3$. This direct blocking delays its execution. The task $\tau_2$ is then indirectly subjected to the blocking of $\tau_1$.

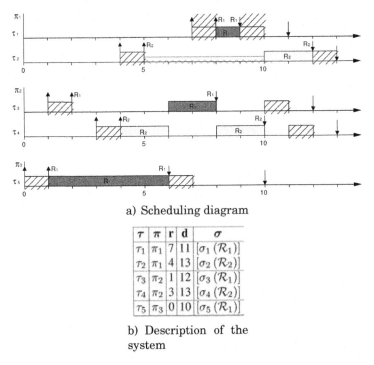

a) Scheduling diagram

| $\tau$ | $\pi$ | r | d | $\sigma$ |
|---|---|---|---|---|
| $\tau_1$ | $\pi_1$ | 7 | 11 | $[\sigma_1\,(\mathcal{R}_1)]$ |
| $\tau_2$ | $\pi_1$ | 4 | 13 | $[\sigma_2\,(\mathcal{R}_2)]$ |
| $\tau_3$ | $\pi_2$ | 1 | 12 | $[\sigma_3\,(\mathcal{R}_1)]$ |
| $\tau_4$ | $\pi_2$ | 3 | 13 | $[\sigma_4\,(\mathcal{R}_2)]$ |
| $\tau_5$ | $\pi_3$ | 0 | 10 | $[\sigma_5\,(\mathcal{R}_1)]$ |

b) Description of the system

**Figure 4.15.** *Blocking due to transitive interferences with MPCP*

Finally, the schedulability analysis has to take into account the fact that a task can be subject to multiple blockings due to priority inversions. We represent in Figure 4.17 an example scenario showing this phenomenon. The obtained scheduling is presented in Figure 4.17(a) and the task parameters are given in Figure 4.17(b). The task $\tau_2$ is preempted by $\tau_3$ or lower priority at time $t = 3$ since $\tau_3$ is notified of the release of $\mathcal{R}_1$ and the priority of $\tau_3$ then becomes the ceiling of $\bar{p}(\mathcal{R}_2)$ higher than $p(2)$. This type of blocking is entirely normal. The fact that the global resources have a higher priority ceiling than the highest priority of the system allows to avoid a task being blocked waiting for the release of a distant resource $\mathcal{R}_k$ on the processor $\pi_j$ and that the release of $\mathcal{R}_k$ being delayed on $\pi_j$ by a higher priority task. The task $\tau_1$ which shares $\mathcal{R}_1$ with $\tau_3$ is activated a second time at time $t = 6$. It executes its critical section $\sigma_1(\mathcal{R}_1)$ from $t = 7$ to $t = 9$. At time $t = 9$, the resource $\mathcal{R}_3$ is released and ready for $\tau_3$ to execute its second critical section $\sigma_{3,2}(\mathcal{R}_1)$, directly blocking $\tau_2$ a second time. In contrast to PCP, in which a task cannot be blocked more than a single time by a lower priority task, multiple blockages have to be considered with MPCP.

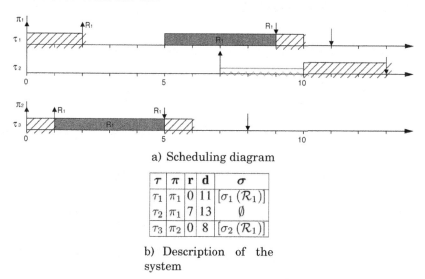

a) Scheduling diagram

| $\tau$ | $\pi$ | r | d | $\sigma$ |
|---|---|---|---|---|
| $\tau_1$ | $\pi_1$ | 0 | 11 | $[\sigma_1(\mathcal{R}_1)]$ |
| $\tau_2$ | $\pi_1$ | 7 | 13 | $\emptyset$ |
| $\tau_3$ | $\pi_2$ | 0 | 8 | $[\sigma_2(\mathcal{R}_1)]$ |

b) Description of the system

**Figure 4.16.** *Blocking due to the multiple executions of a task with MPCP*

In order to guarantee that a task $\tau_i$ complies with its deadline with a fixed-priority scheduling, one approach consists of calculating its worst-case response time $W_i$. In the case of MPCP, $W_i$ is calculated recursively in the following way:

$$
\begin{cases}
W_i^0 = C_i + B_i \\
W_i^n = C_i + B_i + \sum_{p(\tau_h)>p(\tau_i)\wedge\pi(\tau_h)=\pi(\tau_i)} \left\lceil \frac{W^{n-1}+B_h}{T_h} \right\rceil C_h \\
\qquad + s_i \sum_{p(\tau_l)<p(\tau_i)\wedge\pi(\tau_l)=\pi(\tau_i)} \max_{1\leq k<s_l} C'_{l,k}
\end{cases}
$$

where $W_i^n \leq D_i$ and $W^n \neq W^{n-1}$. The value $s_i$ represents the number of non-critical sections of the task $\tau_i$ and $C'_{l,k}$ is the worst-case execution time of the $k$-th critical section of $\tau_l$.

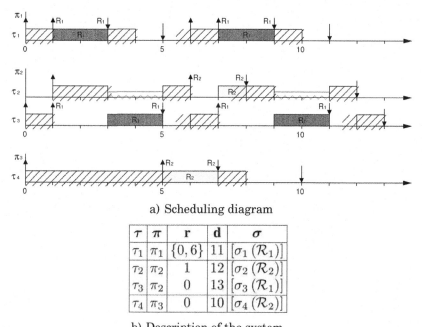

a) Scheduling diagram

| $\tau$ | $\pi$ | r | d | $\sigma$ |
|---|---|---|---|---|
| $\tau_1$ | $\pi_1$ | $\{0,6\}$ | 11 | $[\sigma_1(\mathcal{R}_1)]$ |
| $\tau_2$ | $\pi_2$ | 1 | 12 | $[\sigma_2(\mathcal{R}_2)]$ |
| $\tau_3$ | $\pi_2$ | 0 | 13 | $[\sigma_3(\mathcal{R}_1)]$ |
| $\tau_4$ | $\pi_3$ | 0 | 10 | $[\sigma_4(\mathcal{R}_2)]$ |

b) Description of the system

**Figure 4.17.** *Blocking due to multiple priority inversions with MPCP*

The interested reader is referred to the works of Rajkumar [RAJ 90] and of Lakshmanan, de Niz and Rajkumar [LAK 09] for the details of this calculation.

## 4.4.2.2. *FMLP*

In the case of a fixed-priority partitioned scheduling with FMLP, the blocking factor $B_i$ of a task $\tau_i$ is broken down into 5 terms which we describe below.

First, we show the blockings that can be induced by the utilization of long resources with the scenario represented in Figure 4.18. The obtained scheduling is presented in Figure 4.18(a) and the task parameters are given in Figure 4.18(b). At time $t = 1$, $\tau_1$ and $\tau_3$ are in competition for the use of $\mathcal{R}_1$. The task $\tau_1$, having a higher priority, is allowed to execute its critical section $\sigma_1 (\mathcal{R}_1)$. The task $\tau_3$ is then subjected to a *long blocking* on the interval $[1, 3]$. In order not to delay the tasks which could be blocked waiting for the release of $\mathcal{R}_1$ on other processors, $\tau_3$ benefits from increase of its priority which prevents $\tau_2$ from preempting it. During the execution of the critical section $\sigma_3 (\mathcal{R}_1)$ of $\tau_3$, the task $\tau_2$ is subjected to *boost blocking* on the interval $[3, 5]$.

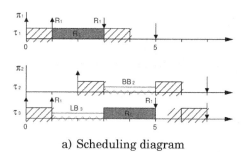

| $T$ | $\pi$ | $r$ | $d$ | $\sigma$ |
|---|---|---|---|---|
| $\tau_1$ | $\pi_1$ | 0 | 5 | $[\sigma_1 (\mathcal{R}_1)]$ |
| $\tau_2$ | $\pi_1$ | 2 | 7 | $\emptyset$ |
| $\tau_3$ | $\pi_2$ | 0 | 7 | $[\sigma_3 (\mathcal{R}_1)]$ |

a) Scheduling diagram          b) Description of the system

**Figure 4.18.** *Boost blocking and long blocking blockages due to the utilization of global long resources with FMLP*

Second, we show the blockings that can occur when short resources are used in the scenario represented in Figure 4.18. The obtained scheduling is presented in Figure 4.19(a) and the task parameters are given in Figure 4.19(b). At time $t = 2$, $\tau_3$ attempts to start the execution of its critical section

$\sigma_3\,(\mathcal{R}_1)$, but $\mathcal{R}_1$ is already being used by $\tau_1$. The task $\tau_3$ is therefore blocked in a state of active waiting and is executed in a non-preemptive manner until it can have access to $\mathcal{R}_1$ and terminated the execution of $\sigma_3\,(\mathcal{R}_1)$. The task $\tau_3$ is therefore subjected to *short blocking* on the interval $[2, 4]$. At time $t = 3$, the task $\tau_2$ is activated but cannot begin its execution since $\tau_3$ cannot be preempted. It is then subjected to *arrival blocking* on the interval $[3, 5]$.

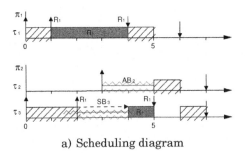

a) Scheduling diagram

| $\tau$ | $\pi$ | r | d | $\sigma$ |
|---|---|---|---|---|
| $\tau_1$ | $\pi_1$ | 0 | 6 | $[\sigma_1\,(\mathcal{R}_1)]$ |
| $\tau_2$ | $\pi_1$ | 3 | 7 | $\emptyset$ |
| $\tau_3$ | $\pi_2$ | 0 | 7 | $[\sigma_3\,(\mathcal{R}_1)]$ |

b) Description of the systeù

**Figure 4.19.** *Arrival blocking and short blocking blockages due to the utilization of global long resources with FMLP*

Finally, we show the impact that could result from the utilization of global resources on the lower-priority tasks in the scenario of Figure 4.20. The obtained scheduling is presented in Figure 4.20(a) and the task parameters are given in Figure 4.20(b). At time $t = 1$, the task $\tau_2$ is blocked waiting for $\mathcal{R}_1$ to be freed. At time $t = 2$, the task $\tau_3$ may begin its execution, but is preempted at time $t = 3$ by $\tau_2$ which is notified of the release of $\mathcal{R}_1$. The delay due to the blocking sustained by $\tau_2$ is reflected on $\tau_3$ which is then subject to *deferral blocking* over the interval $[4, 6]$.

Finally, the blocking factor of the task $\tau_i$ is given by the sum of the 5 terms presented above and is given by the relation:

$$B_i = BB_i + AB_i + SB_i + LB_i + DB_i$$

where $BB_i$ corresponds to *boost blocking*, $AB_i$ to *arrival blocking*, $SB_i$ to *short blocking*, $LB_i$ to *long blocking* and $DB_i$ to *deferral blocking*.

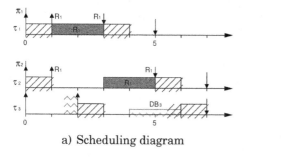

| $\tau$ | $\pi$ | $r$ | $d$ | $\sigma$ |
|---|---|---|---|---|
| $\tau_1$ | $\pi_1$ | 0 | 5 | $[\sigma_1\,(\mathcal{R}_1)]$ |
| $\tau_2$ | $\pi_1$ | 0 | 7 | $\emptyset$ |
| $\tau_3$ | $\pi_2$ | 2 | 7 | $[\sigma_3\,(\mathcal{R}_1)]$ |

a) Scheduling diagram                b) Description of the system

**Figure 4.20.** *Deferral blocking due to the utilization of global long resources with FMLP*

The reader interested in the details of calculating each term is referred to the appendix of the work of Brandenburg and Anderson [BRA 08a].

## 4.5. Conclusion

In this chapter, we have presented the various resource access protocols applicable to uniprocessor (PIP, PCP) and multiprocessor architectures (MPCP, FMLP). We have described their properties. We have described the undesirable and unavoidable effects during the sharing of resources in a real-time system (unbounded priority inversion, interblocking and chained blocking). We have presented these effects in the case of uni- and multiprocessor architectures. We have shown how these effects are controlled (or not) following the access protocol used. Finally, we have described how to quantify the worst-case block durations applicable to resource-sharing tasks and how we have to integrate them into the schedulability analysis of systems.

## 4.6. Bibliography

[BAK 90] BAKER T.P., "A stack-based resource allocation policy for real-time processes", *Proceedings of the 11th IEEE Real-time Systems Symposium (RTSS)*, Lake Buena Vista, FL, IEEE Computer Society, pp. 191–200, December 1990.

[BAK 91] BAKER T.P., "Stack-based scheduling of real-time processes", *Real-time Systems*, vol. 3, no. 1, pp. 67–99, March 1991.

[BLO 07] BLOCK A.D., LEONTYEV H., BRANDENBURG B.B., *et al.*, "A flexible real-time locking protocol for multiprocessors", *Proceedings of the 13th IEEE International Conference on Embedded and Real-time Computing Systems and Applications (RTCSA)*, Daegu, South Korea, IEEE Computer Society, pp. 47–56, August 2007.

[BRA 08a] BRANDENBURG B.B., ANDERSON J.H., "An implementation of the PCP, SRP, D-PCP, M-PCP, and FMLP real-time synchronization protocols in $LITMUS^{RT}$", *Proceedings of the 14th IEEE International Conference on Real-time and Embedded Computing Systems and Applications (RTCSA)*, Kaohsiung, Taiwan, IEEE Computer Society, pp. 185–194, August 2008.

[BRA 08b] BRANDENBURG B.B., CALANDRINO J.M., BLOCK A.D., *et al.*, "Real-time synchronization on multiprocessors: to block or not to block, to suspend or spin?", *Proceedings of the 14th Real-time and Embedded Technology and Applications Symposium (RTAS)*, St. Louis, MO, IEEE Computer Society, pp. 342–353, April 2008.

[BRA 10] BRANDENBURG B.B., ANDERSON J.H., "Optimality results for multiprocessor real-time locking", *Proceedings of the 21st IEEE Real-time Systems Symposium (RTSS)*, San Diego, CA, IEEE Computer Society, pp. 49–60, November–December 2010.

[BRA 11] BRANDENBURG B.B., Scheduling and locking in multiprocessor real-time operating systems, PhD thesis, University of North Carolina, Chapel Hill, 2011.

[BRA 12a] BRANDENBURG B.B., ANDERSON J.H., "The OMLP family of optimal multiprocessor real-time locking protocols", *Design Automation for Embedded Systems*, July 2012.

[BRA 12b] BRANDENBURG B.B., BASTONI A., "The case for migratory priority inheritance in linux: bounded priority inversions on multiprocessors", *Proceedings of the 14th Real-time Linux Workshop (RTLWS)*, Chapel Hill, NC, Real-time Linux Foundation, pp. 67–86, October 2012.

[BRA 13] BRANDENBURG B.B., "A fully preemptive multiprocessor semaphore protocol for latency-sensitive real-time applications", *Proceedings of the 25th Euromicro Conference on Real-time Systems (ECRTS)*, Paris, France, IEEE Computer Society, pp. 292–302, July 2013.

[BUR 13] BURNS A., WELLINGS A.J., "A schedulability compatible multiprocessor resource sharing protocol – MrsP", *Proceedings of the 25th Euromicro Conference on Real-time Systems (ECRTS)*, Paris, France, IEEE Computer Society, pp. 282–291, July 2013.

[BUT 11] BUTTAZZO G.C., *Hard Real-Time Computing Systems: Predictable Scheduling Algorithms and Applications*, vol. 24 of Real-time Systems Series, Springer, 2011.

[EAS 09] EASWARAN A., ANDERSSON B., "Resource sharing in global fixed-priority preemptive multiprocessor scheduling", *Proceedings of the 30th IEEE Real-Time Systems Symposium (RTSS)*, Washington D.C., IEEE Computer Society, pp. 377–386, December 2009.

[FAG 10] FAGGIOLI D., LIPARI G., CUCINOTTA T., "The multiprocessor bandwidth inheritance protocol", *Proceedings of the 22nd Euromicro Conference on Real-Time Systems (ECRTS)*, Brussels, Belgium, IEEE Computer Society, pp. 90–99, July 2010.

[GAI 01] GAI P., LIPARI G., DI NATALE M., "Minimizing memory utilization of real-time task sets in single and multi-processor systems-on-a-chip", *Proceedings of the 22nd IEEE Real-Time Systems Symposium (RTSS)*, London, UK, IEEE Computer Society, pp. 73–83, December 2001.

[LAK 09] LAKSHMANAN K., DE NIZ D., RAJKUMAR R.R., "Coordinated task scheduling, allocation and synchronization on multiprocessors", *Proceedings of the 30th IEEE Real-Time Systems Symposium (RTSS)*, Washington D.C., IEEE Computer Society, pp. 469–478, December 2009.

[LAM 01] LAMASTRA G., LIPARI G., ABENI L., "A bandwidth inheritance algorithm for real-time task synchronization in open systems", *Proceedings of the 22nd IEEE Real-Time Systems Symposium (RTSS)*, London, UK, IEEE Computer Society, pp. 151–160, December 2001.

[RAJ 88] RAJKUMAR R.R., SHA L., LEHOCZKY J.P., "Real-time synchronization protocols for multiprocessors", *Proceedings of the 9th IEEE Real-Time Systems Symposium (RTSS)*, Huntsville, AL, IEEE Computer Society, pp. 259–269, December 1988.

[RAJ 90] RAJKUMAR R.R., "Real-time synchronization protocols for shared memory multiprocessors", *Proceedings of the 10th International Conference on Distributed Computing Systems (ICDCS)*, Paris, France, IEEE Computer Society, pp. 116–123, May–June 1990.

[SHA 87] SHA L., RAJKUMAR R.R., LEHOCZKY J.P., Priority inheritance protocols: an approach to real-time synchronization, Report no. CMU-CS-87-18, Carnegie Mellon University, Department of Computer Science, 1987.

[SHA 90] SHA L., RAJKUMAR R.R., LEHOCZKY J.P., "Priority inheritance protocols: an approach to real-time synchronization", *IEEE Transactions on Computers*, vol. 39, no. 9, pp. 1175–1185, September 1990.

[TAK 97] TAKADA H., SAKAMURA K., "A novel approach to multiprogrammed multiprocessor synchronization for real-time kernels", *Proceedings of the 18th IEEE Real-Time Systems Symposium (RTSS)*, San Francisco, CA, pp. 134–143, December 1997.

[WAR 12] WARD B.C., ANDERSON J.H., "Supporting nested locking in multiprocessor real-time systems", *Proceedings of the 24th Euromicro Conference on Real-Time Systems (ECRTS)*, Pisa, Italy, IEEE Computer Society, pp. 223–232, July 2012.

# 5

# Estimation of Execution Time and Delays

In the previous chapters, the execution time of the programs or tasks was considered as one of the parameters of schedulability analysis. This execution time is denoted by $C_i$ or $E_i$. In this chapter, we explain how it can be estimated, what it represents and why this analysis may be difficult.

The timing constraints of critical real-time systems have to be fully respected under the penalty of severe damage (passenger injuries in a vehicle, for example, if the airbag is not deployed on time). Thus, the execution time given as a reference to the scheduling algorithms must be an upper bound of the execution time for the program to be analyzed. However, in critical real-time systems, programs often use values coming from sensors which may have very large amplitudes (e.g. external temperature of an aircraft). As a result, it is generally impossible to test all the values and therefore impossible to guarantee that an upper bound on the execution time has been measured. This is especially true given that embedded processors are more and more complex,

Chapter written by Claire MAIZA, Pascal RAYMOND and Christine ROCHANGE.

which leads to a large variation of the execution time of the programs. In this chapter, we explain how to estimate the *worst-case execution time* (WCET): a guaranteed upper bound for any execution of the program. We use static timing analysis, in contrast to a dynamic analysis which would be based on execution time measurements.

As explained above, the execution time of a program may depend on the execution path (for instance "then" or "else" branch of a conditional structure) and therefore on the software, but also on the hardware (pipeline processor, cache memories or multi-core, for example). In this chapter, based on a simple example, we first explain the usual methodology used to estimate WCET by static analysis (section 5.1). By "simple example" we mean a short piece of code containing all the specificities which may have an influence on the execution time. We consider a mono-task execution without interference from other programs or interrupt routines and a very simple hardware architecture. In section 5.2, we get more into the details of the analysis by answering three questions:

– How to estimate delays due to interferences caused by another running program in multi-task systems? We present the example of delays due to preemptions.

– How to analyze the execution time for more complex architectures in which the tasks share resources and therefore interfere with one another? We examine several approaches to compute the WCET of a task running on a multi-core architecture.

– What is the influence of the high-level design methods and their compilation on the WCET? This issue is illustrated by the example of the synchronous approach (see Chapter 4, Volume 2), by considering an example designed in the SCADE environment.

Finally, we list some state-of-the-art tools dedicated to the WCET estimation (section 5.2.4).

## 5.1. Worst-case execution time analysis: an example

The program we use as an example is presented in Figure 5.1(a). This program is typical of the control engineering field: it is the functional code of a task being called on a periodic clock. At each call, the `Step` procedure performs a processing cycle: computing the output `S` as a function of the inputs (`X`, `Y`, `idle` and `low`), and updating the memory (`tab` and `init`). The inputs `X` and `Y` are values obtained from sensors (for instance temperature or pressure sensors). The inputs `idle` and `low` are variables which inform about the global state of the system (often referred to as *computation modes*). At the very first call of program, the internal variable `init` is supposed to be true, and thus, the array `tab` is initialized. In standard mode (neither `idle` nor `low`), the program computes the sum of `Y` with the smallest obtained value of `X` while storing the ten smallest values of `X` in the `tab` array. If the system is low on battery (`low` mode), the current value of `X` is used and `tab` is not updated. Moreover, if the system is suspended (`idle` mode), the program does not perform any computation.

Our goal now is to compute the WCET of this program. The code to analyze is not the C source code of Figure 5.1(a) but the code such as it is executed: the binary code obtained after compilation and adaptation to the target hardware. The first step of WCET analysis consists of extracting the structure of the binary code as a *Control Flow Graph* (CFG). The CFG corresponding to the example of Figure 5.1(a) is given in Figure 5.1(b). This graph is composed of basic blocks connected by transitions. A basic block is itself composed of a sequence of machine instructions with a single entry point and a single exit point. For the sake of simplicity, the C program is compiled without optimization, which explains that the control structure of the binary code is similar to that of the C code. For instance, in Figure 5.1, we can easily see that block B0 corresponds to the first "`if (init)`"

statement, that blocks B3 and B4 correspond to the
initialization of the array, and that block B8 corresponds to
the call of the function `insert`.

```
void Step(){
  if(init){
    // initialization of tab
    for(i=0;i<10;i++){
      tab[i]=0;
    }
  }
  if (not(idle)){
    if(low){
      S=X+Y;
    }
    else{
      insert(X,tab);
      S=tab[0]+Y;
    }
  }
  if(init){
    init=false;
  }
}
```

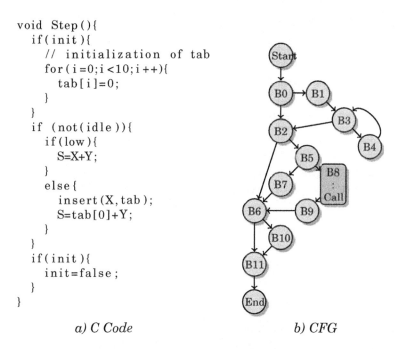

a) C Code                    b) CFG

**Figure 5.1.** *Program to be analyzed: a) C code,*
*b) binary control flow graph*

This control flow graph allows us to represent the code as
a model on which we can perform our analysis. By using the
CFG as input, the WCET analysis consists of estimating the
execution time of each basic block (section 5.1.1), and then
computing the longest path (in execution time) in the graph
(section 5.1.2).

## 5.1.1. *Embedded system architecture analysis*

In this part, we look at the way we can compute the worst-case execution time of each basic block of the CFG [1]. A simple solution would be to sum the execution time of every instruction of the basic block, which would be taken from the processor user manual. While this was possible on old processors, it is no longer the case for modern processors due to pipeline execution, superscalar, out-of-order, speculative architectures associated with advanced internal or external components (memory hierarchy: cache memories, scratchpad memories, etc.). In the next section, we see how these different elements can be analyzed.

### 5.1.1.1. *Pipeline analysis*

In a pipelined execution, the processing of an instruction is split into steps that fit a processor cycle (as much as possible). This is illustrated on Figure 5.2. Every instruction must pass through these steps and, in a cycle, each step is likely to process a different instruction.

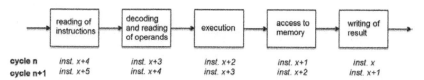

**Figure 5.2.** *Pipeline execution*

Ideally, if we start from a state in which the pipeline is empty, the execution time of the first instruction is equal to the traversal time of all the steps, but the following instructions leave the pipeline at the rate of one per cycle. In practice, the execution of instructions is not always fluid since some instructions have to wait, before the next step, that the previous instructions have reached certain steps in

---

1. In general, this time is expressed as a number of processor cycles.

their processing. For instance, if an arithmetic instruction has as operand the result of a previous memory load, the arithmetic instruction can only access the execution stage when the preceding instruction exits the memory access stage. It is necessary to take these behaviors into account when estimating the worst-case execution time of a basic block. In a simple way (but poorly adapted to complex mechanisms as we see later on), we can represent the execution of a basic block in a reservation table, as shown in Figure 5.3. On the figure, the WCET of the block is 9 cycles and the dependency between instructions (b) and (c) leads to a bubble in the pipeline. With this method, we determine the execution time of a basic block by taking into account the overlapping of the instructions in the pipeline.

In order to be precise, we also have to take into account the overlapping between instructions belonging to different basic blocks executed in sequence. We then compute the execution cost of the block, as illustrated in Figure 5.4, which can be different depending on the predecessor block and is therefore generally associated with the transition edge between the predecessor and the block, instead of the node representing the block. For instance, our block B5 has a cost of 4 cycles after B2, whereas B6 has a cost of 8 cycles when executed after B7 but only 2 cycles when executed after B2 (estimations performed on a compiled version of the code). In order to be precise, we also have to take into account the overlapping between instructions belonging to different basic blocks executed in sequence. We then compute the execution cost of the block, as illustrated on Figure 5.4. A block WCET may vary depending on the which block was previously executed. For instance, the block B6 has a cost of 8 cycles when executed after B7 but only 2 cycles when executed after B2 (estimations performed on a compiled version of the code). It is therefore more accurate to attach the WCET estimation to the transitions between blocks, rather than to the blocks themselves.

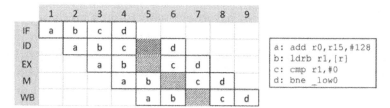

**Figure 5.3.** *Reservation table for basic block B5 of Figure 5.1b)*
*(example of compiled code for this block).*

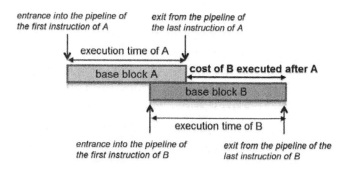

**Figure 5.4.** *Cost of a basic block*

Unfortunately, the implementation of advanced mechanisms which increase the instruction throughput leads to a complex analysis. Firstly, computing the cost of a block depending on its direct predecessor no longer works due to the possibility of the so-called *long-timing effect*: the execution time of a basic block does not only depend on its direct predecessor, but also on basic blocks further away on the execution path leading to the block. A typical source of such an effect is the presence of functional units with a latency longer than one cycle. It is difficult to prove that a processor cannot cause this phenomenon. Therefore, it is necessary to consider a more complete history while analyzing the execution time of a basic block. A possible approach is based on abstract interpretation techniques [COU 77]. Through a fix-point analysis, we compute the set of possible states of the pipeline at each point of the program, and we use these sets to determine a bound on the execution time of each basic block [LAN 02]. This approach also allows us to take advanced mechanisms into account such as superscalar execution (several instructions are processed in parallel in each cycle) or out-of-order execution (the instructions can be executed in a different order than that of the program as far as the data dependencies are respected). If all the instructions of the basic block have a fixed processing time (known statically), its execution time in presence of such complex mechanisms only depends on the state of the pipeline.

### 5.1.1.2. *Execution artifacts: example of cache memories*

The assumption of a statically known execution time of the instructions (at the time of the analysis) is refuted: (i) due to the optimization of certain computing units, which leads to the fact that the processing time of an instruction may depend on the value of its operands, and (ii) due to the use of devices whose behavior depends on a global history. This is the case of cache memories or dynamic branch predictors which try to predict the target instruction of a branch depending on its past behavior (to avoid inserting bubbles into the pipeline). This section presents cache memories in more details.

A cache memory is a fast memory in which we can find instructions or data recently referenced by the program. It can be accessed in one (or several) processor cycles, instead of several tens of cycles for accessing the main memory. However, a cache memory is much smaller: typically from 4 to 64 kilobytes. It allows to reduce memory access times by exploiting the temporal and spatial locality of accesses. It is organized into sets containing a number of lines equal to the associativity (we refer to 4-way set associative cache for instance when a set contains 4 lines). The set into which a line of memory is loaded is determined by its address. If the set is full, a replacement policy is implemented in order to select the line to be replaced. A classical example of such a policy is LRU – *Least Recently Used* – which replaces the least recently used line.

We see below how we can analyze the behavior of a cache. The aim of this analysis is to determine, for every access to an instruction or a piece of data in a basic block, whether the requested information is present (hit) or not (miss) in the cache. The analysis techniques are based on an over-approximation of the cache state and do not allow us to provide a clear response for all the accesses. In case of uncertainty, we may be tempted to consider that the worst case is a miss. However, it has been shown that this was not necessarily true for out of order architectures: this phenomenon is known by the term *timing anomaly*. Therefore, it is safer to consider both possibilities (hit or miss) in this case [REI 09].

In order to present the cache analysis techniques, we will firs consider an instruction cache. We will then give a few elements on the analysis of data caches and cache hierarchies.

The analysis of the cache assigns a category to each instruction, namely:

– *AlwaysHit*: for every execution of the program, the instruction is present in the cache;

– *AlwaysMiss*: the instruction has to be loaded into the cache from higher levels of the hierarchy;

– *NonClassified*: the analysis is unable to predict the behavior of the cache for reading this instruction.

We may also consider a fourth category, *Persistent*, which is applied to an instruction belonging to the body of a loop, absent from the cache at the first iteration and present for the following iterations. These categories are used to determine the fetch latency of these instructions, during the execution time estimation of the basic blocks.

How do we assign a category to each instruction? The usual techniques are based on abstract interpretation. A fix-point analysis allows us to compute the set of possible states of the instruction cache before and after each block. As the number of states is generally very high, we consider abstract states. An *abstract cache state* contains a set $\mathcal{E}$ of lines for each set of the cache. For an $N$-way set associative cache, we assign an *age* $a$ to every line, with $a \in [0..N[ \cup l_\top$ where the virtual age $l_\top$ is the oldest possible age: it is assigned to the lines which have been loaded and then replaced in the cache.

Three analyses are performed: *May*, *Must* and *Persistence*. Update functions define the effect of accessing a line on the abstract cache state. The join function merges several abstract states into a single one at junctions in the CFG [ALT 96].

For the *May* analysis, the set $\mathcal{E}$ contains the lines which *may* be present in the cache, and we consider the smallest possible age for each line. For a cache with an LRU replacement policy, the newly inserted line is assigned the age 0 and every other line is aged by one. The join function performs the union of the input abstract states and keeps the smallest possible age for each line. This is illustrated in Figure 5.5 which considers an LRU 4-way set associative cache.

In a similar way, the *Must* analysis considers the lines which *must* be present in the cache and maintains their highest possible age. The join function computes the intersection between the input abstract states and keeps the oldest possible age for each line. Figure 5.6 illustrates the effects of the update and join functions for the *Must* analysis.

For the *Persistence* analysis, the set $\mathcal{E}$ contains the lines which may be present in the cache with their oldest possible age. Every line which has a lower age than $l_\top$ is ensured to remain in the cache once loaded. The update function is similar to that of the *Must* analysis and the join function computes the union of the input states while keeping the maximum age of each line.

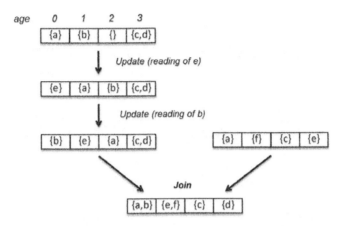

**Figure 5.5.** *Example of May analysis for an LRU 4-way set associative cache*

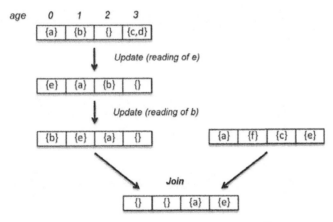

**Figure 5.6.** *Example of Must analysis for an LRU 4-way set associative cache*

Once built, the abstract states are used to assign the categories. A line is marked AlwaysHit (respectively, AlwaysMiss or Persistent) if it is present in the abstract state of the Must analysis (respectively, May or Persistence) and if its age is not equal to $l_\top$. In all other cases, the line is NonClassified.

Figure 5.7 shows the results of the cache analysis for a simple program. The CFG contains three basic blocks, each of them containing a single instruction. We assume that the cache is two-way set associative, with a single set. The input and output states of each block for the Must, May and Persistence analyses are presented. The instruction of block $a$ is not present in the input state May: it is noted AlwaysMiss. The instruction of block $b$ is not in the Must state but is in the May and Persistence states. It is therefore marked Persistent.

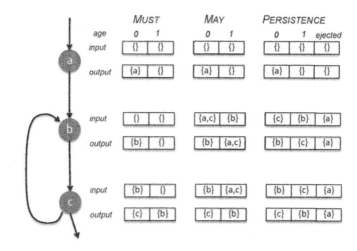

**Figure 5.7.** *Example of cache analysis by abstract interpretation (LRU two-way set associative cache)*

Note that the cache analysis is more complex and less precise when the replacement policy is not LRU [REI 13].

The analysis of a data cache presents an additional difficulty with respect to that of an instruction cache. While the addresses of the instructions fetched by the processor during the execution are known as soon as the placement of the code in the memory space is specified, the addresses of the data are often dynamic:

– access to the stack (function parameters and local variables): a static analysis can allow the evaluation of the value of the stack pointer and therefore the determination of the addresses of these accesses [REG 05];

– access to data through pointers: if the data has been allocated statically, it may be possible to perform an analysis on the value of the pointer; however, this is not possible for dynamically allocated data, which is to be avoided in critical software.

– access to array elements: a load instruction in a loop may access a different element at each iteration. In some cases (regular accesses), it may be possible to take the behavior of the cache into account with respect to such instructions [HUY 11].

Note that every address which cannot be predicted leads to the assumption that the access can touch any set in the cache and replace a line there. This has a huge impact on the precision of cache analysis.

More and more frequently, processors are equipped with a cache hierarchy: if a data/instruction is not present in the first-level cache, it is searched for in the second-level cache (bigger but slower: several megabytes and accessed in a few processor clock cycles), or even in the third-level cache (even bigger – several tens or hundreds of megabytes – and even slower). The analysis of the higher-level caches requires determining which accesses of the processor (loading an instruction or accessing data) reach them and are therefore likely to modify their state [HAR 08].

## 5.1.2. *Execution path analysis*

### 5.1.2.1. *Estimation by graph traversal*

The previous section has shown how to estimate, for each transition between basic blocks, a local WCET (cost), or "weight". Figure 5.8(a) represents the control flow graph of our example with the weight of each transition (in processor clock cycles). From this graph, the idea is now to estimate the execution time of the entire program. The WCET corresponds to the path with the heaviest "weight" in the graph.

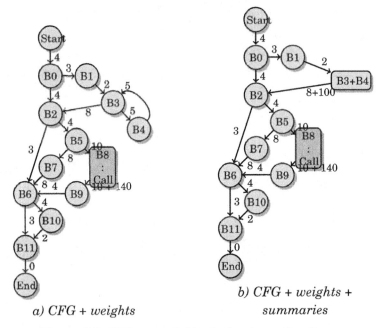

a) CFG + weights

b) CFG + weights + summaries

**Figure 5.8.** *CFG annotated by the local execution times*

The most natural idea is to obtain this WCET by a traversal of the graph that associates each node $B$ with the WCET *starting from B*, denoted by $\pi(B)$. For this, we apply a simple max/plus rule to each branch. For instance, we have $\pi(B2) = max(4 + \pi(B5), 3 + \pi(B6))$. Naturally, such a method only converges if the graph does not contain cycles: every cycle contributes to assigning, in cascade, an infinite WCET to each node, as in our example with the cycle B3 and B4.

In order to guarantee a finite WCET, we have to (1) guarantee that the loop terminates, and (2) find an upper bound on the number of iterations. This step is called *loop bound analysis*, and is intrinsically limited to processing simple cases[2]. We do not present this analysis in detail, but note that, in our simple example with a *for* loop, the analysis succeeds and finds a bound of 10 iterations. This bound allows us to compute a WCET that "summarizes" the execution of the entire loop: it is the WCET of one iteration ($3 + 7 = 10$), multiplied by the upper bound on the number of iterations ($\times 10 = 100$). Figure 5.8(b) represents the modified graph in which the cycle is replaced by a "summary" (block B3+B4) of local weight $100$.

Once all the loops are recursively eliminated, we obtain an acyclic oriented graph where the longest path estimation is guaranteed to terminate. In our example, this path is Start-B0-B1-(B3+B4)$^{10}$-B2-B5-B8-B9-B6-B10-B11-End,   and it corresponds to a WCET of 291 clock cycles.

### 5.1.2.2. *Infeasible paths*

The approximation of the WCET may sometimes be pessimistic, since it takes into account infeasible execution paths, due to provable or assumed semantic properties. For instance, if we refer to the code in our example (Figure 5.1(a)), we may note that the test of the `init` variable is performed twice. On the CFG of the program, these two tests correspond to the blocks B0 and B6: if the test is true (respectively, false) in B0, it is eventually true (respectively, false) in B6. From this, we can deduce that every path that passes through the transition B0-B1 and the

2. Loop bound analysis is limited by the undecidability of the *halting problem*.

transition B6-B11 (respectively, B0-B2 and B6-B10) is impossible. In general, identifying infeasible paths may reject worst case candidates, and thus enhance the estimation, but this is not the case for our particular example.

Not all properties of the program are intrinsic: they often arise from known properties on the inputs of the program. In our example, suppose that we know that, when init is true, low is necessarily true too. On the CFG, this property is translated by the fact that if the transition B0–B1 is fired, then the transition B5-B8 is not. By taking this property into account, the longest path becomes Start-B0-B2-B5-B8-B9-B6-B11-End, which is 179 clock cycles. With this additional information, coming from the system design, we gain more than 40% precision.

### 5.1.2.3. *Estimation by resolution of a numerical system*

The worst-case path estimation method by graph traversal is simple and intuitive. However, it is difficult (or even impossible) to implement when the control structure is less regular (use of *goto* or *break* for instance). This is why the majority of existing tools prefer using a more homogeneous method, called *implicit path enumeration technique* (or IPET) [LI 97]. Figure 5.8(a) illustrates this method for our example program.

The idea is to characterize an execution by the number of times it passes through each transition. For this, we introduce an integer variable for each transition: $x_{i,j}$ corresponds to the number of times the execution passes through the transition from block $B_i$ to block $B_j$. For every execution of a program without cycle, each of these variables is either equal to 1 or 0, and there is not much interest in reasoning on integers. The method is more useful for programs containing cycles.

All these variables, called "counters", are linked by constraints that directly arise from the structure of the program, and which are intuitively summarized by: the number of times the execution enters a block is equal to the number of times it exits it. For example, the structural constraint associated with the block $B2$ is: $x_{0,2} + x_{3,2} = x_{2,5} + x_{2,6}$. We complete this set with the constraints that state that the execution begins and terminates once, which in our example is: $x_{Start,0} = x_{11,End} = 1$.

All these constraints are trivially linear. Moreover, the total weight of an execution can be expressed as a linear function of its counters. This is the sum of the counters multiplied by their weight (denoted by $w_{i,j}$), or: $\sum w_{i,j} \times x_{i,j}$. Finding the WCET is thus reduced to *maximizing* this total weight: this is a classical problem of *integer linear programming* (or ILP), for which there are efficient resolution tools (ILP solver). In our example, the resolution of the linear program leads to an infinite WCET, caused by the B3-B4 loop. As in the case of graph traversal, the additional information on the loop bound has to be taken into account. In the context of ILP, the loop bound is easily integrated: it is sufficient to complete the structural constraints with $x_{3,4} \leq 10$. With this new constraint, the ILP solver obtains the expected solution, which is a worst-case time of $291$ clock cycles.

Taking infeasible paths into account are possible with ILP, under the condition that we can express them using numerical constraints. This is the case in our example, in which the assumption of implication between `init` and `low` may be translated by the constraint: $x_{0,1} + x_{5,8} < 2$ (we traverse at most once B0-B1 or B5-B8). With this additional constraint, the ILP solver gives the expected improved WCET of $179$ clock cycles.

The following articles may be useful for any additional details or references concerning:

– loop bound analysis [DEM 08];

– path analysis [ASA 13].

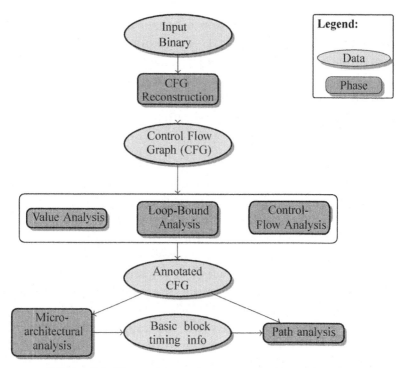

**Figure 5.9.** *Worst-case execution time analysis workflow*

We have shown in the example how an upper bound on the execution time can be estimated. Figure 5.9 summarizes the main steps of WCET analysis. Some steps were not detailed in our example, such as the value analysis that allows us to better take into account the values for the program variables and the memory addresses, the flow analysis that we only presented in infeasible paths analysis. We recommend reading the article [WIL 08] for additional information on the WCET analysis.

In the remainder of this chapter, we explain how the WCET is influenced by the execution context: multitask, multicore and compilation.

## 5.2. Going further

### 5.2.1. *Multi-task: the cost of preemption*

In preemptive systems, the execution of a task can be interrupted at any time when a higher priority task is activated. For example, Figure 5.10 shows a preemption of task $T_2$ by task $T_1$ ($T_2$ is the preempted task, and $T_1$ is the preempting task). Some additional delays are inherent to the preemption mechanism, typically such as the *context switch* cost [YOM 07]. Figure 5.10 shows in dark gray the costs of saving and restoring the context of $T_2$. These delays may vary slightly but are relatively easy to bound, and therefore to take into account in the timing analysis: it is sufficient to find an upper bound on the number of preemptions and to multiply this number by the maximum cost of a context switch.

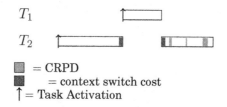

$\blacksquare$ = CRPD
$\blacksquare$     = context switch cost
$\uparrow$ = Task Activation

**Figure 5.10.** *Delays due to preemption*

Certain delays are much more difficult to take into account, since they depend on the exact location of the preemption (preemption point). This is the case when the architecture uses cache memories: the delays depend on the preemption point, and have an effect throughout the execution of the remainder of the task.

In this section, we explain why, and study how, these delays can be bounded and taken into account in the scheduling algorithms. This bound on the delay, due to cache memory, is denoted by CRPD for *cache-related preemption delay.* In Figure 5.10 we can see that the CRPD is composed of several parts (light gray) that represent the situations in which: (1) task $T_2$ loads a block [3] $a$ into the cache; (2) task $T_1$ replaces this block by block $x$ during preemption; (3) task $T_2$ accesses again block $a$ that needs to be reloaded into the cache. In order to evaluate the delays due to preemptions, we need to know how many cache misses are due to preemption (and would not occur during an execution without preemption).

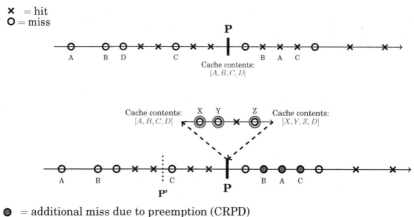

Figure 5.11. *Impact of a preemption at point P on the cache contents*

Let us consider the example of Figure 5.11. The upper part of this figure represents the execution of a task without preemption. Blocks A, B, C and D are loaded into the cache before point P, and therefore constitute the contents of the cache at this execution point. Among these blocks, A, B and C are accessed further on in the execution. Since they are always present in the cache, these accesses are *hits*. In the second scenario, the task is preempted at point P, and the preempting task loads three memory blocks (X, Y and Z) into

---

3. In this section, we use the term *block* instead of cache *line*, but the two terms are equivalent.

the cache, evicting blocks A, B and C. The following accesses to blocks A, B and C are, therefore *misses*, while they would have been *hits* in an execution without preemption: these *misses* constitute the delay due to preemption. Here, the CRPD equals three times the cost of loading a block into the cache. Note that if the preemption would have occurred before the access to block S at point $P'$, the preemption would only have caused two loads into memory instead of three: the CRPD depends on the preemption point.

Let us now give the intuition behind several approaches to estimate the CRPD. We consider two points of view:

– Which blocks of the preempted task are in danger in case of preemption?

– Which blocks of the preempting task may replace some blocks of the preempted task?

The first approach is called UCB, for *useful cache block*, and determines, at a given execution point, which "useful" blocks of the task are being accessed. A block is useful when it is in the cache before the preemption point and is reused afterward. The blocks A, B and C are, therefore, useful at point P. The CRPD can be approximated by counting one load ($t_{cb}$) for each useful cache block. In our example, $CRPD_{UCB} = 3 \times t_{cb}$.

The second approach performs the analysis of the preempting task. In our example, this task loads three blocks into the cache, and can therefore replace three memory blocks. The CRPD can be approximated by counting the number of blocks loaded by the preempting task ($CRPD_{ECB} = 3 \times t_{cb}$): this approach is called ECB, for *evicting cache block*.

In our example, these two approaches are equivalent, since we consider three useful cache blocks to be overwritten by three evicting cache blocks ($CRPD_{UCB} = CRPD_{ECB}$).

However, in the following cases, the two approaches would obtain different results:

– There are four useful blocks A, B, C and D, and three accesses X, Y and Z during the preemption: $(CRPD_{UCB} = 4 \times t_{cb}) > (CRPD_{ECB} = 3 \times t_{cb})$.

– There are three useful blocks and four accesses during the preemption: $(CRPD_{UCB} = 3 \times t_{cb}) < (CRPD_{ECB} = 4 \times t_{cb})$.

None of these approaches dominates the other one: this is why some work has been done in order to analyze the two tasks and better approximate the number of memory reloads due to preemption. The studies mentioned above are all based on static analysis by abstract interpretation [ALT 11].

During the scheduling/schedulability analysis, the CRPD can be added to the WCET: a single entity $C_i = WCET_i + CRPD_i$ represents the WCET including the delays due to preemption. However, the analysis gains in precision whenever the CRPD is taken into account separately: for instance, in [ALT 12], $\gamma_{i,j}$ represents the CRPD due to the preemptions of task i by task j.

The following articles give more detail on the CRPD analysis or references to further related work:

– the UCB, ECB analyses and their complementarity [ALT 11];

– the scheduling analyses taking the CRPD into account [ALT 12].

Note that all of these approaches assume that the CRPD is estimated separately from WCET. This is only possible under the assumption that there are no long-term effects due to complex architecture. These long-term effects are explained in section 5.1.1. In the case of long-term effects, the CRPD can be taken into account with an approach that consists of assuming that the preemptions are possible at any control point of the program [SCH 00].

The CRPD analysis presented in this section is valid for a monocore architecture, timing analysis becomes more complex in the case of multicore architectures. This is explained in the following section 5.2.2.

### 5.2.2. *Multi-core and other complex architectures*

Tomorrow's embedded systems, subject to performance constraints, integration and low-power consumption, will be built around multicore architectures. We will see that this creates new challenges for the analysis of the WCET.

Figure 5.12 presents the general architecture of a multicore processor. Each core has private resources (pipeline, functional units and often a cache level) and shares other resources (buses or other communication networks, second- and sometimes third-level caches and central memory) with the other cores. Due to this sharing, execution times are difficult to predict.

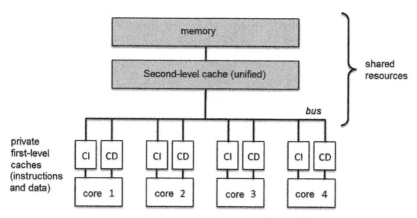

**Figure 5.12.** *General architecture of a multicore processor*

Let us consider, for example, a memory access instruction. In the case of a monocore system, cache analysis allows us to predict whether or not the data are present in the cache. If not, the latency of the operation is the memory access time, including the transfer time of the request on the bus (or the network). Otherwise, it is equal to the access time to the cache. If we want to take into account the precise behavior of the network, the calculation may be a little bit more complex but it is still possible to determine a maximum latency for each access. Things are more complicated in a multicore architecture. First of all, the conclusions of a shared cache analysis are likely to be invalidated by the behavior of another thread, executed on another core. Indeed, this other thread also loads memory blocks into the shared cache, and these blocks can replace other blocks used by the thread for which we are calculating the WCET. Thus, while the cache analysis predicts *hits* for these blocks, it is possible that they are not present in the cache after all. The calculation of the WCET is then erroneous. The other difficulty can be found in the evaluation of the access times to the shared resources such as the bus: it may be that a core which wants to send a request to the memory cannot do so immediately, since the bus is busy with a request of another core. This delay has to be taken into account in the WCET estimation. However, it is in general difficult, or even impossible, to bound it. In the following, we briefly outline the main solutions proposed to date.

The first type of solution aims to design shared resource control mechanisms, in such a way that the possible interferences between cores/threads become predictable. For memory resources (caches and prediction tables), it can be partitioning (each core gets a part of the resource) or locking (for instance, the data present in the cache, for the set of active threads, are selected offline and preloaded before the execution) devices. For other types of resources, the access conflicts between threads have to be arbitrated. For example, a *round-robin* bus arbiter schedules the requests of the different cores in a fair manner, using round-robin priority. This allows us to predict whether a core (among the $n$ cores) sending a request will wait, in the worst case, $n \times L$ cycles before obtaining access to the bus (where $L$ is the maximum occupancy time of the bus by a request, generally around a few processor cycles) [PAO 09]. This is illustrated in Figure 5.13. The use of *time division multiple access* (TDMA) strategies, with variable time slots allocated offline to the different cores, is also possible. Flexibility is increased at the expense of a more complex timing analysis (the position of each request has to be determined relative to the time slots assigned to the core) [KEL 13]. Other approaches constrain the software in order to limit the risk of conflict (with communication phases and computational phases without access to central memory) [PEL 10].

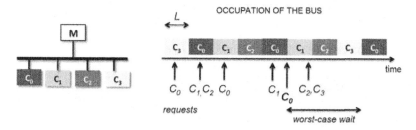

**Figure 5.13.** *Round-robin-type bus arbitration*

Another class of solutions consists of jointly analyzing the set of threads likely to be executed simultaneously (easier to identify if the scheduling is static). For example, the behavior analysis of a shared cache can take into account the memory footprints of each thread [CHA 10]. We can also try to combine the CFGs of the different threads in order to identify their temporal interactions (access conflicts to a shared resource).

Note that the issues raised above for multicore architectures are also present when considering a multithread processor, capable of processing several threads simultaneously: the threads share certain resources, such as the execution units, the pipeline stages, the instruction queues, the caches and the branch prediction tables. The predictability of the execution times is affected in the same manner by the temporal and spatial sharing of resources, which invalidates the analysis of the memory components and makes it difficult to overapproximate latencies.

Several recent works look at the WCET analysis of parallel programs. The main difficulty, besides taking resource sharing into account, results from the synchronizations and communications between threads: they lead to waiting times for some threads, and these delays have to be included in the WCETs [OZA 13].

### 5.2.3. *Influence of critical embedded systems design methods*

The precise analysis of the WCET is particularly important in the field of critical embedded systems (avionics, automotive industry, railway systems and nuclear power). Indeed, all of these control systems exchange inputs and outputs with the physical world, and are therefore subjected to strict timing constraints. We often refer to *hard real-time* systems. The critical nature of these fields leads to the use of particular development methods. Despite the apparent variety of the formal or semi-formal methods used, we can draw a schematic on three levels:

– High-level design uses methods related to (or arising from) control engineering: block diagrams, ladder diagrams, finite-difference equations, etc. The most widely used tool for this level is certainly Matlab/Simulink [4]. It is a very complete tool, a sort of "swiss army knife" for the physicist

---

4. http://www.mathworks.fr/products/simulink/.

and control engineer. In parallel, other tools propose a more computer-based approach of high-level design. This is the case of the so-called *synchronous* approach (see Chapter 4, Volume 2), adopted for instance in the SCADE tool[5], and used, for example, by AIRBUS to design the flight control systems. It is also at this level that the real-time constraints are specified by the specialists of the field.

– The intermediate level corresponds to the moment when the system concretely becomes an executable program (almost always written in the C language). Historically, and even currently in some cases, the transition from the high level to the intermediate level is done by hand. For security reasons (limiting human intervention) but also for cost reasons, the tendency over the last 20 years has been to automatize the translation between the two levels. A tool such as Matlab/Simulink, initially developed for simulation, has since been completed by code generators (e.g. EmbeddedCoder of MathWorks). The SCADE tool is even more representative of this tendency, since it was designed as a programming environment, whose core is the code generator (KCG) that transforms high-level designs into C code.

– The implementation level corresponds to the moment when the code is translated to binary and is effectively run on a given execution platform. Besides the compilation of the intermediary code, the implementation raises specific issues linked to the choice of a specific hardware and operating system: distribution into tasks and onto computing units, scheduling and communication. It is at this level that the temporal analysis has to be performed, in order to find relevant bounds to the WCET for each task, check the feasibility of the scheduling, and then decide whether the high-level temporal constraints are actually satisfied by the implementation.

---

5. http://www.esterel-technologies.com/products/scade-suite/.

After this brief panorama, we may address the core of this section, which is the influence of design methods on the temporal analysis. We will particularly insist on the case of SCADE, but the general ideas presented here can be transposed to other design and code generation methods. The case of SCADE is particularly representative in the domain of critical systems, since its code generator (KCG) has been certified according to the most demanding standard in avionics (DO178-B, *Software Considerations in Airborne Systems and Equipment Certification* [6]).

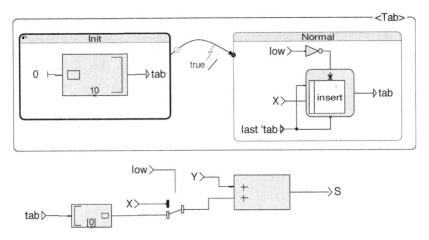

**Figure 5.14.** *Example of a SCADE V6 program*

Figure 5.14 shows an example developed with the SCADE tool. This tool proposes a mix of two classical paradigms: control-flow style (upper part, automaton denoted by <Tab>) and a data-flow style (lower part, and also inside the states of the automaton). The specification of this program is a simplified version of the example in section 5.1, we have simply removed the role of the idle input. The notable points of this example are the following:

---

6. http://www.rtca.org.

– The lower part is a classical data-flow graph that describes the computation of the output S; it is the result of an addition between the input Y and, depending on the value of the input low, either the input X, or the element with index 0 of the tab array.

– The upper part is a two-state automaton that describes the computation of the tab array. The state Init is executed once, then the transition to the state Normal is eventually taken (guarded by the true condition). The execution is then indefinitely continued in the Normal state, which is the default behavior when no transition is defined. Each state contains its own definition of the computation of tab, given in the data-flow style. In the Init state, tab is obtained through a filling operator that copies 10 times the value 0. In the Normal state, tab is the result of the conditional activation of the function insert. The activation condition is a particular Boolean parameter, connected on top of the block, that controls the execution of the block. In the example, the activation condition is the negation of the input low; as a consequence, when low is false, the function insert is executed, and its return value is assigned to tab; when low is true, the function is not executed, and tab keeps its previous value (denoted as last' tab in the design).

The behavior of the SCADE program is implicitly an infinite sequence of input/output reactions. At each reaction, the program receives a value of the inputs (X, Y and low), and reacts by updating its internal memory (the tab array) and producing the corresponding output (S).

Figure 5.15 presents a simplified version of the code generated by the SCADE compiler (KCG). It allows us to illustrate the main characteristics of the code generator:

– The required memory is identified. The precise implementation of the memory can be influenced by compilation options: we have chosen here a basic implementation in which the inputs/outputs are imported

global    variables    (extern int X, Y and S),    and    the
internal memory is a private structure (Ctx).

– The procedure Step implements an atomic reaction of the
program, in other words it computes the current output and
updates the internal memory.

```
static struct { int[10] tab; state_type state; } Ctx;
extern int X, Y, S;

void Step(void) {
  int tmp;
  if (Ctxt.init) {
    Ctx.state = Init;
    Ctxt.init = false;
  }
  switch (Ctx.state) {
    case Normal :
      if (!low) insert(Ctx.tab, X);
      state = Normal;
      break;
    case Init :
      for (tmp = 0; tmp < 10; tmp++) { Ctxt.tab[tmp] = 0; }
      state = Normal;
      break;
  }
  if (low) tmp = X; else tmp = Ctxt.tab[0];
  S = Y + tmp;
}
```

**Figure 5.15.** *C code generated by the SCADE program of
Figure 5.14*

The    implementation    of    the    infinite    behavior,    which
consists of indefinitely iterating calls to the *step* procedure, is
left to the user, since it depends on the execution platform
(hardware and operating system). Typically, the SCADE
program is associated with a periodic system task, executed
concurrently with other tasks. Here, we only consider the
temporal analysis of a single *step* procedure, the result of
which will be used later to check the schedulability of the
entire multitask system.

The fact that the high-level language is deliberately restricted implies that the execution time of the *step* procedure is intrinsically bounded:

– No dynamic memory allocation: the program memory is finite, and its size is known at compile-time (this is the Ctx structure in the example).

– No recursive functions, and therefore no recursive data structures such as lists or trees: only arrays (or structures) whose size is known statically.

– No recursion and no unbounded loops (such as *while* statements): only statically bounded loops (such as simple *for* statements), are used in order to process arrays (initialization of the array tab in the example).

These principles are valid as long as the programmer only uses the high-level features. This is not the case in the example with the imported function insert. The use of external code is fairly common in industrial applications requiring complex data processing or the use of third-party libraries (*device drivers* in particular). In this case, it is up to the programmer to check whether the imported code has the right characteristics to be integrated into a real-time application.

The design method guarantees, by construction, the existence of a bound on the computation time. The temporal analysis must find, for a given platform, a finite quantitative estimation of this bound. Here again, the simplicity of the generated code is an advantage for this search. For instance, the code does not use (or only in a very restrictive way) pointers, which are a source of complexity and approximation in value analysis (*aliasing* problem). Also, the generated code is well-structured (no goto statements), and results in a simple binary control graph, allowing a simpler (and possibly more precise) analysis of the execution paths. Finally, the program analyses that may help to discover infeasible execution paths, are in general easier to implement in higher level programs, instead of machine code or C.

In conclusion, here are some references that will enable the reader to go further on the subject: [FER 08] presents the integration of the WCET analysis tool AiT[7] in the SCADE environment; [KIR 02] and [TAN 09] consider the temporal analysis of Matlab/Simulink models; [RAY 13] aims at pruning infeasible execution paths using the semantic properties extracted from the high-level synchronous model.

### 5.2.4. *Tools*

Table 5.1 presents the main commercial and academic WCET computing tools and indicates their main functionalities as well as the techniques used together with bibliographical references:

– *C/A*: commercial/academic.

– *Flow*: performs a flow analysis.

– *Hardware*: performs a low-level analysis (hardware model).

– *Techniques*: main techniques used (AI = abstract interpretation. PA = Presburger arithmetic, SE = symbolic execution, EG = execution graphs, TA = timed automaton, MC = model checking, IM = instrumentation and measures, S = simulation, RRTP = resolution of recurrence relations and theorem proofs).

The reports of the *WCET Tool Challenge*, which takes place every second year, are also valuable sources of information. [8]

---

7. http://www.absint.com.

8. http://www.mrtc.mdh.se/projects/WTC/.

| Tool | C/A | Flow | Hardware | Techniques | References |
|---|---|---|---|---|---|
| aiT (AbsInt GMbH) | C | x | x | AI, IPET | [FER 04] |
| Bound-T (Tidorum Ltd.) | C | x | x | PA, IPET | [WIL 08] |
| Chronos (Univ. Singapour) | A | x | x | AI, EG, IPET | [LI 07] |
| Heptane (Univ. Rennes) | A | | x | AI, IPET | [WIL 08] |
| Metamoc (Univ. Aalborg) | A | | x | TA, MC | [DAL 10] |
| oRange (Univ. Toulouse) | A | x | | AI | [DEM 08] |
| Otawa (Univ. Toulouse) | A | | x | AI, EG, IPET | [BAL 11] |
| RapiTime (Rapita Systems Ltd.) | C | x | x | IM, IPET | [RAP 13] |
| Sweet (Mlardalen MRTRC) | A | x | x | AI, SE | [GUS 06] |
| r-TuBound (Univ. Tech. Vienne) | A | x | | RRTP | [KNO 12] |

**Table 5.1.** *WCET computing tools*

## 5.3. Conclusion

In this chapter, we have presented the main steps of WCET analysis of critical real-time tasks. This topic is studied in a fairly active community, which is structured around such activities as the organization of an annual seminar (*Workshop on WCET Analysis*) and a research action in the frame of European networks that, among other activities, group *benchmarks* [9] for the evaluation of analysis techniques. More or less complete commercial and academic tools are available and are being used in various domains such as avionics (for several years) or the automotive industry (more recently). The evolution of hardware architectures as well as user requirements brings a large set of research perspectives: improving the existing analysis (or even proposing new ones) or designing predictable architectures which leads to precise and efficient WCET estimation [AXE 13].

## 5.4. Bibliography

[ALT 96] ALT M., FERDINAND C., MARTIN F., *et al.*, "Cache behavior prediction by abstract interpretation", *Static Analysis Symposium (SAS)*, Springer, 1996.

---

9. http://www.tacle.knossosnet.gr/activities/taclebench.

[ALT 11] ALTMEYER S., MAIZA C., "Cache-related preemption delay via useful cache blocks: survey and redefinition", *Journal of Systems Architecture – Embedded Systems Design*, vol. 57, no. 7, pp. 707–719, 2011.

[ALT 12] ALTMEYER S., DAVIS R.I., MAIZA C., "Improved cache related pre-emption delay aware response time analysis for fixed priority pre-emptive systems", *Real-Time Systems*, vol. 48, no. 5, pp. 499–526, 2012.

[ASA 13] ASAVOAE M., MAIZA C., RAYMOND P., "Program semantics in model-based WCET analysis: a state of the art perspective", *WCET*, pp. 32–41, 2013.

[AXE 13] AXER P., ERNST R., FALK H., *et al.*, "Building timing predictable embedded systems", *ACM Transaction on Embedded Computing Systems*, vol. 13, no. 4, December 2013.

[BAL 11] BALLABRIGA C., CASSÉ H., ROCHANGE C., *et al.*, "OTAWA: an open toolbox for adaptive wcet analysis", *Proceedings of Software Technologies for Embedded and Ubiquitous Systems*, Springer, pp. 35–46, 2011.

[CHA 10] CHATTOPADHYAY S., ROYCHOUDHURY A., MITRA T., "Modeling shared cache and bus in multi-cores for timing analysis", *SCOPES*, Page 6, 2010.

[COU 77] COUSOT P., COUSOT R., "Abstract interpretation: a unified lattice model for static analysis of programs by construction or approximation of fixpoints", *Proceedings of the 4th ACM SIGACT-SIGPLAN symposium on Principles of Programming Languages*, ACM, pp. 238–252, 1977.

[DAL 10] DALSGAARD A.E., CHR M., TOFT M., *et al.*, "METAMOC: modular execution time analysis using model checking.", *WCET*, pp. 113–123, 2010.

[DEM 08] DE MICHIEL M., BONENFANT A., CASSÉ H., *et al.*, "Static loop bound analysis of C programs based on flow analysis and abstract interpretation", *14th IEEE International Conference on Embedded and Real-Time Computing Systems and Applications, RTCSA'08*, IEEE, pp. 161–166, 2008.

[FER 04] FERDINAND C., HECKMANN R., "aiT: Worst-case execution time prediction by static program analysis", *Building the Information Society*, pp. 377–383, Springer, 2004.

[FER 08] FERDINAND C., HECKMANN R., SERGENT T.L., *et al.*, "Combining a high-level design tool for safety-critical systems with a tool for WCET analysis on executables", *ERTS2*, 2008.

[GUS 06] GUSTAFSSON J., ERMEDAHL A., SANDBERG C., *et al.*, "Automatic derivation of loop bounds and infeasible paths for WCET analysis using abstract execution", *Real-Time Systems Symposium, 2006. RTSS'06. 27th IEEE International*, IEEE, pp. 57–66, 2006.

[HAR 08] HARDY D., PUAUT I., "WCET analysis of multi-level non-inclusive set-associative instruction caches", *Real-Time Systems Symposium (RTSS)*, 2008.

[HUY 11] HUYNH B.K., JU L., ROYCHOUDHURY A., "Scope-aware data cache analysis for WCET estimation", *Real-Time and Embedded Technology and Applications Symposium (RTAS)*, 2011.

[KEL 13] KELTER T., FALK H., MARWEDEL P., *et al.*, "Static analysis of multi-core TDMA resource arbitration delays", *Real-Time Systems*, 2013.

[KIR 02] KIRNER R., LANG R., FREIBERGER G., *et al.*, "Fully automatic worst-case execution time analysis for Matlab/Simulink models", *ECRTS*, 2002.

[KNO 12] KNOOP J., KOVÁCS L., ZWIRCHMAYR J., "Symbolic loop bound computation for wcet analysis", *Perspectives of Systems Informatics*, pp. 227–242, Springer, 2012.

[LAN 02] LANGENBACH M., THESING S., HECKMANN R., "Pipeline modeling for timing analysis", *Static Analysis Symposium*, 2002.

[LI 97] LI Y.-T., MALIK S., "Performance analysis of embedded software using implicit path enumeration", *IEEE Transactions on Computer-Aided Design of Integrated Circuits and Systems*, vol. 16, no. 12, 1997.

[LI 07] LI X., LIANG Y., MITRA T., *et al.*, "Chronos: a timing analyzer for embedded software", *Science of Computer Programming*, vol. 69, no. 1–3, pp. 56–67, Elsevier North-Holland, Inc., 2007.

[OZA 13] OZAKTAS H., ROCHANGE C., SAINRAT P., "Automatic WCET analysis of real-time parallel applications", *13th International Workshop on Worst-Case Execution Time Analysis*, Page 11, 2013.

[PAO 09] PAOLIERI M., QUIÑONES E., CAZORLA F.J., *et al.*, "Hardware support for WCET analysis of hard real-time multicore systems", *ACM Computer Architecture News*, vol. 37, no. 3, 2009.

[PEL 10] PELLIZZONI R., SCHRANZHOFERY A., CHENY J.-J., *et al.*, "Worst case delay analysis for memory interference in multicore systems", *Design, Automation & Test in Europe Conference & Exhibition (DATE), 2010*, IEEE, pp. 741–746, 2010.

[RAP 13] RAPITA SYSTEMS LTD., "RapiTime White Paper – RapiTime Explained", 2013, available at: http://www.rapitasystems.com/downloads/white-papers/ rapitime-explained.

[RAY 13] RAYMOND P., MAIZA C., PARENT-VIGOUROUX C., *et al.*, "Timing analysis enhancement for synchronous program", *RTNS*, pp. 141–150, 2013.

[REG 05] REGEHR J., REID A., WEBB K., "Eliminating stack overflow by abstract interpretation", *ACM Transactions on Embedded Computing Systems (TECS)*, vol. 4, no. 4, 2005.

[REI 09] REINEKE J., SEN R., "Sound and efficient wcet analysis in the presence of timing anomalies", *Int'l Workshop on WCET Analysis*, 2009.

[REI 13] REINEKE J., GRUND D., "Sensitivity of cache replacement policies", *ACM Transactions on Embedded Computing Systems (TECS)*, vol. 12, no. 1, 2013.

[SCH 00] SCHNEIDER J., "Cache and Pipeline Sensitive Fixed Priority Scheduling for Preemptive Real-Time Systems", *IN Proceedings of the 21st IEEE Real-time Systems 2000*, pp. 195–204, 2000.

[TAN 09] TAN L., WACHTER B., LUCAS P., *et al.*, "Improving timing analysis for Matlab Simulink/stateflow", *ACES-MB*, 2009.

[WIL 08] WILHELM R., ENGBLOM J., ERMEDAHL A., *et al.*, "The worst-case execution-time problem: overview of methods and survey of tools", *ACM Transactions on Embedded Computing Systems (TECS)*, vol. 7, no. 3, Page 36, ACM, 2008.

[YOM 07] YOMSI P.M., SOREL Y., "Extending rate monotonic analysis with exact cost of preemptions for hard real-time systems", *ECRTS*, pp. 280–290, 2007.

6

# Optimization of Energy Consumption

Embedded systems currently have insufficient autonomy, and this situation will worsen over the next few years: the resources which respond to application demands in terms of performance leads to an energy consumption increasing at a rate that is outstripping developments in battery capacity. The aim of this chapter is to identify the sources of energy consumption in a real-time multicore system, and also to propose energy-aware optimization techniques during task scheduling within an operating system (OS). The effectiveness of these techniques will be analyzed in relation to the application context. To get to this point, we will need to characterize the energy consumption of a system at the very first steps of the design flow, by considering both the application aspect and OS services. In order to evaluate the effectiveness of the proposed energy-aware optimization techniques, we will need to identify suitable simulation tools which must offer an acceptable level of accuracy. Then, we will use different experiments to illustrate the relevance of each of the proposed approaches.

---

Chapter written by Cécile BELLEUDY.

## 6.1. Introduction

The increase in the use of electronic equipment in our daily life (often wireless devices) has led to global energy overconsumption. For embedded systems, the subject of this chapter, energy is produced by batteries. To give an idea of the scale of the issue, around 170,000 tonnes of portable batteries for mobile equipment are sold annually in the European Union (EU). These batteries contain components which pollute the environment, and only 25% of batteries are currently recycled in the EU (the EU has set the goal of 45% for 2016). Additionally, consumers tend to discard electronic equipment when its battery loses capacity, because its autonomy becomes too low. This trend is a second source of pollution. The situation will deteriorate over the next few years because of:

– the significant power consumption increase of these devices;

– the low increase of battery capacity;

– the stability of the number of battery recharges.

It should also be noted that this increase in consumption leads to higher thermic dissipation which decreases the reliability of circuits and requires more and more performant cooling systems. This effect on temperature is slowing the development of future circuits for smaller transistor technology, which could challenge Moore's Law and its derivatives.

It has thus become essential to reduce energy consumption both during electronic systems design and through the introduction of adaptive power consumption management techniques. For example, a mobile phone connected in 4G has low autonomy in terms of hours, whereas in standby mode it has a level of autonomy which is acceptable for users. In everyday objects, usually objects which are communicating, the radio and data processing have been identified as significant sources of power consumption. In this chapter, we will focus on data processing, and will analyze this problem for multicore systems.

For over ten years, much work has been carried out with a view to reduce processor power consumption, which has continually increased from one generation of processors to the next. The increase of processor frequency between one generation and the next has exacerbated this problem. In addition, this increase has hindered our response to application data processing demands for new equipment, and has led to thermic heating which reduces reliability. The solution that has been adopted, also taking the particularities of new applications into account, is to introduce parallelism within architectures. According to the forecasts of the ITRS [ITR 13], the number of processing units doubles every two years in System on Chip (SoC). Therefore, it is essential to analyze the power consumption of these units, and then to study energy management techniques, particularly through scheduling policies for multicore systems. The proposed solutions must, among other features, take different operating modes provided by the components into account (e.g. degraded mode and low power mode), and must use these modes in a relevant manner with regard to energy consumption management in function of application requirements.

To achieve this, it is necessary to identify the sources of power consumption by the definition of relevant models, and also to evaluate the potential gains that might be obtained depending on the operating modes used and the penalties for change in mode. Experiments are generally essential during this pre-characterization phase. For example, processors and memories have low power modes and it makes good sense to take advantage of these (DPM: Dynamic Power

Management) if application conditions allow us to do so. Another technique involves adjusting frequency and voltage (DVFS: Dynamic Voltage and Frequency Scaling) according to the performance required by the application. If we use these techniques, we should take into account the expected energy gains, and also the temporal conditions that need to be satisfied. Embedded systems bring together both material and software units, and these interact with each other; as a result, we need to consider all of these elements, including the OS, which provides a large variety of services, including those relating to power consumption management.

Section 6.2 aims to give an overview of different modeling and optimization techniques for energy consumption which have been developed in embedded systems and to analyze both their positive points and the points which require further development. We will consider these issues essentially at the level of the OS, because the expected energy gains can be very high. This is due to the fact that the OS is able to use its knowledge of the state of the entire system, covering both software and equipment aspects, in order to make its decisions. We will pay particular attention to scheduling policies and the limitations to their applicability when they include power consumption management.

Section 6.3 will present power consumption models defined for quantifying energy consumption and also time penalties due to the execution of primary services of an OS. This characterization will be carried out according to the different operating points of processor core. The models established result from the analysis of various experiments conducted on a Cortex-A8 type processor core.

To take these models into account during simulations, the simulation tool of scheduling policy STORM has been modified with a view to take these parameters into consideration and to produce a more realistic estimation of the power consumption of a real-time application. This is described in section 6.4. Two energy-aware optimization techniques (ASDPM and DSF) are also presented in this section.

Section 6.5 begins with the description of an application test, an image processing application (video decoder H264). This application was modeled in the simulation environment STORM. The energy consumed by this application and for the two energy-aware management techniques has been estimated. Both the simulation results and their analysis show variable effectiveness in function of the number of cores and the authorized operating frequencies.

## 6.2. State of the art

### 6.2.1. *General comments*

Power consumption dissipated in a CMOS circuit has two components: the static power, notated as $P_{static}$, and the dynamic power, notated as $P_{dynamic}$. Static power is principally due to leakage currents ($I_{leak}$) of the transistors:

$$P_{static} = I_{leak}.V_{dd}.$$

where $V_{dd}$ is the supply voltage.

These currents are highly dependent on the technology, the threshold voltage and the temperature. The dynamic power consumption is essentially due to the commutation activity, as the following equation shows:

$$P_{dynamic} \cong \alpha.C_L.Vdd^2.f_{clk}.$$

where $\alpha$ is the switching activity factor (the average number of falling transitions per clock cycle), $C_L$ is the charging capacity and $f_{clk}$ the circuit clock frequency.

This equation shows that the dynamic power dissipated in a CMOS circuit is proportional to the average charge capacity per transition, to the switching activity, to the clock frequency and to the square of the supply voltage. The relationship between the two components $P_{static}/P_{dynamic}$ varies depending on the technologies and the circuit types. For example, in processor cores, the switching activity is more significant than in memories, where it is relatively weak. Energy-aware optimization techniques must take this relationship into account so that they can define suitable techniques for energy consumption reduction.

Various methods have been developed in order to estimate the energy consumption of an application. The oldest of these was first introduced by V. Tiwari [TIW 96]. It involves evaluating the power consumption per instruction and then adding the individual consumptions of the instructions executed in a program. To this value is added an overhead power consumption due to data path change and to penalties such as cache miss and pipeline stall. For this method, no pre-existing knowledge of the architecture is required. It allows us to produce a trace of the power and the energy consumed, and in this way to identify which instructions are costly in terms of energy. The downside of this method is the number of measurements that need to be made for it, which can be very high, depending on the instruction set.

Another method, which was first suggested by [QU 00] and further developed by [SEN 02], led to the development of the SoftExplorer tool. This second method is based on the functional analysis of the processor architecture. A set of measures is put in place in order to identify power consumption in relation to the different functional blocks of the processor. The power consumption model is also based on application parameters such as the rate of parallelism, of cache miss, of pipeline stalls, and the type of memory access. This method has been furthered within the OPENPEOPLE project [RET 13], where the modeling was extended to more recent processors. In this project the operating points of the cores were also brought into the model, i.e. the voltage/frequency couple was considered.

### 6.2.2. *Modeling the consumption of an operating system*

When modeling the energy consumption of a system, we need to take the cost linked to the OS into account. In the current chapter, we will focus solely on the services that are employed during task and energy management, i.e. DVFS and DPM.

Various studies have been conducted on power consumption modeling of OS services. The earliest of these were by Dick *et al.* [DIC 00], who suggested a model for the OS μCOS. The services which they studied in more detail are those linked to the management of semaphor, to task scheduling, synchronizations and time. This study primarily showed the significant impact that the power consumption of these services can have. This direction of study was further developed by [KAN 12] several years later, in order to model cache memory management.

Tao and Lizzy, in [TAO 03], introduce a model for OS routines. The energy consumed by a service is thus equal to the sum of energies consumed by the various routines which a service comprises. For this method, all the basic routines need to be modeled and the laws of composition need to be defined.

Many studies have focused on energy models for processor communications with the outside world [DHO 09]. In order to relieve processors of certain services, these may be carried out by hardware accelerators. Energetic and temporal characterizations have been suggested for software or hardware implementations of the basic services of an OS, for example in [PEN 10].

For this study, our aim is to characterize the services that are employed in the management of tasks and energy (DVFS and DPM). To date, few studies have focused on the service consumption of an OS in function of processor operating mode.

### 6.2.3. *Consumption management strategies within multicore systems*

Two main techniques are used to reduce energy consumption within processor cores: DPM, which involves cutting the supply voltage for some parts of the circuit, and DVFS, which makes it possible to adapt the operating speed and the supply voltage depending on requirements such as for example, the workload and the energy available in the battery. For an OS to be able to use these mechanisms (DPM and DVFS), it needs to have a software architecture available to it which is capable of identifying the different operating points of the processor(s) and which is also able to evaluate the application and environmental requirements.

The earliest approaches in this direction were developed with a view of prolonging the autonomy of laptops [ACP 06, IBM 02]. The processor is modeled by a state graph, which has nodes that represent the operating modes (processor + devices), and edges that represent the transition conditions. These graphs usually do not specify certain relevant information such as the transition times between the modes or the power consumed in a certain mode. With a real-time system, this information is essential in order to satisfy the time constraints or to make decisions regarding energy management. Using this graph, the user can define an energy management policy, using the measurable application parameters on the processor such as the number of instructions executed within a certain time window. The application can also limit the operation by the requirements, for example: bandwidth and resources. This is also the case for certain environmental parameters such as battery charge, which may impose a limitation on the current consumed or the minimal functionalities which need to be maintained.

For embedded systems, initiatives specific to different processor families have been developed. For example, ARM [ARM 08] defined a hardware component Intelligent Energy Controller (IEC), which is responsible for gathering information regarding an execution period. This component is coupled with a software component called Intelligent Energy Management (IEM), which defines the system configuration in function of the current and predicted workload.

Also, many theoretical studies have taken place which aim to define low consumption scheduling strategies. Early energy management techniques only exploited the low power modes of a processor: they aimed to optimize processor inactivity time and to reduce the number of returns to active mode. Many studies were first carried out in a monocore context, and then extended to apply to multicores. Most of these approaches are based on task execution history, using it to predict periods of inactivity and thus to select the most suitable low power mode [SRI 96, HWA 97, BEN 00, RON 06]. These approaches cannot always be applied to real-time systems. However, it may be observed that these DPM techniques are becoming more widely used for the regulation of thermic dissipation, as is the case in [MER 06, KLI 13].

Presently, the use of low power modes is often coupled with efficient management of DVFS, which makes it possible to achieve a significant reduction in power consumption, a parameter that is primordial in the battery discharge model.

Among the studies which have already been carried out, some involve a purely static (offline) context [LUO 02, CHE 05, LAN 06, BEN 06]. For these, the number of cores in active mode and the execution speed of the cores are fixed prior to execution, on the basis of the worst case execution time. Other studies [CHO 07] use this offline analysis as a basis and re-evaluate these parameters depending on the dynamic workload, which takes the real-time execution constraints of the tasks into account. Finally, some approaches [ZHU 03, CHE 07, ZHA 12] are essentially defined in a purely dynamic (online) context, without any *a priori* information on the system.

Most of these studies have been developed for homogeneous platforms whose operating speed can be adjusted either globally at all the cores [FUN 01, CHE 07] or locally for each individual core [LUO 02, CHE 05, BEN 06]. The case of heterogeneous systems may be viewed as a set of processor cores which all operate at a given frequency [CHE 07] or as processors which can operate at various different frequencies and whose task execution time also varies depending on the processor type [YAN 09].

These different strategies may be used to achieve different aims. For example, they may be used to minimize the total energy consumed by the execution of a set of tasks [CHE 05, ZHA 12], or they may be used to reduce the power peak in function of constraints linked to battery charge [LUO 01, CHO 05].

Among the scheduling techniques used, some are known as global [ZHU 03, VEN 06]. In these global techniques, all of the tasks may be allocated to different processor cores, which thus makes global management of energy consumption possible; this management performs best if the number of migrated tasks is not too high. Other approaches are known as local [CHE 05]. In these, the allocation of tasks is performed statically and each processor chooses its operating point in function of its own workload. Finally, some approaches are known as mixed [CHE 11]. For these approaches, a part of the tasks is allocated to the processor cores, and the other tasks are distributed globally to processors depending on their individual workloads. Migration is authorized only for the tasks that are distributed globally.

Too many approaches only consider dynamic power as a consumption model. This hypothesis is very restrictive, especially for technologies lower than 90 nm. Static power consumption features in the following works: [LAN 06, YAN 09, AWA 11]. The speed of processors is thus calculated in function of the two energy components.

In these studies, it is demonstrated that, depending on the distribution of static and dynamic power, certain operating points no longer allow energy savings. Additionally, it should be noted that the low level of supply voltage for future technologies (according to ITRS, this is 0.5 V in 2020) will reduce energy gains. However, from the battery point of view, reducing power consumption always has a positive effect on autonomy. It is therefore necessary to take a model into account which will consider both components of dissipated power.

Also, we should note that the time penalty associated with the change in the voltage/frequency couple is rarely taken into account, and where it is, it is fixed at a value far below real values. Transition times in the order of a millisecond up to a tenth of millisecond have been observed. Therefore, this parameter needs to be included in calculation.

For monocore systems, schedulability tests have been defined which determine whether an application can be scheduled. These tests may be used to calculate, both online and offline, a slowing factor. For multicores, the research of [BAK 03] on schedulability analysis shows that the deadlines of real-time tasks cannot be guaranteed for a workload greater than m/2 for a platform of m processors, where we use fixed priority scheduling algorithms for task jobs. This theorem strongly restricts the use of DVFS, at least unless we consider dynamic priority scheduling algorithms. When faced with the set of architecture parameters which have an influence on task execution time, formal schedulability analysis approaches are not applicable, unless the models considered under this approach are significantly extended. Appropriate simulations alone might allow us to verify that a given scheduling policy meets the deadlines. Obviously, a validation achieved in this way would only be partial.

## 6.3. Modeling consumption

### 6.3.1. *Characterization     platform:     hardware     and software*

To have realistic models at our disposal, we chose to carry out our experiments on an ARM Cortex-A8 core, present in an OMAP3530 [OMA 11]. The final aim would be to use this model in a homogeneous multicore context. The EVM_OMAP35x evaluation platform has a set of pins which provide current measurements for different parts of the circuit. The Cortex-A8 has five operating points (voltage/frequency couple) noted OP in the suite, which are described in the table that follows. The data presented in this table have been provided by the manufacturer.

The OS used is a Linux kernel which has been adapted for this platform. Various scheduling policies are available: SCHED_RR, SCHED_FIFO and SCHED_others. As the scheduling policy closest to a real-time kernel is the

SCHED-RR, measurements reported in the rest of this chapter have been effected with this scheduling policy.

| Parameter | OP1 | OP2 | OP3 | OP4 | OP5 |
|---|---|---|---|---|---|
| Frequency (MHz) | 125 | 250 | 500 | 550 | 720 |
| Voltage (V) | 0.975 | 1.05 | 1.2 | 1.27 | 1.35 |
| $P_{average}$ in active mode (mW) | 57 | 130 | 303 | 348 | 550 |
| $P_{idle}$ | 4 | 7 | 16 | 18 | 28 |

**Table 6.1.** *Operation point of OMAP*

### 6.3.2. *Power consumption modeling*

Power consumption linked to the execution of an application (or a group of applications) comprises both the power consumption due to the execution of application tasks and of the different OS services employed.

The model used to evaluate power consumption due to task execution has been defined in the OPENPEOPLE project by the University of Valenciennes (France) [RET 13].

In order to study the efficiency of low power scheduling policies, it is also necessary to characterize the power consumption of the OS services which are called into operation during task management and communication between tasks. We therefore focused on the context switch (CS) at fixed and at variable frequency i.e. when a change in the voltage/frequency couple took place. Also, for communication between tasks, power consumption of OS services involved was characterized for different operating frequencies.

Research conducted in our research laboratory [OUN 11] has shown that scheduling policy execution consumes less than 2% of total power consumption. Therefore, within this chapter, these results will not be presented and this power consumption will not be considered.

### 6.3.3. *Context switch*

CS occurs during a task execution change and comprises saving and restoring processor registers, re-initializing the pipeline of processor core and executing the scheduler. A CS can also lead to address translations in the virtual address space. Additionally, there is a change in the content of the cache memories, which may lead to additional cache miss. We will not consider this final point in our study.

In order to characterize the energy consumption linked to CS, we created a set of threads in a multitask environment, using the POSIX standard [WAL 95]. Execution alternates between several threads. The energy linked to the execution of the tasks is deduced from the energy that is measured in this way. These measures were carried out for the different operating points of the processor core.

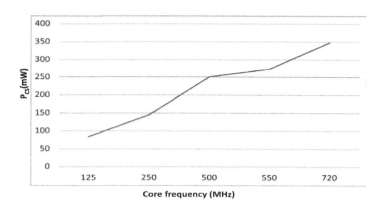

**Figure 6.1.** *Power consumed during context switch at fixed frequency*

The curve in Figure 6.1 shows that the power dissipated is practically proportional to the frequency of the circuit. A linear variation law may be deduced from it:

$$P_{cs}(f) = 0.44 *f + 30.41 \quad (in\ mW)$$

where f is the operating frequency of the core in MHz

Using this formula, we can identify the share of power consumption held by static and dynamic power dissipation. For the frequencies of 125 MHz and 250 MHz, a significant share of the total dissipated power is held by static power. At higher operating frequencies, it becomes negligible. Note that the maximum error observed by this model is less than 3%: this is an acceptable level of accuracy.

These measurements were then extended to CSes during which a frequency change occurs, as shown in Figure 6.2.

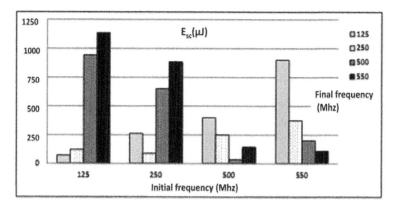

**Figure 6.2.** *Energy consumed by a context switch with possible variation in frequency and voltage*

The energy consumed during a CS depends on the gap between the initial and destination frequency and voltage. When this gap is large, the energy consumed sharply increases. This effect is even more marked when the voltage increases. In fact, charging all the capacities of the core to the desired voltage level leads to additional overconsumption which is not present when voltage decreases. Given these results, it would be difficult to deduce a mathematical law from them, so the energy consumed during a CS will be modeled, in what follows, in a value table. It may be remarked that at fixed frequency, energy diminishes between 125 MHz and 500 MHz. The explanation for this phenomenon lies in the fact that the CS occurs more rapidly here, due to the increase in frequency. However, at 550 MHz the energy increases again, because the dynamic power no longer compensates for the speed of execution.

During a CS where there is a change in the voltage/frequency couple, a higher time penalty (Figure 6.3) may be observed. This should be taken into account, because it may be of a significant scale, depending on task characteristics (period, execution time, etc.). This time penalty is largely due to a change in frequency, which leads to the requirement for resynchronization of the clock with those of the systems in dialogue with the core.

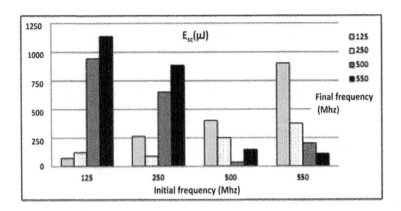

**Figure 6.3.** *Time penalty linked to context switch*

Therefore a CS may be characterized by an energy and time penalty which will depend on the initial and final voltage/frequency couple. These different values also allow us to define the limitations during changes in the voltage/frequency couple. In fact, in order to obtain an energy gain with a change in frequency from $f_1$ to $f_2$ ($f_2 < f_1$) for a task Ti, we need to verify that:

$$E_{Ti}(f_1) > E_{Ti}(f_2) + E_{CS}(f_1,f_2) + E_{CS}(f_2,f_1)$$

and the execution time for this task becomes $T_{run}(T_i) = T_{CS}(f_1,f_2) + T_{Ti}(f2) + T_{CS}(f_2,f_1)$.

For these equations we assume that the core will need to return to its nominal frequency at the end of the execution of the task Ti. If the change in frequency is operated on several tasks, the time and energy penalties will apply to the group of tasks.

## 6.3.4. *Inter-process communication*

Inter-process communication (IPC) allows the threads of a process to share information with the threads of other processes. The OS explicitly copies the information from the emitting process' address space into the receiving process' address space. Various IPC mechanisms have been developed. We have chosen to characterize the following IPC mechanisms:

– by shared memory, which allows the processes to communicate simply by reading or writing in a pre-defined memory location;

– by pipes which allow processes to communicate with each other sequentially using FIFOs. In the case of anonymous pipes, the pipes disappear when the process which has created them finishes. For named pipes, the end of the communication which will be effected by the OS must be explicitly indicated.

To characterize the power and the energy consumption of the IPC, test programs which call up an IPC mechanism several times have been created. The aim here is to measure the extra costs for IPC mechanisms in terms of power consumption and performance during program execution. The parameters studied during these experiments are:

– the processor frequency.

– the quantity of data shared by the IPC (application parameters).

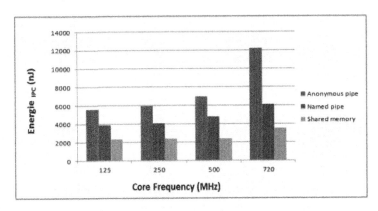

**Figure 6.4.** *Energy consumed during transmission of a message*

Figure 6.4 shows the energy consumed in function of the operating frequency for 800 octets of data. Notice that the power consumption by the communication effected by the shared memory is low compared to the power consumption by the pipe communications.

Following this, we varied the data quantity by changing the frequency to 500 MHz. Figure 6.5 shows the energy measured on the platform.

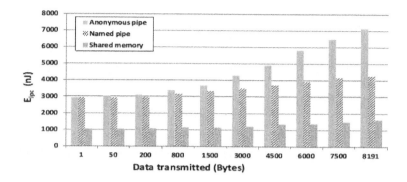

**Figure 6.5.** *Energy consumed by the IPC depending on the size of data*

Analysis of these different curves shows that consumption is lowest for IPC by shared memory. As a result, we will use this communication mechanism in what follows.

The model we will use for this IPC mechanism is the following:

$$E_{IPC} = 82.12 * F * e^{48.9*msz} (nJ)$$

where msz (message size) is the quantity of data (in octets) which needs to be transmitted, and F is the core frequency. Observed error is less than 4% for this model.

## 6.4. Low consumption scheduling

On the basis of the models established previously, we now aim to evaluate the effectiveness of low power scheduling policies in a multicores context. In order to achieve this, we have chosen to use the real-time simulation tool of scheduling policy STORM [STO 14] s, and to integrate the power consumption models previously established.

### 6.4.1. *Simulation environment*

STORM is a real-time scheduling policy simulation tool for a STORM multicores system. It allows us to easily define scheduling policy, with its capacity to integrate energy management mechanisms. Through its simulations, we can identify robustness and energy efficiency for different hardware and software architectures. STORM was developed by IRCCyN [STO 14] during the French project PHERMA.

This simulator has:

– a hardware library which can be assimilated to a catalogue of processors, memories, and the characteristics that are associated with them. For this study, the Cortex-A8 will be defined by the average power consumed (measured value) at each operating point in active mode and in low power mode, along with the time and energy penalties linked to mode change;

– a library of scheduling policy: two low power consumption scheduling policies will be studied. The first, Assertive Dynamic Power Management (ASDPM) is based on the mechanisms for putting processors into low power mode. The second, Deterministic Stretch to Fit (DSF), focuses on conjoint adjustment of voltage and frequency (DVFS). The main characteristics of these policies are described later on in this chapter.

In addition to these libraries, the simulator also has the definition of the hardware and software architecture at its disposal. The hardware architecture is defined by a set of characteristics such as its type (for example Symmetric shared-memory multiprocessor (SMP or SCMP)), the list of types of referenced processors, and the number of processors required for each type of processor. In what follows, we will study an SMP homogeneous multicore architecture based on the Cortex-A8 core.

The software architecture is described by all of the application tasks along with the characteristics associated with these tasks, such as their type (periodic, aperiodic, etc.), the period, and the worst execution time.

On this basis, STORM simulates the behavior of the system using all the characteristics (task execution time, processor operating points, etc.) and provides a trace of task scheduling and the power and energy consumed over time. Using this, we can, in real time, analyze the behavior and the performance of the systems under study.

In order to take the OS services' power consumption into account, we adjoined a module which would allow us to introduce the energy and time costs occasioned by them. Two cases were examined:

– Execution at fixed frequency: the energy consumed corresponds to the sum of the energies consumed by task execution, OS services and during periods of inactivity (low power mode) for a given frequency.

– Execution at variable frequency: the energy consumed corresponds to the sum of the energies consumed by task execution, OS services and during periods of inactivity (rest mode); this is in function of the different frequencies chosen by the scheduler. The time and energy penalties for mode change will also be taken into account.

### 6.4.2. *Low power consumption scheduling policy*

In order to evaluate the efficiency of the low power consumption scheduling policy, two policies developed within our research laboratory were selected for study. The first of these is based on the management of low power modes (ASDPM) and the second operates on conjoint adjustment of voltage and frequency (DSF).

*Low consumption scheduling policy: ASDPM [BHA 09]*

The ASDPM scheduling policy aims to reduce energy consumption by exploiting processor low power modes. This technique is not based on predicting inactivity intervals, as is the case in many other studies, but rather on the principle of grouping tasks on active processors in order to lengthen inactivity slack time. As a result, deeper low power modes with lower energy consumption are used. This principle aims also to reduce the number of transitions, which are costly in terms of time and energy.

The technique consists of adjoining a module named ASsertive Dynamic Power Management (ASDPM) to the scheduler. This module is then responsible for deciding whether ready tasks may enter the scheduler's running task queue. The ASDPM module delays the execution of ready tasks as much as possible and controls the maximum number of active processors in the system at any given time. The operating principle is to extract the intervals of processor inactivity and to gather them together onto a part of these processors, so as to increase the inactivity intervals, or even to completely avoid activating some of the processors. It may be noted that this ASDPM module is independent from the global scheduling policy used. In what follows of this document, a global EDF scheduling has been studied.

An example of scheduling with ASDPM is given below, for a system composed of six tasks. The first two cores are practically working at 100%, and the third can, largely, be placed in low power mode.

This technique is based on the previous definition of the time and energy penalties associated with state transitions between low power modes and active modes. These penalties reduce the energy efficiency of the DPM techniques. With

ASDPM, the penalties are reduced, because the number of transitions becomes as low as possible.

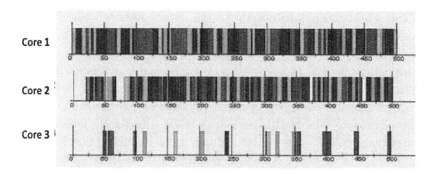

**Figure 6.6.** *Example of scheduling under ASDPM*

This table shows the sleeping and waking times of the Cortex-A8.

| State | Sleeping time (µs) | Waking time (µs) |
|---|---|---|
| Idle | 73.6 | 78 |
| Standby | 163 | 182 |
| Sleep | 366 | 800 |
| Deepsleep | 4300 | 12933 |

**Table 6.2.** *Sleeping and waking times for the Cortex-A8*

## Deterministic Stretch-to-Fit scheduling policy

Low power scheduling techniques have greatly developed in the last few years because they provide significant gains in power consumption and energy, through voltage and frequency scaling in function of application requirements. The DSF technique, suggested in [BHA 10], is based on this principle.

This technique comprises three algorithms: the Dynamic Slack Reclamation (DSR) algorithm, the Online Speculative speed adjustment Mechanism (OSM) algorithm, and the m-Tasks Extension (m-TE) algorithm. The principle of the DSR algorithm is to attribute the time interval which is not used by a task to the next ready task which has a suitable priority level and which can be executed on the same processor. For this algorithm, unused time intervals are not shared with other processors from the system. A time unit which is not used by a task is entirely consumed by the processor to which the task has been allocated. This greedy attribution of intervals allows the DSR algorithm to calculate a greater slowing factor, thus reducing both the operating frequency and voltage of a single task. The final result of this is an increase in energy gains. The OSM and the m-TE algorithms are extensions of the DSR algorithm.

The OSM algorithm is an adaptive and speculative online mechanism for the adjustment of operating speed. It forecasts the dates for the task execution's end by calculating an average execution time and adequately slows the processor speed. In addition to an additional energy economy compared to the DSR algorithm, OSM also contributes to avoiding dramatic changes in supply frequency and voltage. This has the effect of reducing the power peak and, as a result, it leads to an increase in battery life. The m-TE algorithm extends the On-Task Extension (OTE) [AYD 04] technique for monoprocessor systems to multiprocessor systems. The principle consists of considering a group of m tasks rather than one task alone. This technique means that time penalties due to change in the voltage/frequency couple can be more easily taken into account. The value of the parameter m depends on the relationship between the runtime of the application tasks and the time penalties linked to mode change.

Note that the decision for change in the voltage/frequency couple requires advance verification of the time constraints linked to change in the voltage/frequency couple.

The DSF technique is generic in the following sense: if there is a scheduling for a target real-time application, and it is based on the worst case workload using a global scheduling algorithm, then the same scheduling can be reproduced using the real workload with a lower consumption of power and energy. Thus, DSF can work in collaboration with various different scheduling algorithms. In our study, we used an EDF scheduling.

DSF is based on the principle of following canonical execution of tasks at the moment of execution, that is, for an optimal offline scheduling in which the worst case execution time for all task jobs is considered. An execution trace for all the optimal static scheduling tasks must be kept so that it can be followed during execution. However, the establishment and the memorization of this canonical scheduling in its entirety is very difficult in the case of multiprocessor systems because the allocation of preemptive and migrant tasks to the processors is not necessarily known. As a result, we suggest a model for producing online canonical scheduling ahead of practical scheduling, which imitates the canonical execution of tasks only for future m-tasks. This characteristic reduces extra execution costs linked to the scheduler, which makes DSF an adaptive technique.

## 6.5. Experimental results

### 6.5.1. *Application test: H.264 decoder*

In order to validate the approach developed we have selected the H.264 video decoder as an example. This high-quality compression application is based on efficient extraction strategies for spatial dependencies (within an image) and time dependencies (between images). It offers flexible coding and high compression, while still maintaining good image quality. Our aim is to integrate this standard into embedded systems and thus to suggest hardware and software architectural solutions which could maintain a sufficient service quality level while having the lowest possible energy consumption level.

H.264 decoding comprises of two main tasks:

– with a video flow as its starting point, the first task extracts the compression parameters and the data which represent the compressed image;

– the second task is the decoding of the compressed image.

The H.264 video decoder can be parallelized by breaking the image down into several parts, called "slices", to which the decoding treatments are then applied. To enable parallel execution of an image broken down in this way, we need to introduce a first task which breaks down the coded image and a second which, after treatment, puts the decoded image back together again, as shown in Figure 6.7.

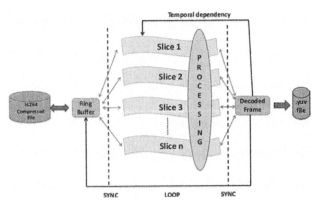

**Figure 6.7.** *H.264 decoder, "slice" version*

Breaking the image down in this way may lead to border effects on each sub-part of the image. In order to limit the appearance of these, while still allowing parallel execution to occur, the image has been broken down into four sub-images. Our application thus comprises four types of tasks:

– NEW_FRAME (T1), which can only sequentially access the buffer memory of input data;

– NAL_DISPATCH (T2), which is responsible for breaking the image down into sub-images;

– the SLICE_PROCESSING tasks (T3, T4, T5 and T6), which are executed in parallel, and which decode each sub-part of the image. Due to the time dependencies between the images, it is not possible to begin the next frame if the one preceding it has not been fully decoded;

– REBUILD_FRAME (T7): this task is responsible for synchronizing previous treatments and constructing the decoded image.

The execution times for these tasks are in Table 6.2.

| Name of the task | WCET (ms) | Period (ms) | Activation date (ms) |
|---|---|---|---|
| New_frame (T1) | 1 | 19 | 0 |
| Nal_Dispatch (T2) | 2 | 5 | 0 |
| Slice1_processing | 38 | 66 | 0 |
| Slice2_processing | 38 | 66 | 1 |
| Slice3_processing | 38 | 66 | 2 |
| Slice4_processing | 38 | 66 | 3 |
| Rebuild_frame | 2 | 66 | 66 |

**Table 6.3.** *Description of the tasks of the H.264 decoder*

The frame rate has been fixed at 15 images per second. This rate allows us to deduce both the period for each task and the activation date. In what follows, we will assume that the period is equal to the task deadline. The execution times listed correspond to the frequency of 500 MHz on the Cortex-A8. The execution time for these tasks for a frequency other than $F_{init}$ = 500 MHz is calculated as follows:

$T(f_i) = T_{finit} * f_{init}/f_i.$

Thus, the energy consumed is given by the following formula:

$E(f_i) = P(f_i) * T(f_i)$

### 6.5.2. Analysis of the simulation results

To evaluate the energy cost linked to the execution of an application, an H.264 video decoder was modeled using the STORM environment. The application is described with the characteristics listed in Table 6.2. The frame rate has been assumed to equal 15 images per second. The hardware architecture is composed of identical cores linked to a single shared main memory, which have complete access to all the input/output devices, and which are controlled by a global OS. This is an SMP type architecture. Each core can execute different tasks and is able to share common resources (memory, input/output devices, etc.) with other cores. The cores are linked with each other using a bus system. The core type considered is the Cortex-A8. The scheduling policies studied are ASDPM and DSF.

*Impact of OS modeling on energy gains*

The number of cores is firstly fixed at four, and the operating frequency at 500 MHz. For DSF, this frequency is the initial frequency.

| Without an OS model | Global EDF | DSF | ASDPM |
|---|---|---|---|
| E (mJ)/frame | 79.2 | 44.1 | 50.77 |
| Gain on E | | 1.8 | 1.56 |

**Table 6.4.** *Energy consumed by the H.264 application alone*

| With an OS model | Global EDF | DSF | ASDPM |
|---|---|---|---|
| E (mJ)/frame | 108.7 | 78.2 | 74.45 |
| Gain on E | | 1.39 | 1.46 |
| % of OS | 27.1% | 43.6% | 31.8% |

**Table 6.5.** *Energy consumed by the H.264 application, taking the operating system into account*

Tables 6.4 and 6.5 show that the power consumption of the OS is far from negligible, and can reach 43% in the case of the DSF policy where changes in the voltage/frequency couple lead to extra energy cost. Time and energy penalties linked to mode change reduce the energy savings, which nonetheless remain significant.

*Impact of the frequency with ASDPM scheduling technique*

With the ASDPM technique, the aim is now to analyze the energy consumption for four cores with a different operating frequency.

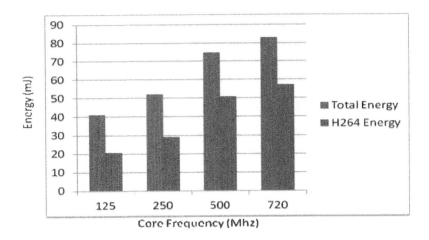

**Figure 6.8.** *Energy consumed by the H.264 application with the ASDPM algorithm at different frequencies*

Figure 6.8 shows that energy consumption rises as operating frequency increases. The extension of low power modes is not sufficient to reduce energy consumption. It should be noted that for the frequencies 125 MHz and 250 MHz, the time constraints are not met.

*Analysis of the influence of the consumption of the OS services with DSF and ASDPM in function of the core number*

In order to study the impact of the OS services on the total energy consumed with DSF, Table 6.6 shows the distribution of energy consumption across a variable number of cores.

| Number of cores | CS (%) | IPC (%) |
|:---:|:---:|:---:|
| 1 | 49.6 | 50.4 |
| 2 | 47.5 | 52.5 |
| 4 | 52.9 | 47.1 |
| 6 | 30.3 | 61.7 |
| 8 | 27.6 | 72.4 |

**Table 6.6.** *Distribution of energy consumed by the operating system services under DSF*

Time analysis shows that the deadlines are not respected for a number of cores that is less than four. The operating frequency therefore remains at the nominal value, and does not lead to a change in frequency. For a number of cores greater than or equal to four, Table 6.6 shows that, when the number of cores increases, the number of changes in the voltage/frequency couple decreases, leading to a decrease in CS energy.

In order to analyze the distribution of the energy consumption by OS services under the ASDPM policy, the number of cores is now fixed at four, and the processor frequency at 500 MHz.

|  | CS (%) | IPC (%) |
|:---|:---|:---|
| ASDPM (4 cores) | 28.67 | 71.3 |

**Table 6.7.** *Distribution of the energy consumed by the operating system services under ASDPM*

In Table 6.7 we can see that, for an equivalent number of cores, the CS has less of an influence on energy than is the case with DSF. In fact, changes occur in the voltage/frequency couple more often than the cores enter in low power mode. This is because ASDPM gathers together periods of inactivity on certain cores, and thus reduces the number of entries into low power mode and reactivations.

## 6.6. Conclusion

In this chapter, a methodology for modeling OS services was presented, which is of particular interest for modeling CS and inter-process communications, at different processor operating speeds. These models were input into the simulation tool of scheduling policies STORM in order to evaluate the power consumption of the application and that of the OS. Two low power scheduling techniques, ASDPM and DSF were used in these experiments. For an H.264 video decoding application, the simulation results show significant energy gains and they also show that the OS services consume a significant share of the energy. In addition, it may be observed that, through frequency changes, the DVFS techniques lead to time penalties which may become significant if changes occur often. In this way, energy gains may be reduced. In future studies, these models should be extended to take the battery into account, and in particular its level of charge, and also to consider energy harvester systems in order to increase the lifetime of electronic equipment. Most of the relevant equipment includes a radio circuit which would also need to be modeled in this simulation environment.

## 6.7. Bibliography

[ACP 06] ACPI, Advanced Configuration and Power Interface, available at: http: //www.acpi.info/, 2006.

[ARM 08] ARM, "Intelligent energy controller technical reference manual", ARM Limited, available at: http: //in-fo-center.arm.com/, 2008.

[AYD 04] AYDIN H., MELHEM R., MOSSÉ D., et al., "Power-aware scheduling for periodic real-time tasks", IEEE Transactions on Computers, vol. 53, pp. 584–600, May 2004.

[AWA 11] AWAN M.A., PETTERS S.M., "Enhanced race-to-halt: a leakage-aware energy management approach for dynamic priority systems", Proceedings of the 23rd ECRTS, 2011.

[BAK 03] BAKER T.P., "Multiprocessor EDF and deadline monotonic schedulability analysis", Proceedings of 24th IEEE International Real-Time Systems Symposium, RTSS'03, 2003

[BEN 00] BENINI L., BOGLIOLO A., MICHELI G.D., "A survey of design techniques for system-level dynamic power management", IEEE Transaction on Very Large Scale Integration System, pp. 299–316, 2000.

[BEN 06] BENINI L., BERTOZZI D., GUERRI A., et al., "Allocation, scheduling and voltage scaling on energy aware MPSoCs", LNCS Integration of AI and OR Techniques in Constraint Programming for Combinatorial Optimization Problems, vol. 3990/2006, pp. 44–58, June, 2006.

[BHA 09] BHATTI M.K., FAROOQ M., BELLEUDY C., et al., "Assertive dynamic power management (AsDPM) strategy for globally scheduled RT multiprocessor systems", Lecture Note in Computer Science, Integrated Circuit and System, Springer, vol. 5953, pp. 116–126, 2009.

[BHA 10] BHATTI M.K., BELLEUDY C., AUGUIN M., "Power management in real-time embedded systems through online and adaptive interplay of DPM and DVFS policies", Proceedings of International Conference on Embedded and Ubiquitous Computing, EUC'10, Hong Kong, SAR, China, December 2010.

[CHE 05] CHEN J., TEI WEI K., "Energy efficient scheduling of periodic real-time tasks over homogenous multiprocessors", *Proceedings of PARC'05*, 2005.

[CHE 07] CHEN J., YANG C.Y., KUO T., *et al.*, "Energy efficient real-time system task scheduling in multiprocessor DVS systems", *Proceedings of ASP-DAC*, January, 2007.

[CHO 02] CHOU P.H., LIU J., LI D., *et al.*, "IMPACCT: methodology and tools for power aware embedded systems", *Design Automation for Embedded Systems*, Kluwer International Journal, *Special Issue on Design Methodologies and Tools for Real-Time Embedded Systems*, pp. 205–232, 2002.

[CHO 05] CHOWDHURY P., CHAKRABARTI C., "Static task-scheduling algorithms for battery-powered DVS systems", *IEEE Transactions on Very Large Scale Integration (VLSI) Systems*, vol. 13, no. 2, February 2005.

[CHO 07] CHOWDHURY P., CHAKRABARTI C., KUMAR R., "Online dynamic voltage scaling using task graph mapping analysis for multiprocessors", *VLSI Design*, 2007.

[DIC 00] DICK R.P., LAKSHMINARAYANA G., RAGHUNATHAN A., *et al.*, "Power analysis of embedded operating systems", *Proceedings of In Design Automation Conference*, Los Angeles, CA, 2000.

[DHO 09] DHOUIB S., SENN E., DIGUET J.-P., *et al.*, "Model driven high-level power estimation of embedded operating systems communication services", *Proceedings of International Conference on Embedded Software and Systems*, 2009.

[FRE 14] Freescale, http://www.freescale.com/files/32bit/doc/fact_sheet/MC9328MX31FS.pdf, 2014.

[FUN 01] FUNK S., GOOSENS J., BARUAH S., Energy minimization techniques for real-time scheduling on multi-processor platforms, Technical Report UNC-CS TR01-030, University of North Carolina, Chapel Hill, 2001.

[HWA 97] HWANG C.-H., WU A., "A predictive system shutdown method for energy saving of event-driven computation", *Proceedings of International Conference on Computer-Aided Design*, pp. 28–32, November 1997.

[IBM 02] IBM, MontaVista, "Dynamic power management for embedded systems", 2002.

[INT 04] INTEL, Wireless intel speedstep power manager, White paper, 2004.

[INT 05] INTEL, "Intel PXA270 processor, electrical, mechanical, and thermal specification", available at: http://www.in-tel.com, 2005.

[ITR 13] ITRS 2013 available at: http://www.itrs.net/Links/2013ITRS/Home2013.htm.

[KAN 02] KANDEMIR M., KOLCU I., KADAYIF I., "Influence of loop optimizations on energy consumption of multi-bank memory systems", *Proceedings of Compiler Construction*, April 2002.

[KAN 12] KANG K., PARK K.-J., KIM H., "Functional-level energy characterization of µC/OS-II and cache locking for energy saving", *Bell Labs Technical Journal*, vol. 17, no. 1, pp. 219–227, 2012.

[KLI 13] KLIAZOVICH D., BOUVRY P., KHAN S.U., "DENS: data center energy-efficient network-aware scheduling", *Cluster Computing*, vol. 16, no. 1, pp. 65–75, Springer, March 2013.

[LAN 06] DE LANGEN P., JUURLINK B., VASSILIADIS S., "Multiprocessor scheduling to reduce leakage power", *Proceedings of 17th International Conference on Parallel and Distributed Symposium*, IPDPS'06, 2006.

[LUO 01] LUO J., JHA N.K., "Battery-aware static scheduling for distributed real-time embedded systems", *Proceeedings of DAC 2001*, Las Vegas Nevada, June 18–22, 2001.

[LUO 02] Luo J., Jha N.K., "Static and dynamic variable voltage scheduling algorithms for real-time heterogeneous distributed embedded systems", *Proceedings of International Conference on VLSI Design*, January 2002.

[MER 06] Merkel A., Bellosa F., "Energy power consumption in multiprocessor systems", *Proceedings of EuroSys2006*, 2006.

[OMA 11] OMAP35x Evaluation Module (EVM), 2011. Available at: http://focus.ti.com/docs/toolsw/folders/print/tmdsevm3530.html.

[OUN 11] Ouni B., Belleudy C., Bilavarn S., *et al.*, "Embedded operating systems energy overhead", DASIP '11, *Proceedings of the Conference on Design and Architectures for Signal and Image Processing*, Tampere, Finland, November 2011.

[OUN 13] Ouni B., High-level energy characterization, modeling and estimation for OS-based platforms PhD Thesis, July 2013.

[PEN 10] Penolazzi S., Sander I., Hemani A., "Predicting energy and performance overhead of real-time operating systems". *Proceeding of In Design, Automation and Test in Europe*, p. 1520, Dresden, Germany, March 2010.

[QU 00] Qu G., Kawabe N., Usami K., *et al.*, "Function level power estimation methodology for microprocessors", *Proceedings of the Design Automation Conference 2000*, pp. 810–813, 2000.

[RON 06] Rong P., Pedram M., "Determining the optimal timeout values for a power-managed system based on the theory of Markovian processes: offline and online algorithms", *Proceedings of Design Automation and Test in Europe*, 2006.

[RET 13] Rethinagiri S.K., System level power estimation methodology for MPSoC based platforms, PhD Thesis, March 2013.

[SEN 02] Senn E., Julien N., Laurent J., *et al.*, "Power consumption estimation of a C program for data-intensive applications", *Proceedings of the PATMOS Conference*, pp. 332–341, 2002.

[SRI 96] SRIVASTAVA M., CHANDRAKASAN A., BRODERSEN R., "Predictive system shutdown and other architectural techniques for energy efficient programmable computation", *IEEE Transactions on VLSI Systems*, vol. 4, pp. 42–55, March 1996.

[STO 14] STORM, available at: http://storm.rts-software.org, 2014.

[TAO 03] TAO L., LIZY KURIAN J., "Run-time modeling and estimation of operating system power consumption", *Proceedings of the International Conference on Measurement and Modeling of Computer Systems (SIGMETRICS)*, San Diego, CA, 2003.

[TIW 96] TIWARI V., MALIK S., WOLFE A., "Instruction level power analysis and optimization of software", *Journal of VLSI Signal Processing*, pp. 1–18, 1996.

[VEN 06] VENTROUX N., On-line control for embedded heterogeneous multiprocessors systems: architecture design and validation, PhD Thesis, 2006.

[YAN 09] YANG C., JIAN-JIA C., TEI-WEI K., *et al.*, "An approximation scheme for energy-efficient scheduling of real-time tasks in heterogeneous multiprocessor systems", *Proceeding of 2009*, April 2009.

[WAL 95] WALLI S.R., "The POSIX family of standards", *Standard View*, vol. 3, no. 1, pp. 11–17, March 1995.

[ZHA 12] ZHAO B., AYDIN H., ZHU D., "Energy management under general task-level reliability constraints", *Proceedings of RTAS*, 2012

[ZHU 03] ZHU D., MELHEM R., CHILDERS B., "Scheduling with dynamic voltage/speed adjustment using slack reclamation in multi-processor real-time systems", *IEEE Transactions on Parallel & Distributed Systems*, vol. 14, no. 7, pp. 686–700, 2003.

# List of Authors

Cécile BELLEUDY
LEAT Laboratory
University of Nice
Sophia-Antipolis
France

Maryline CHETTO
IRCCyN Laboratory
University of Nantes
France

Frédéric FAUBERTEAU
ECE Engineers School
Paris
France

Laurent GEORGE
LIGM Laboratory
University of Paris
Est-Créteil
Vitry sur Seine
France

Joël GOOSSENS
Computer Science Department
Université Libre de Bruxelles
Belgium

Emmanual GROLLEAU
LIAS Laboratory
ISAE-ENSMA
Poitiers
France

Jean-François HERMANT
INRIA
Rocquencourt
France

Claire MAIZA
VERIMAG Laboratory
ENSIMAG
Grenoble
France

Serge MIDONNET
LIGM Laboratory
University of Paris
Est-Marne la Vallée
France

Pascal RAYMOND
VERIMAG Laboratory
CNRS
Grenoble
France

Pascal RICHARD
LIAS Laboratory
University of Poitiers
France

Christine ROCHANGE
IRIT Laboratory
Paul Sabatier University
Toulouse
France

# Index

## A

ABS, 3
access protocol, 151
actuator, 9
allocation
    best-fit, 121
    first-fit, 121
    longest processing time
        first, 128
    reasonable, 126
    worst-fit, 121
anomaly, 25
asymptotic ratio, 124, 127

## B

bin packing, 120
blocking, 150
    chained, 170
    direct, 150
    indirect, 150
    multiple, 170
blocking factor, 150, 158
busy period, 56
BWI, 153

## C

cache memory, 6
clairvoyant, 113
critical scaling factor, 78
critical section, 149

## D

deadline
    arbitrary, 19, 44
    constrained, 19
    constraint, 44
    implicit, 19, 44, 105
    relative, 43, 105
deadlock, 164
demand bound function, 49
dispatcher, 107

## E

EDF, 54
EDL server, 47
embedded system, 2
ESP, 3
execution time, 105

## F

feasibility conditions, 64

# Summary of Volume 2

# Contents

Other titles from

in

Networks and Telecommunications

## 2014

CAMPISTA Miguel Elias Mitre, RUBINSTEIN Marcelo Gonçalves
*Advanced Routing Protocols for Wireless Networks*

EXPOSITO Ernesto, DIOP Codé
*Smart SOA Platforms in Cloud Computing Architectures*

MELLOUK Abdelhamid, CUADRA-SANCHEZ Antonio
*Quality of Experience Engineering for Customer Added Value Services*

OTEAFY Sharief M.A., HASSANEIN Hossam S.
*Dynamic Wireless Sensor Networks*

TANWIR Savera, PERROS Harry
*VBR Video Traffic Models*

VAN METER Rodney
*Quantum Networking*

XIONG Kaiqi
*Resource Optimization and Security for Cloud Services*

# 2013

ASSING Dominique, CALÉ Stéphane
*Mobile Access Safety: Beyond BYOD*

BEN MAHMOUD Mohamed Slim, LARRIEU Nicolas, PIROVANO Alain
*Risk Propagation Assessment for Network Security: Application to Airport Communication Network Design*

BEYLOT André-Luc, LABIOD Houda
*Vehicular Networks: Models and Algorithms*

BRITO Gabriel M., VELLOSO Pedro Braconnot, MORAES Igor M.
*Information-Centric Networks: A New Paradigm for the Internet*

BERTIN Emmanuel, CRESPI Noël
*Architecture and Governance for Communication Services*

DEUFF Dominique, COSQUER Mathilde
*User-Centered Agile Method*

DUARTE Otto Carlos, PUJOLLE Guy
*Virtual Networks: Pluralistic Approach for the Next Generation of Internet*

FOWLER Scott A., MELLOUK Abdelhamid, YAMADA Naomi
*LTE-Advanced DRX Mechanism for Power Saving*

JOBERT Sébastien *et al.*
*Synchronous Ethernet and IEEE 1588 in Telecoms: Next Generation Synchronization Networks*

MELLOUK Abdelhamid, HOCEINI Said, TRAN Hai Anh
*Quality-of-Experience for Multimedia: Application to Content Delivery Network Architecture*

NAIT-SIDI-MOH Ahmed, BAKHOUYA Mohamed, GABER Jaafar, WACK Maxime
*Geopositioning and Mobility*

PEREZ André
*Voice over LTE: EPS and IMS Networks*

## 2012

AL AGHA Khaldoun
*Network Coding*

BOUCHET Olivier
*Wireless Optical Communications*

DECREUSEFOND Laurent, MOYAL Pascal
*Stochastic Modeling and Analysis of Telecoms Networks*

DUFOUR Jean-Yves
*Intelligent Video Surveillance Systems*

EXPOSITO Ernesto
*Advanced Transport Protocols: Designing the Next Generation*

JUMIRA Oswald, ZEADALLY Sherali
*Energy Efficiency in Wireless Networks*

KRIEF Francine
*Green Networking*

PEREZ André
*Mobile Networks Architecture*

## 2011

BONALD Thomas, FEUILLET Mathieu
*Network Performance Analysis*

CARBOU Romain, DIAZ Michel, EXPOSITO Ernesto, ROMAN Rodrigo
*Digital Home Networking*

CHABANNE Hervé, URIEN Pascal, SUSINI Jean-Ferdinand
*RFID and the Internet of Things*

GARDUNO David, DIAZ Michel
*Communicating Systems with UML 2: Modeling and Analysis of Network Protocols*

LAHEURTE Jean-Marc
*Compact Antennas for Wireless Communications and Terminals: Theory and Design*

RÉMY Jean-Gabriel, LETAMENDIA Charlotte
*Home Area Networks and IPTV*

PALICOT Jacques
*Radio Engineering: From Software Radio to Cognitive Radio*

PEREZ André
*IP, Ethernet and MPLS Networks: Resource and Fault Management*

TOUTAIN Laurent, MINABURO Ana
*Local Networks and the Internet: From Protocols to Interconnection*

## 2010

CHAOUCHI Hakima
*The Internet of Things*

FRIKHA Mounir
*Ad Hoc Networks: Routing, QoS and Optimization*

KRIEF Francine
*Communicating Embedded Systems / Network Applications*

## 2009

CHAOUCHI Hakima, MAKNAVICIUS Maryline
*Wireless and Mobile Network Security*

VIVIER Emmanuelle
*Radio Resources Management in WiMAX*

## 2008

CHADUC Jean-Marc, POGOREL Gérard
*The Radio Spectrum*

GAÏTI Dominique
*Autonomic Networks*

LABIOD Houda
*Wireless Ad Hoc and Sensor Networks*

LECOY Pierre
*Fiber-optic Communications*

MELLOUK Abdelhamid
*End-to-End Quality of Service Engineering in Next Generation Heterogeneous Networks*

PAGANI Pascal *et al.*
*Ultra-wideband Radio Propagation Channel*

## 2007

BENSLIMANE Abderrahim
*Multimedia Multicast on the Internet*

PUJOLLE Guy
*Management, Control and Evolution of IP Networks*

SANCHEZ Javier, THIOUNE Mamadou
*UMTS*

VIVIER Guillaume
*Reconfigurable Mobile Radio Systems*

CPSIA information can be obtained at www.ICGtesting.com
Printed in the USA
BVOW08*1123241014

372147BV00001B/3/P